ENVIRONMENTAL SCIENCE, ENGINEERING AND TECHNOLOGY

MARSHES

ECOLOGY, MANAGEMENT AND CONSERVATION

ENVIRONMENTAL SCIENCE, ENGINEERING AND TECHNOLOGY

Additional books in this series can be found on Nova's website under the Series tab.

Additional E-books in this series can be found on Nova's website under the E-books tab.

ENVIRONMENTAL SCIENCE, ENGINEERING AND TECHNOLOGY

MARSHES

ECOLOGY, MANAGEMENT AND CONSERVATION

DEMARCO C. ABREU
AND
SAVANNAH L. DE BORBÓN
EDITORS

Nova Science Publishers, Inc.
New York

QH
541.5
.M3
M37
2012

Copyright © 2012 by Nova Science Publishers, Inc.

All rights reserved. No part of this book may be reproduced, stored in a retrieval system or transmitted in any form or by any means: electronic, electrostatic, magnetic, tape, mechanical photocopying, recording or otherwise without the written permission of the Publisher.

For permission to use material from this book please contact us:
Telephone 631-231-7269; Fax 631-231-8175
Web Site: http://www.novapublishers.com

NOTICE TO THE READER

The Publisher has taken reasonable care in the preparation of this book, but makes no expressed or implied warranty of any kind and assumes no responsibility for any errors or omissions. No liability is assumed for incidental or consequential damages in connection with or arising out of information contained in this book. The Publisher shall not be liable for any special, consequential, or exemplary damages resulting, in whole or in part, from the readers' use of, or reliance upon, this material. Any parts of this book based on government reports are so indicated and copyright is claimed for those parts to the extent applicable to compilations of such works.

Independent verification should be sought for any data, advice or recommendations contained in this book. In addition, no responsibility is assumed by the publisher for any injury and/or damage to persons or property arising from any methods, products, instructions, ideas or otherwise contained in this publication.

This publication is designed to provide accurate and authoritative information with regard to the subject matter covered herein. It is sold with the clear understanding that the Publisher is not engaged in rendering legal or any other professional services. If legal or any other expert assistance is required, the services of a competent person should be sought. FROM A DECLARATION OF PARTICIPANTS JOINTLY ADOPTED BY A COMMITTEE OF THE AMERICAN BAR ASSOCIATION AND A COMMITTEE OF PUBLISHERS.

Additional color graphics may be available in the e-book version of this book.

Library of Congress Cataloging-in-Publication Data

Marshes : ecology, management and conservation / editors, Demarco C. Abreu and Savannah L. de Borbsn.
 p. cm.
 Includes index.
 ISBN 978-1-61942-715-0 (hardcover)
 1. Marsh ecology. 2. Wetland management. 3. Marsh conservation. 4. Wildlife management. 5. Marshes. I. Abreu, Demarco C. II. Borbsn, Savannah L. de.
 QH541.5.M3M37 2011
 577.68--dc23
                                                                                          2011052306

Published by Nova Science Publishers, Inc. † New York

CONTENTS

Preface		**vii**
Chapter 1	Reconsidering Climatic Roles of Marshes: Are they Sinks or Sources of Greenhouse Gases? *Serena Moseman-Valtierra*	**1**
Chapter 2	The Introduction, Impacts, and Management of a Large, Invasive, Aquatic Rodent in the United States *Gary Witmer, Trevor R. Sheffels and Stephen R. Kendrot*	**49**
Chapter 3	The Mesocosm Marsh Ecology of Two Southwestern Spanish Estuaries: Applications *M. L. González-Regalado, F. Ruiz, J. Borrego, M. Abad, E. X. García and A. Toscano*	**91**
Chapter 4	Factors Conditioning the Vegetation in the Salt Marshes of the Atlantic Coast of the Iberian Peninsula *José M. Sánchez*	**103**
Chapter 5	Nutrient Cycling in Salt Marshes: An Ecosystem Service to Reduce Eutrophication *A. I. Lillebø, A. I. Sousa, M. R. Flindt, M. E. Pereira, A. C. Duarte, M. A. Pardal and I. Caçador*	**129**
Index		**163**

PREFACE

Marshes, both tidal and non-tidal, are productive and complex ecosystems. The water in these systems ranges from fresh, to brackish, to saline as one moves from inland to coastal areas. Marshes are an interface between upland and aquatic habitats. In this book, the authors present current research in the study of the ecology, management and conservation of marshes including the climatic roles of marshes; the mesocosm marsh ecology of two southwestern Spanish estuaries; factors conditioning the vegetation in the salt marshes of the Atlantic Coast of the Iberian Peninsula; and nutrient cycling in salt marshes.

Chapter 1 - Marshes are exceptionally productive ecosystems that constitute significant global carbon sinks. Particularly along coasts, marshes are prime targets for efforts that aim to enhance biological carbon sequestration. However, the net climatic impact of ecosystems depends not only on carbon sinks but also on sources of carbon and nitrogen to the atmosphere. Carbon dioxide (CO_2), methane (CH_4), and nitrous oxide (N_2O) strongly influence climate together; CH_4 and N_2O wield 25 and 298 times the global warming potential per molecule as CO_2, respectively, over 100 year time periods. Yet, the magnitude of all three greenhouse gases has rarely been measured simultaneously in marshes, and controls on these fluxes are not well understood. Anthropogenic impacts such as nutrient loading and other changes in environmental conditions may substantially alter the greenhouse gas emissions from marsh ecosystems. Recent manipulative experiments show that short-term nitrate loading (at concentrations found in anthropogenically enriched groundwater) can significantly enhance emissions of N_2O from salt marsh sediments. These fluxes are substantial enough in terms of global warming potential to offset as much as half of the daily C sequestration rates in coastal marshes. This is in striking contrast to negative fluxes (sinks) of

N_2O that are consistently observed in the absence of nitrate (Moseman-Valtierra et al. 2011). In general, studies so far suggest that the highest N_2O fluxes are found in marshes experiencing significant anthropogenic nutrient loading. Since nitrate loading affects many riparian and coastal marshes worldwide, the net global warming potential of marshes may be substantially altered on local scales, with potential consequences for global climate. However, in several marshes N_2O and CH_4 fluxes show high spatial heterogeneity that suggests complex controlling factors. Current research is reviewed herein to identify known environmental controls of N_2O and CH_4 production, consumption, and emission from fresh and coastal marshes. This information is used to develop hypotheses regarding potential shifts in greenhouse gas sinks and sources in response to rising sea levels, increasing temperatures, and biological invasions. Information regarding anthropogenic and environmental factors that affect greenhouse gas emissions in marsh ecosystems is essential in order to prioritize areas for conservation and to guide restoration activities across dynamic fresh-marine transition zones and shifting biomes. As restoration activites proceed, the ability of marsh ecosystems to not just passively respond to global climate change but also to actively influence climate through carbon sequestration and greenhouse gas emissions, needs to be recognized, especially as these abilities may be significantly altered by human activities.

Chapter 2 - Marshes, both tidal and non-tidal, are productive and complex ecosystems. The water in these systems ranges from fresh, to brackish, to saline as one moves from inland to coastal areas. Marshes are an interface between upland and aquatic habitats, and many biotic and abiotic processes lead to increased species richness and diversity (Gedan et al., 2009). Marshes provide many ecological services, including recharge and discharge of ground water; water quality control; retention, removal, and transformation of nutrients; habitats for many floral and faunal species; biomass production and exports; flood control and storm buffering; and stabilization of sediments and slowing of erosion (Southwick Associates, 2004; Woodward et al., 2001). Marshes also provide for human activities such as hiking, wildlife viewing, hunting, trapping, fishing, etc. (Bounds and Carowan, 2000; Southwick Associates, 2004).

Marshes in North America, and elsewhere in many parts of the world, have been greatly affected by human activities, including dredging, filling, water diversions, flood control structures, contamination by pollutants, conversion to agricultural cropland and urban centers, introduction of invasive species, salinization, habitat fragmentation, and other factors (Bounds and

Carowan, 2000; Takekawa et al., 2006; Pathikonda et al., 2008; McFalls et al., 2010). Sea level rise and hurricanes also affect marshes and species interactions (Pathikonda et al., 2008; Pyke et al., 2008). Additionally, many marshes have been invaded by exotic species, upsetting normal physical and ecological functions, species richness, and species interactions. Much has been studied and published about invasive plants invading marshes (e.g., Guntenspergen and Nordby, 2006; Pathikonda et al., 2008), but much less has been reported about invasive herbivore impacts in marshes.

Nutria, or coypu (*Myocastor coypus*), are semi-aquatic rodents native to southern South America. In the first half of the 20th century, nutria were widely promoted as a farmable fur bearer and introduced to more than 20 US states, beginning in California in 1899 (Carter and Leonard, 2002). Through a series of accidental and intentional releases, to establish fur resources or to control aquatic weeds, feral populations have since become established in 17 states and are considered an invasive species causing detrimental impacts to native habitats, agricultural resources, and water control structures. In the United States, nutria impacts have mainly occurred in the mid-Atlantic, Southeast, and Pacific Northwest regions of the country. The feeding activities of these herbivores can damage agricultural crops and aquatic vegetation, leading to altered aquatic ecosystems. Their burrowing habits can weaken water control structures, and they are a host for some infectious diseases.

Management of nutria and the damage they cause can be problematic for natural resource managers. Nutria are habitat generalists, prolific breeders, and are capable of long-distance dispersals – all characteristics of successful invaders. Eradication or local extirpation may be feasible and desirable in areas where risk of reinvasion can be minimized, but a number of challenging criteria must be met for eradication efforts to succeed. However, in contiguously occupied habitats, control through population suppression may be the only viable alternative for protecting high priority resources. Both management strategies are labor intensive and require specialized equipment to reach nutria populations in wetland environments with limited access. Control efforts can be further complicated where nutria are considered a valuable resource and regulated harvest occurs, such as in Louisiana. This chapter discusses nutria biology, ecology, introductions, impacts as an invasive species, and management and eradication efforts.

Chapter 3 - This paper analyzes the foraminiferal and ostracod assemblages of marsh environments in two estuaries of southwestern Spain. High and low marsh deposits may be differentiated according to the percentages of some foraminiferal species (*Jadammina macrescens*,

Trochammina inflata), the presence/absence of other foraminifers (mainly miliolids) or the presence/absence of ostracods. These features and some varia-tions observed in different estuarine environments (fluvial, middle, marine) are directly applicable in the detection of (palaeo-)eustatic changes, salinity variations or hydrodynamic gradients.

Chapter 4 - The zonation of saltmarsh vegetation is a universal phenomenon related to apparently simple physical and chemical gradients. Nonetheless, the relationship between these factors and the vegetation is seldom a direct one, but mediated through a number of other correlated variables. Of these ultimate variables, documentation shows that elevation, salinity and redox potential are correlated with the vegetation gradient. Some possible factors have been considered are anoxia due to waterlogging (inundation of vegetated parts of the saltmarsh), direct toxic effect of salts or the formation of potentially toxic ions (at low redox potential values).

Interacting with those simple physical factors, there are some other factors that arise by the action of the biota itself. Therefore a number of biotic interactions contribute to the final result of plant distribution in salt marshes. Among them (many times, above them) the anthropogenic influence is conditioning the salt marsh vegetation through different kinds of impacts.

Chapter 5 - Salt marshes are classified as sensitive habitat under the Habitats Directive (92/43/EEC), which aims to promote the maintenance of biodiversity. Worldwide, the reduction of salt marsh areas, as a result of anthropogenic disturbance is of major concern, and several studies on the ecology of estuaries have emphasized the negative consequences of its disappearance. In addition, as a result of increasing global population and increasing human activities, salt marshes, estuaries and other coastal waters have been subjected to increasing nutrient loadings with anthropogenic origin. This chapter aims to draw attention to the sequestration capacity of salt marshes for the excess of nutrients, and to evaluate the ecological services provided by salt marsh halophytes by regulating the biogeochemical cycles of nitrogen (N) and phosphorus (P). In this context, two case studies will be presented and discussed: By comparing young and mature marshes colonised by *Saprtina maritima*, the author evaluates their behaviour as sink or source of nutrients; By comparing two halophytes with distinct life cycles (*Spartina maritima* and *Scirpus maritimus*), the author evaluates species-specific N and P cycling and sequestration in salt marshes. This chapter will thus emphasise that salt marsh halophytes have a crucial role on nutrient cycling and sequestration, providing ecological services that contribute to maintain the ecosystem health.

In: Marshes
Editors: D. C. Abreu et al.

ISBN 978-1-61942-715-0
© 2012 Nova Science Publishers, Inc.

Chapter 1

RECONSIDERING CLIMATIC ROLES OF MARSHES: ARE THEY SINKS OR SOURCES OF GREENHOUSE GASES?

Serena Moseman-Valtierra
University of Rhode Island, Department of Biological Sciences,
Kingston, RI, US

ABSTRACT

Marshes are exceptionally productive ecosystems that constitute significant global carbon sinks. Particularly along coasts, marshes are prime targets for efforts that aim to enhance biological carbon sequestration. However, the net climatic impact of ecosystems depends not only on carbon sinks but also on sources of carbon and nitrogen to the atmosphere. Carbon dioxide (CO_2), methane (CH_4), and nitrous oxide (N_2O) strongly influence climate together; CH_4 and N_2O wield 25 and 298 times the global warming potential per molecule as CO_2, respectively, over 100 year time periods. Yet, the magnitude of all three greenhouse gases has rarely been measured simultaneously in marshes, and controls on these fluxes are not well understood. Anthropogenic impacts such as nutrient loading and other changes in environmental conditions may substantially alter the greenhouse gas emissions from marsh ecosystems. Recent manipulative experiments show that short-term nitrate loading (at concentrations found in anthropogenically enriched groundwater) can significantly enhance emissions of N_2O from salt marsh sediments. These fluxes are substantial enough in terms of global warming potential to offset as much as half of the daily C sequestration rates in coastal marshes. This is in striking contrast to negative fluxes (sinks) of N_2O that are consistently observed in the absence of nitrate (Moseman-Valtierra et al. 2011). In general, studies so far suggest that the highest N_2O fluxes are found in marshes experiencing significant anthropogenic nutrient loading. Since nitrate loading affects many riparian and coastal marshes worldwide, the net global warming potential of marshes may be substantially altered on local scales, with potential consequences for global climate. However, in several marshes N_2O and CH_4 fluxes show high spatial heterogeneity that suggests complex controlling factors. Current research is reviewed herein to identify known environmental controls of N_2O and CH_4 production, consumption, and emission from fresh and coastal marshes. This information is used to develop hypotheses regarding potential shifts in greenhouse gas sinks and sources in response to rising sea levels, increasing temperatures, and biological invasions. Information regarding anthropogenic and environmental factors that affect greenhouse gas emissions in marsh ecosystems is essential in order to prioritize areas for conservation and to guide restoration activities across dynamic fresh-marine transition zones and shifting biomes. As restoration activites proceed, the ability of marsh ecosystems to not just passively respond to global climate change but also to actively influence climate through carbon sequestration and greenhouse gas emissions, needs to be recognized, especially as these abilities may be significantly altered by human activities.

INTRODUCTION

In wetlands spanning a range of ecosystems and latitudes, from the fringes of boreal lakes and rivers to temperate coastal salt marshes, vascular plants dominate and define marsh landscapes. Marsh grasses and sedges display impressive productivity given the relatively stressful wetland environment that results from regular inundation of soils (Mitsch and Gosselink 2001). Salt marshes, in particular, rank among the world's most productive ecosystems (Mitsch and Gosselink 2001). This remarkable productivity is supported, in part, by regular tidal flushing that reduces the accumulation of reduced toxins in salt marsh soils while also delivering limiting nutrients from coastal waters.

The significance of coastal wetland productivity to surrounding ecosystems was historically described in Odum's classic hypothesis that these ecosystems produce an excess of organic matter which is exported to the sea, where it supports coastal fisheries (Odum 1980). For decades since, researchers tested this hypothesis by evaluating the C budgets of marsh ecosystems and the relationship between marsh primary production and coastal fisheries (i.e. Morris and Whiting 1986, Dela Cruz 1973, Teal 1962). However, evidence was not conclusive that all coastal wetlands represent significant sources of carbon to the adjacent ocean. Rather, C exports from coastal marshes seemed to be contingent upon factors such as tidal amplitude and hydrology, and the hypothesis continues to be evaluated, particularly, in the context of wetland subsidence and hypoxia (Das et al. 2011). In contrast to the relative emphasis on evaluating marshes as potential sources of carbon to adjacent waters via lateral fluxes (outwelling), the role of marshes in vertical (soil-atmosphere) biogeochemical fluxes has been relatively ignored- until now.

Growing concern over anthropogenic impacts on global climate, via emissions of greenhouse gases, has led to efforts to identify potential sites for biological C sequestration, and attention is increasingly turning to coastal marshes. Wetlands store at least 44.6 Tg C y^{-1} globally (Chmura et al. 2003), representing the largest terrestrial biological carbon pool. Initial attention was directed to freshwater wetlands as carbon sinks, particularly northern peatlands, however salt marshes (and mangroves) have been found to store carbon more rapidly per unit area (Chmura et al. 2003). The estimated average rate of carbon sequestration in salt marshes and mangrove swamps (which did not significantly differ from each other) is 201 g CO_2 m^{-2} y^{-1}, which is an order or magnitude higher than C sequestration in peatlands (20-30 g CO_2 m^{-2} y^{-1}) (Chmura et al.2003, Roulet 2000).

An additional attraction of coastal marshes as potential sites of biological sequestration is that they have been considered to produce insignificant emissions of the potent greenhouse gases, methane and nitrous oxide. Like CO_2, methane and nitrous oxide have increased significantly above pre-industrial levels, rising by 48% and 18%, respectively. In contrast, however, they wield 25 and 298 times the global warming potential per molecule as CO_2 over a 100 year period (Forster et al. 2007), which raises concerns about anthropogenic and natural sources of these gases. Salt marshes are thought to constitute small sources of methane because methanogens cannot compete with sulfate-reducing bacteria that thrive in coastal marsh soils (Fenchel and Blackburn 1979, Morris and Whiting 1986). They have also not been considered major sources of N_2O, at least in part because this is a minor product of denitrification (Seitzinger 1988, Kaplan et al. 1979). However, measurements of N_2O and CH4 in European coastal waters have frequently revealed that estuaries, which include marshes, are a net source of N_2O to the atmosphere, contributing up to 26% of global oceanic N_2O emissions, and a significant source of CH_4 as well (Bange 2006). Specific measurements in coastal marshes within such estuaries have rarely been made and thus their contributions to estuarine greenhouse gas emissions remain largely unknown. Thus, the assumption that coastal marshes do not constitute major sources of greenhouse gases has persisted despite relatively few *in situ* measurements.

Given that biological C sequestration in coastal marshes could be substantially offset by such greenhouse gas emissions from these ecosystems, the relative significance of these processes needs to be quantified and understood. As management decisions regarding wetland restorations are made, cost-benefit analyses will need to consider the potential for enhancement of greenhouse gas emissions in estuaries where wetland area is expanded (Andrews et al. 2006), and the environmental factors that would maximize or minimize those emissions need to be better understood (Huang and Pant 2009, Andrews et al. 2006).

The purpose of this review is to summarize what is known about the magnitude and controls of greenhouse gas emissions from marshes. As few measurements have been made in coastal salt marshes, I compare greenhouse gas emissions from a range of fresh and marine marshes to those of other ecosystems in which significant fluxes have been reported. At least one recent review has focused on greenhouse gas emissions from relatively pristine coastal ecosystems (Dalal and Allen 2009), so this review intentionally includes greenhouse gas fluxes from anthropogenically-impacted marshes which may substantially differ from undisturbed marshes. Given growing human populations and their indelible roles in many ecosystems, estimates of greenhouse gas emissions and our understanding of their controls will need to be based on studies that incorporate human impacts.

MICROBIAL SOURCES OF GREENHOUSE GASES IN MARSH SOILS

Marsh soils provide a heterogeneous environment with combinations of aerobic and anaerobic niches in which microbial respiration proceeds (Sutton Grier et al. 2011). While CO_2 is produced from most respiratory processes (by microbes, plants and animals), N_2O and CH_4 are produced by more specific microbial guilds. The net product of production and consumption of these gases, by both aerobic and anaerobic processes, is their emission from marsh soils to the atmosphere.

N$_2$O: Nitrous oxide is a byproduct of very diverse nitrogen transformations, although the two main sources in coastal marshes are thought to be nitrification and denitrification. Nitrification is generally an aerobic pathway by which NH$_4^+$ is oxidized in two steps, first to NO$_2^-$, and then to NO$_3^-$. Both bacteria and archaea perform the first step of nitrification (oxidation of ammonium), which is the rate limiting step of the process due to close coupling of nitrite-oxidizing bacteria with the ammonia oxidizers (Ward 2005, Ward et al 2007, Konneke et al. 2005). The pathways of N$_2$O production by nitrifiers are not well understood. One is nitrifier denitrification in which nitrite is reduced to nitric oxide (NO) and N$_2$O under microaerobic conditions (Wrage et al. 2001, Arp and Stein 2003). While nitrification by autotrophs is an aerobic process, the process of nitrifier denitrification (also by autotrophs) seems to be enhanced as O$_2$ levels decrease, perhaps because it is a mechanism for acquiring energy under O$_2$- limited conditions (Arp and Stein 2003, Wrage et al. 2001). Ammonium provides the electron source for nitrifier denitrification (Kool et al. 2011, Ritchie and Nicholas 1972; Bock et al., 1995). Polypeptides capable of catalyzing the reduction of nitrite in nitrifier denitrification include the blue copper cytochrome c oxidase (Miller and Nicholas 1985) and an unidentified copper-containing enzyme (Arp and Stein 2003, Ritchie and Nicholas 1974). Potential controls on nitrifier-denitrification have been reviewed elsewhere (Wrage et al. 2001) and are thought to include high N content of soils or sediments, low organic C content, and possibly low pH, based on thermodynamic considerations (Wrage et al. 2001). Depending upon availability of various electron acceptors, denitrification can be a major respiratory pathway by which anaerobic heterotrophs respire organic carbon after oxygen has been exhausted as a terminal electron acceptor. N$_2$O is an intermediate prior to the last step in denitrification, with the complete process proceeding as follows: NO$_3$→ NO$_2^-$ → NO → N$_2$O → N$_2$ (Hochstein and Tomlinson 1988, Wrage et al. 2001). Typically N$_2$ is the dominant product of denitrification, with N$_2$O:N$_2$ ratios being less than 0.5% in estuarine sediments (Seitzinger and Kroeze 1998), but this varies with environmental conditions (discussed further below). Denitrification can be performed by diverse microbes including archaea and eukarya (Zumft 1997), although most studies of the microbial communities in marsh soils have focused on patterns of functional bacterial genes involved in denitrification (Bowen et al. 2011, Cao et al. 2008, Dandie et al. 2011) which have been found to be similar among bacteria and archaea (Cabello et al. 2004).

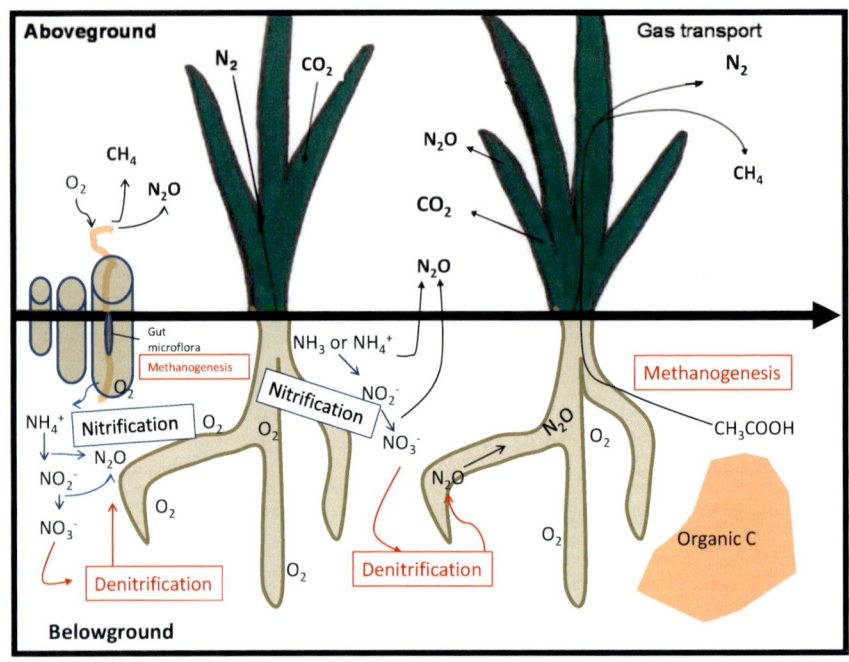

Figure 1. Diagram of major processes producing greenhouse gases in marsh soils, including plant-mediated transport of gases to the atmosphere and faunal production of greenhouse gases. Red text (and boxes) indicate anaerobic processes. Blue text (and boxes) indicate anaerobic processes.

In coastal ecosystems, nitrification and denitrification are frequently coupled, with nitrifiers providing the NO_3^- that denitrifiers reduce to N_2O and then N_2 (Hamersley and Howes 2005, Jenkins and Kemp 1984). Important sites where this coupling occurs include rhizospheres (roots and immediately surrounding soils), where sufficient oxygen is introduced to sediments by plant photosynthesis to enable nitrification to occur (Lovell 2005), and in microniches such as animal burrows and tubes (Kristensen and Kostka 2005) (Figure 1). Due to the coupling of nitrification and denitrification, the relative importance of each as sources of the greenhouse gas N_2O can be tricky to determine. Further, the significance of each process is likely to vary in response to shifts in environmental conditions. For example, in laboratory manipulations of inundation regimes with intertidal sediment cores, nitrification was found to be the dominant source of N_2O during relatively dessicated conditions, while denitrification was the major source under waterlogged or reflooded conditions, and highest N_2O concentrations were observed in the sediments under the latter conditions (Hou et al. 2007). In addition to variation with water levels, rates of nitrification can show seasonality that is distinct from denitrification, as observed in a freshwater marsh where the former was maximal in May while the latter reached highest rates in September (Gribsholt et al. 2006). Other processes that can produce nitrous oxide include dissimilatory reduction to ammonium (DNRA) (Smith and Zimmerman 1981) and assimilatory nitrate reduction although the relative significance of these sources, and nitrifier denitrification (Wrage et al. 2001), has not been well quantified compared to nitrification and denitrification in marshes. In soils, assimilatory nitrate reduction is less than 6% of total nitrate reduction, indicating that it may also be an insignificant source of N_2O (Venterea and Rolston 2000, Dalal and Allen 2009).

CH_4: Methanogenesis constitutes the last terminal respiratory pathway by which organic matter is degraded, because it yields less energy than alternative pathways. Methanogens include a diverse range of bacteria and archaea that use a wide array of various carbon sources and range in habitats from soils to microbial mats and animal guts. The carbon substrates that methanogens convert into methane have been determined predominantly via cultures and can be classified into 3 groups: CO_2-type substrates, methyl substrates, and acetotrophic substrates (Madigan and Martinko 2006). These substrates are made available by fermentative bacteria that degrade polymeric material into labile forms. The predominant substrate supporting methanogenesis in marsh soils can vary with temperature (Wagner and Pfeiffer 1997). Much of the methane in saline marshes is thought to be derived from methyl compounds, such as trimethylamine and dimethylsulfide, although H_2 is an important substrate in surfaces of microbial mats in a salt marsh (Buckley et al. 2008). In salt marshes, groups of methanogenic bacteria have been found to vary in their use of different substrates, with some using trimethylamine but not H_2 or acetate, others using H_2 but not trimethylamine or acetate, and some that could use isopropanol, H_2, and formate (Franklin et al. 1988), which suggests that niche partitioning may occur among them. In freshwater sediments, methanethiol, dimethyl sulfide, and methanol are known to be degraded by methanogens (Lomans et al. 2001). There is evidence that groups of methanogens using different substrates may compete with each other, which includes the finding that addition of acetates to peatland soils inhibited hydrogenotrophic methanogenesis (Brauer et al. 2004, Liu et al. 2011).

Although methanogenesis is an anaerobic process, methanogens have been found in oxic marsh soil layers (Wagner and Pfeiffer 1997), and they likely interact with aerobic and anaerobic methanotrophs. Methanogenic archaea have been found to be most abundant in surface soils of multiple freshwater marshes (Liu et al. 2011). Abundance estimates of methanogens in the latter study were based on real-time PCR analyses of DNA and thus may reflect dead or inactive archea (Liu et al. 2011), so further studies are needed to determine whether methanogens can be active in what seem to be aerobic sediments (possibly by residing in anaerobic microniches). The overall flux of methane from marsh soils will represent the interaction of methanogens with methanotrophic bacteria that oxidize methane, in aerobic microhabitats such as rhizospheres, as well as in anoxic environments where sulfate reduction can be coupled to methane oxidation (Conrad 1996). Anaerobic methane oxidation has also relatively recently been found to occur via consortia that couple the process to denitrification (Dalal and Allen 2009, Raghoebarsing et al. 2006, Islas-Lima 2004) as well as to iron reduction (Sivan et al. 2011).

Current knowledge regarding environmental controls on nitrous oxide production and consumption as well as methanogenesis and methane oxidation are discussed further in the following sections.

OVERVIEW OF THE MAGNITUDE OF GREENHOUSE GASES IN MARSHES

A summary of N_2O fluxes reported from a range of northern hemisphere freshwater marshes are provided in Table 1, and studies which measured N_2O fluxes (along with CO_2 and CH_4) in coastal marshes are found in Table 2. The studies summarized in these tables are not exhaustive of all published literature addressing greenhouse gas production, but they do represent the geographical range of marshes in which *in situ* fluxes are mostly being measured. All of the studies that are summarized in Tables 1-3 were conducted via *in situ* closed chamber techniques, and units have been converted to enable comparison of the greenhouse gas fluxes. One exception is Roobroeck et al. 2010 (which used core-based incubations of marsh soils) which is included because no comparable *in situ* studies of fens with N enrichment are known. CO_2 fluxes are included where they were reported, although controls on CO_2 are not the focus of this review because they have been relatively well characterized (Wigand et al. 2009, Rocha and Goulden 2008, Drake et al. 1996, Morris and Whiting 1986, Morris and Whiting 1985).

Table 1. N₂O fluxes (μg N$_2$O m^{-2} h^{-1}) from freshwater marshes (standard errors in parentheses)

Source	dominant plant(s)	Wetland description	Location	average N2O flux
Jordan et al. 2007	n/a	FW, FT, NT; spring	USA Chesapeake Bay	0.2 (0.3)
		FW, FT, NT; summer	USA Chesapeake Bay	0.7 (0.4)
		FW, FT, NT; fall	USA Chesapeake Bay	1.2 (0.8)
		FW, RV, NT; spring	USA Chesapeake Bay	4.2 (3.1)
		FW, R, NT; summer	USA Chesapeake Bay	1.6 (1.2)
		FW, R, NT; fall	USA Chesapeake Bay	5.4 (2.8)
Weller et al. 1994		FW, RP, FST	USA Maryland	4.4
Yu et al. 2007	*Deyeuxia angustifolia*	FW	NE China	4.45 to 6.85
		FW	NE China	-1.00 to -0.76
Roobroek et al. 2010	*Carex appopringuata, Peucedanum palustre*	FW, F	Biebrza, Poland	2.1 (0.3)
		FW, F	Biebrza, Poland	-3.0 (0.1)
		FW, F	Biebrza, Poland	2.7 (0.4)
Hefting et al. 2003	*Alnus glutinosa*	FW, FST, +N	Netherlands	358 maximum: 4167
	Glyceria maxima	FW, G, +N	Netherlands	36 to 72
Liikanen et al. 2009		B,C	Baltic Sea	-5.5

Minimum and maximum values are included where they have been provided by the sources. The key to the wetland descriptions, which are based on the respective authors' evaluations of their field sites, is as follows: FW=Freshwater, C= Coastal, SM= salt marsh, BRK= Brackish marsh, CRK= Tidal creek, F=fen, FST= Forested, RV=Riverine, RP= Riparian, G=grassland, FT= Flat, B=Boreal, +N= Fertilized with nitrogen, SAND= sandy intertidal.

Table 2. Average fluxes of greenhouse gases from coastal and freshwater marshes and wetlands (with standard errors in parentheses)

Source	dominant plant(s)	Wetland description	Location	average N_2O flux ($\mu g\,N_2O\,m^{-2}\,h^{-1}$)	min. N_2O	max. N_2O	average CH_4 flux ($mg\,CH_4\,m^{-2}\,h^{-1}$)	min. CH_4	max. CH_4	average CO_2 flux ($mg\,CO_2\,m^{-2}\,h^{-1}$)	CO_2 min	CO_2 max	Notes
Roobroek et al. 2010	Carex appopinquata Peucedanum palustre	FW, F	Biebrza, Poland	2.1 (0.3)						35(3)			Tussock
		FW, F	Biebrza, Poland	-3.0 (0.1)						21(9)			Hollows
		FW, F	Biebrza, Poland	2.7 (0.4)						36(9)			Tussock +1N nitrate
		FW, F	Biebrza, Poland	16 (2.9)						20(8)			Hollows + 0.1N nitrate
Hopfensperger et al. 2009		FW, RP, FST	USA New York	5.4 (2.8)		10		-0.06	0.15		37	367	
Moseman-Valtierra et al. 2011	Spartina patens	C, SM, +N	USA(MA)	71 (24)	0	224	0.14 (0.1)	0	0.56				Transparent chambers + 300 µM nitrate
		C, SM	USA(MA)	-6 (8)	-94	56	0.05 (0.05)	-0.24	0.32	380 (47)			Controls, dark and transparent chambers

Reference	Species	Habitat	Location	191 (74)	4	410	0.3(0.1)	0	0.64	380 (158)			Dark chambers + 300 μM nitrate
Moseman-Valtierra et al in prep.	Spartina patens	C, SM, +N	USA(MA)	191 (74)	4	410	0.3(0.1)	0	0.64	380 (158)			
		C, SM	USA(MA)	1.81(12.1)	-18.3	94	0.01 (0.004)	-0.04	0.1	294 (117)	100	425	fertilized marsh
		C, SM	USA(MA)	2.37(2.4)	0.0	9	0.01 (0.007)	0	0.03	163 (127)	37	314	reference marsh, see Deegan et al. 2007
Hirota et al. 2007	Carex rugulosa, Phragmites australis	C, SM	Japan	20	-10	60		91	245		-320	-23	
		C, SM	Japan	-10	-30	1			35			725	
		SAND	Japan	30	20	50		0.01	0.34		14	75	
Ferron et al. 2007		C, CRK	Spain		44	114		0.02	0.1		134	325	
Magenheimer et al. 1996		C, SM	USA east coast				0.1	0.01	0.5	104	13	154	
DeLaune et al. 1983		C, BRK	USA east coast						11.1				
Kristensen et al. 2008		MNG, FST	Tanzania					0.00	0.06		51	211	
		MNG, CRK	Tanzania					0.01	0.1		2	11	high tide
		MNG, CRK	Tanzania					0.07	0.2		55	147	low tide
Morris and Whiting 1985		C, SM	USA east coast (North Inlet, SC)				0.4			226 (46)			

Minimum and maximum values are included if provided by the sources. The key to the wetland descriptions, which are based on respective authors' evaluations of their field sites, is as follows: FW=Freshwater, C= Coastal, SM= salt marsh, BRK= Brackish marsh, CRK= Tidal creek, F=fen, FST= Forested, RV=Riverine, RP= Riparian, G=grassland, FT= Flat, B=Boreal, +N= Fertilized with nitrogen, SAND=sandy.

Table 3. Average methane fluxes in marshes (with standard errors in parentheses)

Source	Dominant plant(s)	Wetland description	Location	Average CH$_4$ flux (mg CH$_4$ m^{-2} h^{-1})	min. CH$_4$	max. CH$_4$	Notes
Bartlett et al. 1987	S. alterniflora	C, SM	USA Chesapeake Bay	2.1 (0.66)	1.9		
	S. alterniflora and S. cynosuroides	C, BRK	USA Chesapeake Bay	2.6 (0.39)			
	S. cynosuroides	C, BRK	USA Chesapeake Bay	0.6 (0.08)		11	
DeLaune et al. 1983		C, BRK	USA (Louisiana)	0.7			salinity 18
		C, BRK	USA (Louisiana)	11.1			salinity 1.4
		C, BRK	USA (Louisiana)	24.3			salinity 0.4
Ding et al. 2005	Carex muliensis, Carex meyeriana	FW	China	3.0	0.16	10	
	Carex spp.	FW	China	19.6	1.18	55	
Flury et al. 2010	Phragmites australis	FW	Switzerland		0.1	20	

Source	Species	Wetland type	Country				Notes
Sha et al. 2011	Not reported but see Altor and Mitsch 2006	FW, RV	Switzerland		0.3	86	
		FW, CRT	Switzerland		0.02	20	
		FW, OX	Switzerland		-0.04	0.1	
Kankaala et al. 2004	Phragmites australis	B, LK	Finland		0.5	49	
	Typha latifolia and Phragmites australis	B, LK	Finland		1.3	47	
	Typha latifolia and Phragmites australis	B, LK	Finland		1.4	19	
VanDerNat and Middleberg 2000	Scirpus lacustris	BRK	Belgium	0.5			
	Phragmites australis	BRK	Belgium	9			
Mitsch et al. 2010	Not reported	TROP	Costa Rica	60			Seasonally flooded tropical site
	Raphia taedigera	TROP	Costa Rica	7 to 15			Humid tropical site

Minimum and maximum values are included where they have been provided by the sources. The key to the wetland descriptions, which are based on authors' evaluations of their field sites, is as follows: FW=Freshwater, C= Coastal, SM= salt marsh, BRK= Brackish marsh, CRK= Tidal creek, F=fen, FST= Forested, RV=Riverine, RP= Riparian, G=grassland, FT= Flat, B=Boreal, +N= Fertilized with nitrogen, SAN D= sandy intertidal.

Table 4. Conceptual summary of impacts of several environmental factors on N₂O production (via aerobic and anaerobic processes), N₂O consumption, and CH₄ production and consumption in marsh soils

Environmental factor	Aerobic N2O production (nitrification)	Anaerobic N2O production (incomplete Denitrification)	N2O consumption (complete denitrification)	Methane production	Methane consumption
Reactive N	+	+	+/0	+/0	-
oxygen	+	-/+	-	-	+
Water level (inundation)	-	-/+	+	+	-
Salinity	-?	-?	-	-/+??	?
Sulfate/Sulfide	?	+	-?	-/+?	+?
Temperature	+	+	+?	+	+?

"+" indicates a positive relationship, "-" denotes a negative relationship. "?" indicates cases where relationships are unclear due to lack of investigation or contradictory results thus far.

Among the papers reviewed, the largest N_2O fluxes have been found in systems in which anthropogenic N loading is occurring (Hefting et al. 2003, Table 1; Moseman-Valtierra et al. 2011 and Ferron et al 2007 in Table 2). In un-enriched fresh and coastal marshes, N_2O emissions are generally low, and even negative, while significant positive N_2O fluxes are found in N enriched marshes (discussed further below). Although marshes are replaced by mangroves at lower latitudes, and mangroves are not included in this review, there is generally a lack of measurements of greenhouse gas emissions in tropical coastal ecosystems, as discussed elsewhere (Dalal and Allen 2009). Most studies have not yet been able to attribute the N_2O fluxes to specific microbial sources, although the importance of various N transformation is known to vary with water content of the soils (Hou et al. 2011, Dalal and Allen 2009), as described further below.

CH_4 emissions from marshes (in Tables 2 and 3) show a considerable range in magnitudes both across and within marshes. The prevalent notion that salt marshes constitute small sources of methane relative to their freshwater counterparts is not always consistently supported. Within an estuarine system, CH_4 fluxes from marshes do show inverse relationships with salinity (Bartlett et al. 1987, DeLaune et al. 1983, Table 3) but across marshes, several freshwater systems show small methane emissions (Sha et al. 2011, Hopfensperger et al. 2009) including tropical mangroves (Kristensen et al. 2008, Table 2), while some notably high CH_4 fluxes have been measured in coastal salt marshes (Hirota et al. 2007, DeLaune et al. 1983).

Many environmental factors co-vary in space and time in dynamic marsh environments. The following section will address some of the key factors that affect greenhouse gas emissions from marshes, with the understanding that isolating the influence of a single variable is challenging, and that many factors interactively influence the biogeochemistry and ecology of marshes. A summary of the general relationships between the discussed environmental factors and production or consumption of N_2O and CH_4 is provided in Table 4.

ROLES OF ANTHROPOGENIC N LOADING ON GHGS IN MARSHES

A recent review of greenhouse gas (GHG) emissions from more than 100 studies in terrestrial ecosystems revealed that although anthropogenic N enrichment increases the terrestrial C sink, it stimulates CH_4 and N_2O

emissions to an extent that can largely offset that effect in multiple ecosystems (Liu and Greaver 2009). Global N_2O emissions from aquatic ecosystems were estimated to be 1.9 Tg N yr^{-1}, using nitrification and denitrification rates from rivers, estuaries, and continental shelves along with models of N loading from 177 watersheds (Seitzinger and Kroeze 1998). These estimates were based on measurements of $N_2O:N_2$ ratios produced by denitrification in mesocosms with estuarine sediments exposed to different N loading rates (Seitzinger and Nixon 1985). In that estuarine study, $N_2O:N_2$ ratios were found to increase linearly with N loading over a range of 100 µmol N m^{-2} h^{-1} to 3645 µmol N m^{-2} h^{-1} (Seitzinger and Nixon 1985). In many estuarine sediments, $N_2O:N_2$ ratios are generally within 0.1-0.5%, with highest ratios (about 6%) observed in heavily polluted sediments (Seitzinger and Kroeze 1998). This ratio is significant because it indicates the extent to which denitrification is completed, and if there are large increases in the production of the greenhouse gas N_2O relative to the unreactive gas N_2 in ecosystems with high rates of denitrification, then they may have significant feedbacks on climate.

Notably, no specific estimates of marsh contribution to global N_2O emissions have been made. Relatively few studies have actually measured impacts of anthropogenic N loading on GHG fluxes or $N_2O:N_2$ ratios of gases emitted from marshes, despite their key roles in water purification as they intercept nutrient loads in rivers, run-off, groundwater, and atmospheric deposition. In salt marsh sediments, the ratio of $N_2O:N_2$ produced by denitrification has been observed to vary greatly, between 5% and 50%, (Lee et al. 1997). The lowest ratio (<5%) was observed in sediments collected from a salt marsh experiencing the highest inputs of 624 kg N ha^{-1} yr^{-1} (Lee et al. 1997). This pattern of decreasing $N_2O:N_2$ ratios in marshes with increasing N loads, suggests that although N_2O production increases with NO_3^- loading, the release of N_2O relative to N_2 may decrease. N loads in this study varied by an order of magnitude (with maximal rates in Childs River, MA) and lowest at Sage Lot Pond, Waquoit Bay (MA) where N loads were estimated to be only 64 kg N ha^{-1} y^{-1} (Lee et al. 1997). More research is needed to understand what controls the tremendous variability in N_2O yields in coastal ecosystems and to ascertain what factors besides N may make the $N_2O:N_2$ ratio vary greatly in marshes in particular.

Methane emissions show less of a clear response to nitrogen inputs. In an experimental nitrate enrichment experiment within a freshwater marsh, no change in methane emissions was observed, although high variability in diffusive and ebullitive fluxes was noted (Flury et al. 2010). However, ammonium is known to be able to inhibit methane oxidation in soils and cultures (Conrad 1996, Steudler et al. 1989). The mechanism for this inhibition involves similarities of the enzyme that catalyzes methane oxidation (methane monooxygenase) with ammonium monooxygenase (used by nitrifying bacteria). Ammonium can be oxidized via the methane monooxygenase enzyme, and if it does so, then it decreases enzymes available for methane oxidation (Bodelier and Laanbroek 2004). Nitrifying bacteria are known to be able to oxidize methane at atmospheric concentrations, and that activity declines at ammonium concentrations equivalent to or higher than those present in temperate forest soils (Steudler et al. 1989). Additional studies are needed to determine conditions under which such an inhibition of methane oxidation may exist in marshes, but it is important for understanding what controls the size of methane sinks (and therefore the magnitude of methane sources) of these ecosystems. Possibly, ammonium inhibition of methane oxidation is restricted to marshes created for wastewater treatment and microniches in which ammonium concentrations are quite high (Laanbroek 2010).

Principal factors influencing the extent to which N_2O and other greenhouse gas emissions vary in response to N loading include the magnitude and duration of the N inputs to marsh ecosystems. Experimental nitrate pulses (single additions equivalent to 1.4 g N m^{-2}) added to *Spartina patens* marsh plots were found to significantly increase N_2O fluxes over 3 dates (Moseman-Valtierra et al 2011, Table 2). As control (unfertilized plots) and background N_2O fluxes were consistently low or negative, the addition of nitrate (at levels comparable to highly enriched groundwater that is found in anthropogenically-impacted estuaries in region) constituted a shift of the wetland sediments from sinks of N_2O to sources of N_2O in response to this short-term fertilization. In sediment cores collected from hollows of a *Carex appoprinquata*-dominated fen, single nitrate amendments (at levels near daily atmospheric nitrate deposition) changed hollows from sinks to sources of N_2O as well. Responses to nitrate additions produced only a minor increase in N_2O in cores collected from tussocks of the same site, which was thought to be due to the influence of plant roots in competing more strongly for mineral N in those sediments than in those collected from relatively bare hollows (Roobroeck et al. 2010).

Responses of sediments to pulsed nutrients may differ substantially from those to chronic N inputs for several reasons. Microbial responses to pulse nutrients may reflect changes in enzymatic activities, while population sizes and possibly community composition may shift over time periods involved in chronic N loading or other long term changes such as land use regimes (Ma et al. 2008). Further, plant competition may limit microbial responses to nutrient inputs over short terms, but over longer periods of time, chronic N loads can cause shifts in plant community composition, or diminish plant biomass allocation belowground (Langley et al. 2009), which could reduce the extent of interaction or competition between microbes and plants. Chronic nutrient loading may also lead to shifts in many environmental properties that indirectly influence microbial responses to nitrogen inputs, such as oxygen levels, oxidation-reduction potential of soils, and marsh elevation or inundation levels if chronic nutrient loading contributes to marsh subsidence.

Chronic nitrogen loading currently affects many ecosystems, and thus its impact on marsh biogeochemistry and greenhouse gas emissions needs to be better understood. Exceptionally high N_2O fluxes were observed in chronically nitrate-loaded riparian buffer zones, where nitrous oxide fluxes in forested zones (dominated by *Alnus glutinosa*) with higher nitrate concentrations (23-30 mg N L^{-1}) in groundwater exceeded those in grassland buffer zones (with *Glyceria maxima*) with lower nitrate concentrations (4-9 mg N L^{-1}) (Hefting et al. 2003, Table 1). Similarly, in Narragansett Bay, RI, soil respiration rates were found to significantly increase across salt marshes experiencing a gradient of watershed nitrogen loads (from 10 kg N ha^{-1} y^{-1} to 6727 kg N ha^{-1} y^{-1}) (Wigand et al. 2009). In *Spartina alterniflora* zones of these marshes, surface soils declined in %C and %N content as respiration rates increased, suggesting that some of the labile organic matter in these soils was being turned over by microbial activities (Wigand et al. 2009). However, in contrast to studies of pulsed nutrient inputs, nitrous oxide fluxes in a chronically fertilized *S. patens* marsh with more than 7 years of experimental fertilization via enrichment of tidal creek waters (Deegan et al. 2007) did not significantly differ from an adjacent reference (unfertilized) marsh (Moseman-Valtierra et al. in prep., Table 2).

Physical factors of the environment may constrain impacts of chronic nutrient loading on marshes. The heavily nutrient-loaded Child's River in Cape Cod, MA, which is enriched by septic tank effluent, was found to be supersaturated with N_2O in surface waters, but due to stratification of the water, benthic sediments displayed consumption of N_2O in most flux measurements and were thought to have only limited exposure to nitrate-rich surface waters (LaMontagne et al. 2003). Likewise, if hydrological and physical characteristics of rivers or estuaries constrain the extent of interaction between nutrient-rich water and marsh soils, then emissions of N_2O may not be significantly enhanced (Groffman et al. 1998).

Recognizing the extent of anthropogenic alteration of greenhouse gas fluxes will be important in marshes that have high nutrient loads. Significant

N_2O fluxes were estimated from a salt marsh in Spain, in which fish farm effluent was draining into the tidal creek (Ferron et al. 2007). Groundwater in coastal and riparian marshes is frequently found to have high concentrations of N_2O and CH_4 (Kroeger et al. in prep., Groffman et al. 1998), as well as high levels of anthropogenic N (Kroeger et al. 2006, Kroeger et al. 2007), and when it intercepts marshes, it can be difficult to determine whether the gases were produced in marsh sediments or subterranean groundwater (Groffman et al. 1998). Recognizing the site of production would be a key first step in mitigating the emissions. Tropical coastal margins, where marshes may be largely replaced by mangrove forests, may face particularly high levels of N loading due to rapid urban growth and large human populations. In the Adyar River in SE India, organic rich and ammonium-enriched regions were found to have high methane and nitrous oxide fluxes, with annual estimates being equivalent in global warming potential to one month of CO_2 emissions from motor vehicles in the region (Rajkumar et al. 2008).

Summary

Some of the highest N_2O fluxes have been observed in marsh ecosystems with significant N loading, and they are sufficient to substantially offset C sinks (as observed in several other ecosystems) (Liu and Greaver 2009). Marshes show much wider ranges in $N_2O:N_2$ ratios produced by denitrification compared to other ecosystems, and impacts of N loading and other environmental factors on this ratio need to be better understood. Methane emissions in theory could be enhanced by higher ammonium levels, due to inhibition of methane oxidation, but field studies have not yet demonstrated this relationship. The magnitude and duration of anthropogenic N inputs exerts a considerable influence on net N_2O, CO_2, and CH_4 emissions, and the fundamental influence of human impacts on release of these greenhouse gases from marsh ecosystems should be recognized. In particular, shifts in GHG fluxes need to be compared to changes in net C sequestration (that may also vary in response to anthropogenic N loading), in order to estimate potential net feedbacks of marshes on global climate change.

OXYGEN AND WATER INUNDATION

Tidal inundation influences the extent and depth to which oxygen penetrates marsh soils. Nutrient enrichment of tidal or groundwater inputs (discussed above) can result in hypoxic or anoxic conditions via eutrophication, and nutrient loading may possibly exacerbate physical limitations (such as tidal inundation) on oxygen availability in marshes. Photosynthetic activities of plants and other primary producers (micro- and macroalgae, cyanobacteria) introduce oxygen to marsh soils (in mats on the sediment surface or deeper in plant rhizospheres, see "Plant Influences"). These photosynthetic activities respond to changes in light levels on diel and seasonal time scales. Animal burrows and tubes and biogenic irrigation activities (associated with feeding) can also increase the depth to which oxygen penetrates marsh soils as well as increase the area of oxic-anoxic boundaries across which nutrients and other solutes are exchanged (Kristensen and Kostka 2005, Figure 1). These are the microenvironments in which microbial respiration, potentially yielding or consuming greenhouse gases, takes place.

Oxygen is commonly manipulated in laboratory experiments to test its influence on N_2O emissions. For example, the oxygen content of purging gas used in experiments with fen soil cores was found to significantly affect N_2O emissions (Roobroeck et al. 2010). Among soils purged with no O_2, 1%, or 5% O_2, N_2O production was greatest in soils with the highest amount of oxygen, regardless of soil type (Roobroeck et al. 2010), and this was attributed to the inhibition of nitrous oxide reductase by oxygen (McKenney et al. 1994).

In the field, several studies have supported relationships between oxygen availability and nitrous oxide emissions, due to the influence of oxygen on nitrification and/or denitrification rates. Oxygen is known to be a proximal controller of denitrification, although direct measurements of oxygen in the environment have been limited (Burgin et al. 2010). Differences in oxygen availability were used to explain higher N_2O emissions found at night than during the day in estuarine sediments using closed chamber techniques (Jensen et al. 1984). Parallel studies had shown maximal denitrification rates in these sediments at night when oxygen-generating photosynthetic activities ceased (Andersen et al. 1984, Jensen et al. 1984). Thus denitrification was thought to be the major source of N_2O emissions from these sediments (Jensen et al. 1984). The aerobic process of nitrification, on the other hand, has been thought to only be possible in soils with oxidation-reduction potentials above 200 mV (Wanderborght and Billen 1975), which has been used to explain the limited vertical distribution of nitrification to the top cm of intertidal sediment cores (Hou et al. 2007), although marsh sediments *in situ* will have more complexity due to the influence of plants and animals. Positive relationships between nitrous oxide consumption in coastal sediments and oxygen uptake (measured in terms of flux rates, La Montagne et al. 2002) were observed and attributed to use of N_2O as an electron acceptor during hypoxic conditions (LaMontagne et al. 2003). Thus fully anaerobic conditions seemed to favor the most complete denitrification of nitrate to N_2. Likewise, in a freshwater wetland, N_2O fluxes were higher in *Deyeuxia* marsh plots with no water logging than in seasonally waterlogged plots (Yu et al. 2007). Although neither were major sources of N_2O, the seasonally waterlogged marsh plots acted as sinks of N_2O, in contrast to the plots that were not water logged (which were always net sources of N_2O). Several studies have suggested that because wetland soils are less dry (and less oxic) than other aerated soils, N_2O fluxes may be smaller because denitrification proceeds more completely with a larger percent of N_2O going to N_2 (Yu et al. 2010, Lindau et al. 1991, Samuelsson 1985, Schiller and Hastie 1994, Smith et al. 1983).

Oxygen is also strongly related to methane production and emissions in marshes, given that methanogenesis is an anaerobic process. When oxygen is introduced to marsh sediments by plant roots or animal burrows and tubes, it sustains alternative electron acceptors in the sediment that can be used in mineralization and thereby represses methanogenesis (reviewed in Laanbroek 2010). Methane emissions have shown diel variation (Kaki et al. 2001). Also, methane fluxes have been found to be higher in continuously inundated zones of a created freshwater marsh than zones with pulsed flooding (Altor and Mitsch 2008). In field measurements, dissolved methane concentrations in marsh water and ebullition of methane from the sediment of a *Phragmites australis* freshwater marsh were both negatively related to water column dissolved oxygen (Flury et al. 2010). Further, methane release from these marsh sediments was suggested to form a positive feedback in which dissolved oxygen was reduced in the water column above the marsh, thereby reducing oxygen fluxes into the sediment where methane was formed, which could positively influence methane production (Flury et al. 2010).

Manipulations of soil inundation regimes offer indirect tests of the effects of oxygen on CH_4 and N_2O production. Mesocosms with *S. alterniflora* plants in salt marsh sediments that were permanently inundated produced higher CH_4 fluxes than others which were only intermittently inundated (Ding et al. 2010). In this experiment, inundation was sustained for one growing season and did not significantly affect plant biomass or stem density, but it did significantly reduce sediment redox potential (Ding et al. 2010). Therefore, the increase in CH_4 fluxes from inundated sediments was attributed to a favorable (reduced) environment for methanogenesis. In contrast, at least one study found that periodically inundated *S. alterniflora* mesocosms released more CH_4 (7-86% more) than permanently inundated mesocosms (Cheng et al. 2007). However, the standing water in mesocosms of that study was 10 cm, in contrast to the 5 cm depth maintained by Ding et al. (2010), and the difference in results may have been in part due to the role of water in acting as a barrier of gases, slowing their diffusion to the atmosphere (Cheng et al. 2007), rather than a fundamental difference in response to oxygen availability. In a core-based test of the impact of inundation on N_2O in intertidal sediments, highest N_2O concentrations were observed in reflooded sediments following a 10day period of emersion (under a ventilating fan) rather than in those with long term (5 day) immersion or emersion (10 days) alone. These time periods reflected average periods of immersion during spring tides in high intertidal flats. Measurements of nitrification and denitrification rates in these cores revealed that during emersion, most N_2O was produced by the former, while during immersion the latter process dominates (Hou et al. 2007), which is consistent with the control of oxygen availability on both processes. Nitrate concentrations were also highest in the reflooded sediments than in other treatments. As in intertidal sediments, moisture levels strongly mediate the sources of observed N_2O fluxes from soils, with N_2O coming predominantly from nitrification up to a threshold of about 65% water-filled pore space in soils (Dalal and Allen 2009, Dalal et al. 2003.). Combinations of isotopic enrichments and inhibition techniques have been applied successfully in silt loam soils, showing that denitrification can account for all of N_2O with 70% water filled pore spaces, but that nitrification can account for up to 81% of all N_2O emitted from soils with only 60% water filled pore spaces (Bateman and Baggs 2005). Such techniques seem to remain to be applied in marsh sediments.

Effects of oxygen on greenhouse gas emissions have also been inferred from manipulations of light levels. In contrasts of transparent (light) and opaque (dark) chambers, N_2O consumption (via denitrification) was significantly less in transparent (light) chambers placed over unvegetated coastal sediments than in opaque (dark) chambers (LaMontagne et al. 2003). This is in contrast however to observations of higher N_2O fluxes (and thus less consumption) in opaque rather than transparent chambers within a *S. patens* marsh during a short-term nitrate enrichment experiment (Moseman-Valtierra et al. 2011). Possibly the presence of plants in the latter study, which would compete more strongly with microbes for nitrogen in the presence of light, explains why N_2O fluxes were lower than they were in opaque chambers. In the case where plants are absent and thus microbes may have less competition for nutrients, oxygen may exert a stronger influence on N_2O fluxes than nitrogen availability.

Summary

Oxygen may stimulate N_2O production from aerobic processes (nitrification), which due to coupling with denitrification in many coastal marshes, may indirectly favor anaerobic N_2O production as well (Table 4). However, as oxygen levels increase, overall rates of denitrification (an anaerobic process) decline. Under completely anoxic conditions, denitrification tends to proceed completely to N_2 rather than N_2O (Table 4). Therefore, intermediate levels of oxygen likely result in highest N_2O fluxes. The relationship of methane to oxygen is simpler, as oxygen inhibits methanogenesis but promotes methane oxidation (Table 4).

PH

The pH level of marsh soils can be a function of oxygenation and inundation, with pH decreasing as oxygen levels decline and sulfide compounds accumulate, and pH is known to strongly influence greenhouse gas emissions from soils. Historical legacies of nutrient enrichment or acidification from atmospheric inputs to aquatic ecosystems can also influence pH levels in riparian and coastal marshes (Monteith et al., 2007, Fenner et al. 2011).

Due to the influence of pH on microbial nitrogen transformations, it may alter N_2O emissions. In soils, pH is known to affect overall rates of denitrification as well as the ratio of $N_2O:N_2$ produced by denitrification (Cuhel and Simek 2011, Simek and Cooper 2002). Based on studies of cultures of denitrifiers, optimal denitrification rates have been found near neutral pH (Van Den Heuvel 2011, Tomsen et al. 1994) while the portion of N_2O produced by denitrification has been seen to increase as pH declines (Van den Heugel et al. 2010, Thomsen et al. 1994). Likewise, in soils, higher denitrification rates have been found in alkaline soils than in acidic ones, while the fraction of gaseous product represented by N_2O (relative to $N_2O + N_2$) was highest in acidic soils (Cuhel and Simek 2011). The increase in proportion of

N_2O produced in denitrification has been attributed to negative effects of low pH (at values of pH=5) on genes for nitrite reductase (*nir*S) and nitric oxide reductase (*cnor*B) Saleh-Lakha *et al.* 2009) and is thought to involve a post-transcriptional mechanism (Liu *et al.* 2010). In organic-rich and nitrate-amended riparian soils, a longer period of N_2O production was observed in slurries with pH values adjusted to 4 rather than slurries with pH values of 7 (Van den Heuvel 2011). These results were supported by field studies in the riparian site, where N_2O emissions were highest (comprising 77% of all N_2O emissions) in spots with pH ranging from 4-5 (with an overall site pH ranging from 3.9 to 6.6). However, not all field studies have shown the same relationships to pH (Cuhel et al. 2010, Bandibas *et al.* 1994), likely because multiple factors influence whether N_2O production translates into N_2O emissions, including changes in N_2O reduction and physical barriers of gas transport to the atmosphere (Van den Heuvel 2011). Interestingly, manipulations of pH in slurries of pasture soils revealed that current pH levels of soils affected ratios of N_2O: (N_2O+N_2) more strongly than historical pH conditions (which reflected different soil management regimes), although the latter showed significant relationships to potential denitrification (DEA) rates (Cuhel and Simek 2011). Further studies are needed to discern how pH changes differentially affect other nitrogen transformations and the source of N_2O emissions from marshes. Mechanistic understanding may necessitate characterization of the major microbial communities, as the diverse microbes involved in processes such as nitrification may show different responses to pH (i.e. Cao et al. 2011).

Methane emissions from marshes also show some relationships with pH. In contrast to N_2O, lower methane emissions have been found in northern acidic (pH<5.5) tundra ecosystems of Alaska than in relatively neutral (pH>6.5) southern ecosystems. As with N_2O, however, the importance of pH has not yet been isolated from other co-varying factors in these ecosystems. In particular, the northern tundra ecosystems also have less heat flux, shallower thaw depths, and smaller C sinks (Zona et al. 2011) than their southern counterparts. Nonetheless, within a recently re-flooded *Sphagnum* and *Juncus* wetland, methane and dissolved organic C "hotspots" were observed in sites with high pH values (pH 5.1 to 5.3) relative to other sites (pH 4.8 to 4.9) (Fenner et al. 2011). Also, on a smaller scale, pH was found to be higher in low centers of "polygons" in the Arctic tundra soils, and that corresponded to higher dissolved CO_2 levels in the wet surface soils. This counter-intuitive pattern was possibly caused by trapping of CO_2 by the water (which acted as a diffusion barrier) or by accumulation of vascular plant material in the center of the microtopographic structure which reduced redox (Zona et al. 2011). Negative relationships are known to exist between oxidation of soils and pH (Reddy and DeLaune 2008). Methane emissions were not measured in that particular study (Zona et al. 2011). Finally, the relationship between methane emissions and pH are known to vary between temperate and tropical wetlands (Inubushi et al. 2005). In a temperate wetland in Japan, where pH values ranged between 5 and 7, methane emissions were positively related to pH, but that was not the case in a tropical forested wetland in Indonesia where soils had been drained and the pH was less than 5 (Inubushi et al. 2005). Positive relationships between pH and methane emissions have been described also in Canadian wetlands (Valentine et al. 1994). In general, however, studies are needed to characterize the response of all major greenhouse gases to changes in pH, and manipulative approaches may be essential for understanding mechanism by which pH mediates greenhouse gas emissions.

Summary

The effect of pH varies for N_2O and CH_4 emissions in marshes. Denitrification, a major source of N_2O emissions from marsh soils, is highest at neutral pH, however the N_2O yield of denitrification (relative to N_2) increases in acidic pH conditions. Further studies need to determine how pH changes affect the variety of other nitrogen transformations that can produce N_2O emissions in marshes. For methane, in contrast, higher emissions have been observed in marshes (tundra) when pH is closer to neutral than in acidic soils. However, the positive relationship between pH and methane emissions is not observed in tropical wetlands where pH values were below 5. The lack of consistent relationships between pH and greenhouse gas emissions may thus involve differences in the ranges of pH between sites (and latitudes) and well as the influence of numerous co-varying factors (moisture, oxidation reduction potential) that also modify greenhouse gas emissions *in situ*.

SALINITY

Methane fluxes display strong inverse relationships with salinity in the porewater of marsh soils (Magenheimer et al. 1996) due to the dominance of sulfate-reducing bacteria over methanogens in saline waters. For this reason, methane fluxes from salt marshes have predominantly been considered to be negligible, based on relatively few *in situ* measurements (i.e. Ding et al 2004, Magenheimer et al. 1996). Nonetheless, methane fluxes from marshes have been found to be highly variable, often for reasons that are not well understood (Table 3). For example, in a salt marsh in the Bay of Fundy, the combination of salinity and water table position could only explain 29% of the variance in CH4 emissions (in contrast to CO_2 emissions for which 63% of variance could be correlated with aboveground plant biomass and water table position) (Magenheimer et al. 1996). Further, somet measurements of methane fluxes in salt marshes are not insignificant (Hirota et al. 2007, Table 2), and recent experiments suggest that responses of methane to salt water intrusion may be complex (Weston et al. 2011).

Salinity has a less direct effect on nitrous oxide fluxes. Concentrations of dissolved greenhouse gases in the tidal creek of a salt marsh receiving effluent from a fish farm were always highest during low tides (Ferron et al. 2007), which is when salinity levels tend to be lowest. However, that low salinity (reflecting freshwater input from the fish farm effluent) also coincides with higher nitrogen inputs to the marsh (Ferron et al. 2007), and thus the effect of salinity cannot be determined in isolation. Similar correlations of N_2O with low salinity and high nitrate concentrations have been described in numerous estuaries (Wang et al. 2009, LaMontagne et al. 2003, Barnes and Owens 1998). In laboratory studies with oligohaline estuarine sediment, cores incubated with higher salinity water were found to have higher ammonium fluxes than those with about 8-9 psu lower salinity levels (with overall salinity ranges between 0 and 19 psu), although N_2O fluxes were not measured. These differences were sustained for 6 days despite no overall difference in respiration rates between the salinity treatments (Giblin et al. 2010). Relationships between salinity and denitrification rates were observed on seasonal scales, with higher denitrification rates generally being found in spring than summer (Giblin et al. 2010). The opposite pattern was observed for dissimilatory nitrate reduction to ammonium, which was very low in the spring but higher in the summer, following patterns of salinity in the estuary (Giblin et al. 2010). Given the significant changes in estuarine nitrogen transformations in response to salinity shifts, further research ought to address the relative significance of DNRA, denitrification, and other nitrogen transformations as sources of N_2O in order to determine how temporal shifts in these processes affect overall N_2O emissions.

One particularly timely topic, as marshes along an estuarine gradient face rising sea levels, is the potential role of salinity and associated sulfate concentrations in what have historically been freshwater marshes. Strong potential exists for salt water intrusion to fundamentally alter the biogeochemistry of fresh marshes by increasing rates at which organic matter is mineralized by microbes (Weston et al. 2011). Contrary to the dogma that methane fluxes are low in saline marshes, an experimental test of salt water intrusion on tidal freshwater marsh soils resulted in a significant increase in CH_4 and CO_2 flux rates for periods of 5-6 months, respectively (Weston et al. 2011). By the end of that one year experiment, the total inorganic C flux (as CH_4 and CO_2) out of salt-water amended cores was about 37% greater than from freshwater cores. This increase in total inorganic C flux (as CO_2 and CH_4) out of the salt-water amended cores, representing salinity intrusion, than their freshwater counterparts (Weston et al. 2011). Although this is contrary to current understanding of the competitive interactions between methanogens and sulfate-reducing bacteria, the observed increase in CH_4 fluxes could potentially be explained by the presence of substrates, such as methanol and methylamines, that sulfate-reducing bacteria do not use, the abundance of organic substrates in general, or heterogeneity in distributions of various electron acceptors and donors in the sediments (Weston et al. 2011). Theoretically, declines in methane oxidation could have contributed to the enhanced CH_4 fluxes, but this process was not measured. Increases in sulfate (with salinity) might be expected to support anaerobic oxidation of methane (Conrad et al. 1996), although the significance of this process relative to aerobic oxidation pathways is not known. Notably, sediment cores were collected prior to plant emergence in the marsh (Weston et al. 2011), in order to focus on understanding microbial mediation of soil C mineralization, but the effects of salt water intrusion on marsh ecosystems and the net greenhouse gas emissions released from them will likely be significantly mediated by plant-microbe interactions (discussed further below). Another significant consequence of the increase in sulfide availability in freshwater marshes that accompanies salt water intrusion, is that sulfide is known to block complete denitrification (Seitzinger et al. 1983, Sorensen et al. 1980), and may thus result in increases in N_2O fluxes. A major potential mediator of such effects of sulfide on denitrifying organisms will be the availability of oxidized iron, which can ameliorate levels of sulfide that accumulate in marsh sediments (Kristensen and Kostka 2005).

Summary

N_2O production via aerobic processes shows negative relationships to salinity, as high N_2O concentrations are frequently observed in fresh portions of estuaries (with anthropogenic N inputs). However, in estuarine sediments, increases in salinity can increase NH_4^+ fluxes from sediments, which may indirectly promote nitrification, while denitrification rates were found to decline (Giblin et al. 2010). Work is needed to characterize the impacts of such salinity changes on N_2O fluxes, but hypothesized results are summarized in Table 4. Also, sulfide (which accompanies increases in salinity) is known to block complete denitrification, yielding higher N_2O fluxes (Table 4). For methane, increased salinity has conventionally been thought to inhibit methanogens, although recent work suggests that methane fluxes from the salt marshes can be substantial (Moseman-Valtierra et al. 2011, Table 2) and a laboratory study has found significant, prolonged increases in methane following increases in salinity (Weston et al. 2011). Methane consumption, on the other hand, is known to be linked in some cases to sulfate reduction in microbial consortia (Conrad 1996), although direct links to salinity are not well characterized and have not been isolated from impacts on methanogenesis.

TEMPERATURE

Because microbial respiration rates increase with higher temperatures (Kirwan and Blum 2011), greenhouse gas emissions that result from respiration would be reasonably expected to increase in response to warming of marshes. Several studies have documented seasonal patterns of respiration, methane (Sha et al. 2011, Hirota et al. 2007, Gross et al. 1993, Bartlett et al. 1987), and nitrous oxide fluxes in marshes (Moseman-Valtierra et al. 2011, Ferron et al. 2007) that are consistent with higher gas emissions in fall and summer months when temperatures are warmest. For instance, in riverine wetlands, methane emissions in fall and summer were significantly higher than winter or spring but did not significantly differ from each other (Sha et al. 2011). A significant positive relationship was observed overall between soil temperate and methane emissions in 3 of 4 wetlands studied (Sha et al. 2011) while it was not observed in a created oxbow wetland with low methane fluxes. The positive relationship between methane and temperature has been described repeatedly in prior studies (Kim et al. 1999, Chen et al. 2008, Nahlik and Mitsch 2010). Positive relationships have also been found between N_2O fluxes and either air or soil temperatures at 5 cm depths (Yu et al. 2007) in freshwater marshes. Soil temperatures in that marsh ranged from close to 0 °C to nearly 20 °C over the course of the year (Yu et al. 2007).

Preliminary studies have also shown that organic matter decomposition rates increase by about 20% per each degree of warming, which is about 6 times faster than observed stimulation of marsh productivity (Kirwan and Blum 2011), although no measurements were made of the greenhouse gases produced by that respiration. Surprisingly, an experimental warming of a freshwater *Phragmites australis* marsh found no effect of a 2.8-2.9 °C increase in water temperature. This temperature increase, though significant, is just a fraction of the range experienced over seasonal cycles in temperate marshes (which can range from 0 to 25 °C, as in Sha et al. 2011), which may explain the lack of relationship between temperature and methane, and the warming seemed to be maintained for just a few weeks at a time. However, other factors besides temperature (such as labile C availability) were suggested to have limited methanogenesis (Flury et al. 2010).

The effects of temperatures on greenhouse gas emissions may also manifest via freeze-thaw processes. In sediments of a freshwater marsh, a peak in N_2O emission was observed under low redox conditions (0 to -150 mV), and were attributed to freezing-thawing effects in the soil. Specifically, the ice layer above the marsh surface was thought to limit oxygen transport from the atmosphere to the soil, sealing an organic rich, anoxic layer beneath the surface, where denitrification could occur (Yu et al. 2007). N_2O is known to be able to be produced at temperatures around 0 °C (Sommerfeld et al. 1993), and some studies have found that N_2O at -4 °C is not different than that at 10-15 °C (Oquist et al. 2004). Thawing of soils then releases N_2O that has been stored beneath ice in unfrozen sub-surface soils (Bremner et al. 1980). Any impacts of freeze-thaw cycles on dissolved inorganic nitrogen or labile C availability would also affect nitrous oxide and possibly methane release from marsh soils.

Summary

Positive relationships have typically been found between temperature and net greenhouse gas fluxes in the field (Table 4), suggesting that over the time and space scales of those studies, that increases in temperature may stimulate microbial production more than microbial consumption of N_2O and CH_4. In part, some stimulation of gas fluxes may occur during thawing of ice, which physically releases gases from marsh soils. Experimental manipulations of temperature by just a few degrees Celsius have not significantly influenced methane emissions although few studies overall have been conducted.

PLANT INFLUENCES

Microbial communities that produce greenhouse gas emissions interact intimately with vascular plants. Plants release between 20-90% of methane emissions from wetlands (King et al. 1998). The interactions of macrophytes and soil microbial processes in methane emission from wetlands have been reviewed in detail elsewhere (Laanbroek 2010) and will be only briefly addressed here. The adaptations that have enabled plants to thrive in water saturated soils of wetlands, aerenchyma and internal gas lacunas, by transporting oxygen from the atmosphere to soils also play key roles in their abilities to facilitate transport of gases in the opposite direction (from soils to the atmosphere). In the wetland reed, *Phragmites australis*, advective methane transport was coarsely estimated to be comparable to ebullition rates (Flury et al. 2010). By oxygenating the soils, plants may also inhibit methanogenesis because the methane may be oxidized before it reaches the atmosphere (Laanbroek 2010). Oxygenation also replenishes alternative electron acceptors which fuels more energetically efficient (and more competitive) respiratory pathways in the marsh microbial communities (Laanbroek 2010). Specifically, iron cycling can be notably enhanced in plant rhizospheres and where this is the case, methane production is likely to be repressed. Potential iron reduction rates are higher in washed excised roots of freshwater plants (*P. cordata, S. eurycarpum*, and *T. latifolia*) than in salt marsh plants (*S. alterniflora*) and seagrasses (*Zostera marina*) (Laanroek 2010, King and Garey 1999). Iron-reducing bacteria are thought to outcompete methanogens and other heterotrophic bacteria (sulfate reducers) for the organic carbon in rhizospheres (Laanbroek 2010), although studies in wetlands suggest that recent photosynthetic products are less significant sources of C fueling methane production than those derived from plant litter (Megonigal et al. 1996, Juutinen et al. 2003, Laanbroek 2010). In Patuxuent River (Maryland) iron reduction rates were higher in tidal freshwater marshes dominated by *Peltandra virginica, Pontederia cordata*, and *Nuphar lutuem* than in brackish marshes with *S. alterniflora, S. patens*, and *Distichlis spicata* (Neubauer 2005). Active iron reduction, influenced by plant rhizosphere effects, translated into limited rates of methanogenesis within the freshwater marsh (Neubauer 2005).

Several studies have addressed the influence of plants by examining relationships between the presence or absence of vegetation and greenhouse gas emissions. When emergent vegetation was removed from one zone of an experimental freshwater marsh and compared to a zone with intact plants, no impact on methane emissions was observed (Altor and Mitsch 2008), however methane fluxes were positively related to net primary productivity in a naturally colonizing marsh (Sha et al. 2011). In mesocosm studies of a brackish marsh in China, *S. alterniflora* (an invasive) and native P. australis plants were both found to contribute significantly to methane emissions from soils (Cheng et al. 2007). Plant biomass and density was significantly correlated with CH_4 emissions, although methane fluxes did not differ between the species (Cheng et al. 2007). However, when plants of both species were clipped, N_2O emissions increased (Cheng et al. 2007). This suggests that plants can influence N_2O emissions via competition with microbes for nitrogen in marsh soils.

In general, plant species are known to vary in the magnitude of their rhizosphere effects, and therefore changes in plant community composition can influence the greenhouse gas emissions that they facilitate (Laanbroek 2010, Ding et al. 2005, Van der Nat and Middleburg 2000). For example, in comparisons of the effects of three freshwater marsh plants on methane emissions, cyperaceous plants (*Carex lasiocarpa* and *Carex meyeriana*) were found to have higher gas transport capacity than a gramineous plant (Deyeuxia angustifola) (Ding et al. 2005). Native plants differ in their effects on greenhouse gas emissions from invasive plants also. In mesocosm studies, the native plant of a coastal salt marsh in China, *Suaeda salsa*, was found to support much lower rates of methane emissions than Spartina alterniflora, which is invasive in that region (Zhang et al. 2010). Similar results were found for both CH_4 and N_2O emissions, which were higher in mesocosms of a brackish marsh with invasive *Spartina alterniflora* than a native, *Phragmites australis*. The main reason for these differences, in both studies, was higher plant biomass of *S. alterniflora* (Zhang et al. 2010). The plant biomass was thought to be related to more organic C for methanogens in the invaded marsh soil than in that with the native plant (Zhang et al. 2010). Enhancement of the biomass and stem density of *S. alterniflora*, via N addition, resulted in stimulation of CH_4 emissions by 71.7% (Zhang et al. 2010).

Although vascular plants stimulate greenhouse gas emissions through exudation of labile carbon, they might-alternatively- limit them via oxygenation of rhizospheres in cases where anaerobic processes dominate production of N_2O and CH_4. Research is needed to clarify which factors control the relative balance of these seemingly opposing processes.. In some cases, oxygenation can actually promote N_2O emissions, as in a wetland constructed for wastewater removal in which plant species stimulated nitrification to in their rhizospheres, with *Zizania latifolia* promoting more nitrification and N_2O emissions than *Phragmites australis* and *Typha latifolia* (Wang et al. 2008). Overall, the direction of plant impacts on GHG fluxes could be determined not only by plant species composition, but also by the physiological states of the plants, which can alter relative levels of oxygenation or C exudation (Lovell 2005). The net influence of plants on greenhouse gas emissions likely also depends upon the composition of microbial communities that reside in marsh sediments (including the prevalence of autotrophs versus heterotrophs) at a given time. Further studies are needed to describe the distribution and controls on microbial populations involved in production or consumption of methane and nitrous oxide. What seems clear is that, on successional time scales, marshes with more developed plant communities (and higher primary production) constitute bigger net sources of methane than those with less accumulated organic matter (Nahlik and Mitsch 2010), but it is less well known how N_2O emissions vary with marsh succession. The latter may depend mostly on anthropogenic N loading (discussed above). Thus the general relationship between plant productivity and the net global warming potential of marsh ecosystems is not yet clear.

Intriguingly, relationships between plant biomass or productivity metrics and greenhouse gas emissions may facilitate landscape-scale estimates of these emissions. For example, positive relationships between Typha biomass in brackish marshes and dissolved methane porewater concentrations have been proposed for use in remote sensing estimates of CH_4 (Gross et al. 1993). Successful implementation of such measurement approaches will require better understanding of the relationships between plant physiology and greenhouse gas emissions in marshes.

Compared to vascular plants, relatively fewer studies seem to have addressed the role of algae or epiphytes in mediating greenhouse gas emissions from marshes. Algae may have interesting indirect effects on greenhouse gas emissions by influencing oxygen levels of sediments, or contributing to organic C sources in marsh soils, particularly as algal litter is less refractory than that of vascular plants. In contrasts of chambers with and without algal mats, in coastal sediments influenced by anthropogenic nitrogen inputs, more N_2O consumption was found in the presence of algae

(LaMontagne et al. 2003). The hypoxic conditions created by the algal mat were thought to promote use of N_2O as an electron acceptor by microbes (completing denitrification) (LaMontagne et al. 2003). Epiphytes on macroalgal fronds have also been found to produce N_2O when exposed to high nitrate concentrations of 550-950 µM (Law et al. 1993). Microniches may exist in which nitrate concentrations occasionally reach those levels, perhaps if nutrient inputs from groundwater are sealed beneath algal mats, limiting dilution with overlying water. Also, epiphytes on dominant macrophytes were found to have comparable denitrification potentials to those measured in sediments (Bourgues and Hart 2007), which suggests that N_2O production might be notable by these organisms. In contrast, no known studies have documented strong links between algae and methane emissions in marshes.

FAUNAL INFLUENCES

Animals in marshes may directly constitute sources of greenhouse gases, although their largest effects may be via indirect influences associated with feeding activities that change the structure, texture, and chemical composition of marsh soils and sediments. In coastal sediments, burrowing macrofauna can reach sufficient densities to significantly contribute to N_2O emissions from sediments (Stief et al. 2009). Microbes in the guts of these animals were found to be major sources of N_2O emissions, and although similar studies are not known to have examined this for methane in marshes specifically, certainly methanogens thrive among gut microflora. In environments with high densities of macrofauna, gut microbes may rival or exceed their sedimentary counterparts as sources of greenhouse gases, but their overall contribution to fluxes in marshes and other wetlands remain to be quantified. In coastal sediments, bioirrigation activities of animals introduce oxygen into otherwise anoxic sediments, increasing the area and depth of oxic-anoxic boundaries across which nitrification and denitrification can be coupled (reviewed in Kristensen and Kostka 2005, Figure 1). Macrofauna also excrete ammonium, urea, and organic-rich deposits (of feces and pseudofeces) that fuel microbial populations in sediments, or tubes or burrows (Barnes and Owens 1998, Mermillod-Bloadin et al. 2008). High denitrification rates have repeatedly been found in sites with high densities of macrofauna (i.e. Barnes and Owens 1998), and these may be sources of N_2O.

For methane, oxic-anoxic boundaries may promote methane oxidation, thereby decreasing net CH_4 emissions relative to coastal sediments or marsh soils that are relatively depauperate of macrofauna. Swan foraging, for example, was found via field enclosures, to decrease methane production in freshwater temperate wetlands because the bioturbation increased methane oxidation rates while decreasing methanogenesis (Bodelier et al. 2006). The grazing activities may have a role in stimulating release of methane from sediments, however, which may partially compensate for the reduction in methane emissions due to those effects (Bodelier et al. 2006, Dingemans et al. 2011). The swans also indirectly diminished methane emissions by reducing the density of a fennel pondweed, *Potamogeton pectinatus*, which would have stimulated methane production via exudation of labile C (Bodelier et al. 2006). Although the swans had no effect on ammonium oxidation, activities of muskrats (grazing, burrowing, lodging construction), were found to stimulate potential net nitrogen mineralization and nitrification in a freshwater tidal marsh (Connors et al. 2000). The latter indicates that N_2O fluxes can potentially be affected by large grazers. In contrast to the effects of swans, methane and CO_2 emissions were found to be higher at low tides from tropical coastal sediments with fiddler crab burrows and mangrove pneumatophores (aerial roots) than they were in bare sediments (Kristensen et al. 2008), likely because these structures act as conduits through which the gases are released. Indirect trophic effects of animals on plants that mediate greenhouse gas emissions are also possible, although current work is needed to first better understand the mechanisms and magnitudes of direct effects of both plants and animals on these biogeochemical processes.

PREDICTIONS FOR THE FUTURE

Mechanistic understanding of greenhouse gas emissions from ecosystems is vital for predicting ways that management practices may help to ameliorate anthropogenic climate change and sustain marshes against multiple aspects of global change. As marshes continue to be considered for emerging carbon markets, incentives to maximize biological carbon sequestration will increase, along with the need to predict, monitor, and minimize losses of CO_2, N_2O, and CH_4 from marsh soils and waters to the atmosphere. Meanwhile, the microbial, plant, and animal communities in marshes may be shifting in response to biological invasions, warming climates, rising sea levels, salt water intrusion, and anthropogenic nitrogen inputs. Current research needs to address how these factors independently and interactively affect wetland communities and biogeochemical functions of marshes.

Anthropogenic perturbations to the global nitrogen cycle are likely to enhance greenhouse gas emissions from marshes, particularly CO_2 and N_2O, by stimulating respiration (Wigand et al. 2009) and denitrification rates in marsh soils (Moseman-Valtierra et al. 2011), as they have in numerous other ecosystems (Liu and Greaver 2009). In marsh soils that are highly ammonium enriched, methane emissions may also increase, if methane oxidation is inhibited, although the response may be constrained by pH (given that methane emissions are highest near neutral pH). Over the long periods in which most coastal ecosystems are experiencing eutrophication from anthropogenic N inputs, both plant and microbial communities can shift, which may change the magnitude of greenhouse gas emissions from particular marshes or zones, as well as they way that those gas fluxes vary with changing environmental conditions. One remaining challenge is predicting how much greenhouse gases will change in marshes in response to N loading is to specifically identify the microbial communities and particular pathways that are responsible for the emissions. Doing so may help to explain some of the remarkable heterogeneity observed in N_2O and CH_4 fluxes, for instance, particularly in chronically fertilized marshes (Moseman-Valtierra et al. in prep).

Although marsh community composition may be varying in response to anthropogenic N loading, the "face" of marshes is also rapidly changing as invasive species spread. Particularly in coastal marshes, biological invasions may dramatically alter the structure and function of the ecosystem, including greenhouse gas emissions. Studies reviewed above indicate that the massive, dominant invasive plants that are spreading in marshes tend to facilitate greater greenhouse gas emissions than the native species that they outcompete. Nutrient loading is known to facilitate several biological invasions (Bennett et al. 2011, Marton and Wasson 2008, Rickey and Anderson 2004) and thus as N loading is enhancing greenhouse gas production in soils, invasive plants may further promote transmission of those gases from anoxic muds to the atmosphere. Invasive animals, particularly those which generate biogenic structures, such as crabs or burrowing isopods, are also very likely to be changing greenhouse gas emissions, although more studies are needed to be able to quantify the extent and direction of those alterations. Hypoxic conditions in coastal sediments reduce the numbers and size of burrowing infauna (Diaz and Rosenberg 1999), which would minimize the oxygenated surface areas and lead to increases in sulfide, and possibly decreased in pH, in coastal marshes. This may increase N_2O emissions, due to incomplete denitrification, and favor methanogenesis via the loss of oxic microniches.

Further, as rising sea levels increase the extent and duration of marsh inundation they may reduce oxygen levels in marsh soils along lower elevation zones and increase the spatial extent of sulfate (and sulfide) along estuarine gradients, further stimulating greenhouse gas emissions (Larsen et al. 2011). Although more studies are needed to predict how sea level rise will affect marshes, in terms of shifting plant and animal communities, data thus far have surprisingly shown that increases in salinity can increase methane emissions from marsh soils and accelerate organic matter remineralization rates (Weston et al. 2011). Thus the carbon that is intended to be stored in wetlands may not be neatly sealed beneath the rising sea, but rather it may be emitted back to the atmosphere in the form of greenhouse gases, potentially exacerbating anthropogenic climate change.

To test hypotheses such as these, regarding the biogeochemical responses of marshes to complex environmental changes, interdisciplinary approaches and innovative technology are needed which can not only detect dynamic changes in greenhouse gas emissions but also quantify, manipulate, and model those gas fluxes. Automated sampling platforms that can simultaneously detect changes in CO_2, CH_4, and N_2O at high spatial and temporal resolutions will be required to constrain the heterogeneity of these greenhouse gas emissions from dynamic marsh ecosystems. Such systems need to be precise but also economical, so that resource managers can accurately assess impacts of restoration projects and other watershed management practices on greenhouse gas emissions. Although relatively few studies thus far have simultaneously quantified all 3 greenhouse gases in marshes, they do need to be measured together in order to ascertain the net global warming potential (GWP) of these ecosystems. Ideally these measurements would be coordinated, in tandem with climatic measurements and studies of C sequestration rates, across a range of marsh types through coordinated research networks that span latitudinal and climatic gradients. While challenging, this area of research offers a promising opportunity for scientists to think and work across spatial and temporal scales, explicitly considering the interactions of microbial cells with plant and animal assemblages in marshes that may ultimately exert influences on global climate.

REFERENCES

Altor, A. E.; Mitsch, W. J., Methane flux from created riparian marshes: Relationship to intermittent versus continuous inundation and emergent macrophytes. *Ecological Engineering* 2006, *28* (3), 224-234.

Andersen, T. K.; Jensen, M. H.; Sorensen, J., Diurnal-variation of nitrogen cycling in coastal marine sediments. 1. Denitrification. *Marine Biology* 1984, *83* (2), 171-176.

Andrews, J. E.; Burgess, D.; Cave, R. R.; Coombes, E. G.; Jickells, T. D.; Parkes, D. J.; Turner, R. K., Biogeochemical value of managed realignment, Humber estuary, UK. *Science of the Total Environment* 2006, *371* (1-3), 19-30.

Arp, D. J.; Stein, L. Y., Metabolism of inorganic N compounds by ammonia-oxidizing bacteria. *Critical Reviews in Biochemistry and Molecular Biology* 2003, *38* (6), 471-495.

Bange, H. W., Nitrous oxide and methane in European coastal waters. *Estuarine Coastal and Shelf Science* 2006, *70* (3), 361-374.

Barnes, J.; Owens, N. J. P., Denitrification and nitrous oxide concentrations in the Humber estuary, UK, and adjacent coastal zones. *Marine Pollution Bulletin* 1998, *37* (3-7), 247-260.

Bartlett, K. B.; Bartlett, D. S.; Harriss, R. C.; Sebacher, D. I., Methane emissions along a salt marsh salinity gradient. *Biogeochemistry* 1987, *4* (3), 183-202.

Bateman, E. J.; Baggs, E. M., Contributions of nitrification and denitrification to N2O emissions from soils at different water-filled pore space. *Biology and Fertility of Soils* 2005, *41* (6), 379-388.

Bennett, A. E.; Thomsen, M.; Strauss, S. Y., Multiple mechanisms enable invasive species to suppress native species. *American Journal of Botany* 2011, *98* (7), 1086-1094.

Bock, E., Schmidt, I., Stüven, R., Zart, D., Nitrogen loss caused by denitrifying *Nitrosomonas* cells using ammonium or hydrogen as electron donors and nitrite as electron acceptor. *Archives of Microbiology* 1995, 163, 16-20.

Bodelier, P. L. E.; Stomp, M.; Santamaria, L.; Klaassen, M.; Laanbroek, H. J., Animal-plant-microbe interactions: direct and indirect effects of swan foraging behaviour modulate methane cycling in temperate shallow wetlands. *Oecologia* 2006, *149* (2), 233-244.

Bodelier, P. L. E.; Laanbroek, H. J., Nitrogen as a regulatory factor of methane oxidation in soils and sediments. *Fems Microbiology Ecology* 2004, *47* (3), 265-277.

Bourgues, S.; Hart, B.T.H., Nitrogen removal capacity of wetlands: sediment versus epiphytic biofilms. Water Science & Technology 2007, 55 (4): 175–182.

Brauer et al. 2004. Brauer, S. L.; Yavitt, J. B.; Zinder, S. H., Methanogenesis in McLean Bog, an acidic peat bog in upstate New York: Stimulation by H-2/CO2 in the presence of rifampicin, or by low concentrations of acetate. *Geomicrobiology Journal* 2004, *21* (7), 433-443.

Bremner, J. M.; Blackmer, A. M.; Waring, S. A., Formation of nitrous oxide and dinitrogen by chemical decomposition of hydroxylamine in soils. *Soil Biology & Biochemistry* 1980, *12* (3), 263-269.

Buckley, D. H.; Baumgartner, L. K.; Visscher, P. T., Vertical distribution of methane metabolism in microbial mats of the Great Sippewissett Salt Marsh. *Environmental Microbiology* 2008, *10* (4), 967-977.

Burgin, A. J.; Groffman, P. M.; Lewis, D. N., Factors Regulating Denitrification in a Riparian Wetland. *Soil Science Society of America Journal* 2010, *74* (5), 1826-1833.

Cao, H. L.; Hong, Y. G.; Li, M.; Gu, J. D., Diversity and abundance of ammonia-oxidizing prokaryotes in sediments from the coastal Pearl River estuary to the South China Sea. *Antonie Van Leeuwenhoek International Journal of General and Molecular Microbiology* 2011, *100* (4), 545-556.

Cao, Y., Green, P.G., Holden, P.A., Microbial community composition and denitrifying enzyme activities in salt marsh sediments. *Applied and Environmental Microbiology* 2008, 74(2), 7585-7595.

Cabello P., Roldan M.D., Moreno-Vivian, C., Nitrate reduction and the nitrogen cycle in archaea. *Microbiology* 2004, 150(11), 3527-3546.

Chen, H.; Yao, S. P.; Wu, N.; Wang, Y. F.; Luo, P.; Tian, J. Q.; Gao, Y. H.; Sun, G., Determinants influencing seasonal variations of methane emissions from alpine wetlands in Zoige Plateau and their implications. *Journal of Geophysical Research-Atmospheres* 2008, *113* (D12).

Cheng, X. L.; Peng, R. H.; Chen, J. Q.; Luo, Y. Q.; Zhang, Q. F.; An, S. Q.; Chen, J. K.; Li, B., CH(4) and N(2)O emissions from *Spartina alterniflora* and *Phragmites australis* in experimental mesocosms. *Chemosphere* 2007, *68* (3), 420-427.

Chmura, G. L.; Anisfeld, S. C.; Cahoon, D. R.; Lynch, J. C., Global carbon sequestration in tidal, saline wetland soils. *Global Biogeochemical Cycles* 2003, *17* (4).

Connors, L. M.; Kiviat, E.; Groffman, P. M.; Ostfeld, R. S., Muskrat (Ondatra zibethicus) disturbance to vegetation and potential net nitrogen mineralization and nitrification rates in a freshwater tidal marsh. *American Midland Naturalist* 2000, *143* (1), 53-63.

Conrad, R., Soil microorganisms as controllers of atmospheric trace gases (H-2, CO, CH4, OCS, N2O, and NO). *Microbiological Reviews* 1996, *60* (4), 609-629.

Cuhel J., Simek, M., Proximal and distal control by pH of denitrification rate in a pasture soil. *Agriculture, Ecosystems and Environment* 2011, 141, 230-233.

Dalal, R.C.; Allen, D. E., Greenhouse gas fluxes from natural ecosystems. *Australian Journal of Botany* 2008, 56 (5), 369-407.

Das A., Justic, D., Swensen E., Turner, R.E., Inoue, M., and D. Park. 2011. Coastal land loss and hypoxia: the 'outwelling' hypothesis revisited. *Environmental Research Letters* 6: 025001. Doi: 10.1088/1748-9326/6/2/025001.

Deegan, L. A.; Bowen, J. L.; Drake, D.; Fleeger, J. W.; Friedrichs, C. T.; Galvan, K. A.; Hobble, J. E.; Hopkinson, C.; Johnson, D. S.; Johnson, J. M.; Lemay, L. E.; Miller, E.; Peterson, B. J.; Picard, C.; Sheldon, S.; Sutherland, M.; Vallino, J.; Warren, R. S., Susceptibility of salt marshes to nutrient enrichment and predator removal. *Ecological Applications* 2007, *17* (5), S42-S63.

De la Cruz, A. A. The role of tidal marshes in the productivity of coastal waters. *Assoc. Southeastern Biologists Bull.* 1973, 20: 147-156.

Delaune, R. D.; Smith, C. J.; Patrick, W. H., Methane release from Gulf-coast wetlands. *Tellus Series B-Chemical and Physical Meteorology* 1983, *35* (1), 8-15.

Diaz, R. J.; Rosenberg, R., Spreading dead zones and consequences for marine ecosystems. *Science* 2008, *321* (5891), 926-929.

Ding, W. X.; Zhang, Y. H.; Cai, Z. C., Impact of permanent inundation on methane emissions from a Spartina alterniflora coastal salt marsh. *Atmospheric Environment* 2010, *44* (32), 3894-3900.

Ding, W. X.; Cai, Z. C.; Tsuruta, H., Diel variation in methane emissions from the stands of Carex lasiocarpa and Deyeuxia angustifolia in a cool temperate freshwater marsh. *Atmospheric Environment* 2004, *38* (2), 181-188.

Ding, W. X.; Cai, Z. C.; Tsuruta, H., Plant species effects on methane emissions from freshwater marshes. *Atmospheric Environment* 2005, *39* (18), 3199-3207.

Dingemans, B. J. J.; Bakker, E. S.; Bodelier, P. L. E., Aquatic herbivores facilitate the emission of methane from wetlands. *Ecology* 2011, *92* (5), 1166-1173.

Drake, B. G.; Muehe, M. S.; Peresta, G.; GonzalezMeler, M. A.; Matamala, R., Acclimation of photosynthesis, respiration and ecosystem carbon flux of a wetland on Chesapeake Bay, Maryland to elevated atmospheric CO2 concentration. *Plant and Soil* 1996, *187* (2), 111-118.

Fenchel, T.; Blackburn, T.H., Bacteria and mineral cycling. Academic Press: New York, N, 1979. 225p.

Ferron, S.; Ortega, T.; Gomez-Parra, A.; Forja, J. M., Seasonal study of dissolved CH4CO2 and N2O in a shallow tidal system of the bay of Cadiz (SW Spain). *Journal of Marine Systems* 2007, *66* (1-4), 244-257.

Flury, S.; McGinnis, D. F.; Gessner, M. O., Methane emissions from a freshwater marsh in response to experimentally simulated global warming and nitrogen enrichment. *Journal of Geophysical Research-Biogeosciences* 2010, *115*.

Forster, P.; Ramaswamy, V.; Artaxo, P;, Berntsen, T.; et al., Changes in atmospheric constituents and in radiative forcing. In: Solomon, S.; Qin, D.; Manning, M.; Chen, Z.; et al., Eds.; Climate Change 2007: *The Physical Science Basis, Contribution of Working Group I to the Fourth Assessment Report of the Intergovernmental Panel on Climate Change;* Cambridge University Press: New York, NY, 2007.

Franklin, M.J.; Wiebe, W.; Whitman, W.B., Populations of methanogenic bacteria in a Georgia salt marsh. Applied and Environmental Microbiology 1988, 54(5), 1151-1157.

Giblin, A. E.; Weston, N. B.; Banta, G. T.; Tucker, J.; Hopkinson, C. S., The Effects of Salinity on Nitrogen Losses from an Oligohaline Estuarine Sediment. *Estuaries and Coasts* 2010, *33* (5), 1054-1068.

Gribsholt, B.; Struyf, E.; Tramper, A.; Andersson, M. G. I.; Brion, N.; De Brabandere, L.; Van Damme, S.; Meire, P.; Middelburg, J. J.; Dehairs, F.; Boschker, H. T. S., Ammonium transformation in a nitrogen-rich tidal freshwater marsh. *Biogeochemistry* 2006, *80* (3), 289-298.

Groffman, P. M.; Gold, A. J.; Jacinthe, P. A., Nitrous oxide production in riparian zones and groundwater. *Nutrient Cycling in Agroecosystems* 1998, *52* (2-3), 179-186.

Gross, M. F.; Hardisky, M. A.; Wolf, P. L.; Klemas, V., Relationships among *Typha* biomass, porewater methane, and reflectance in a Delaware (USA) brackish marsh. *Journal of Coastal Research* 1993, *9* (2), 339-355.

Hamersley, M.R.; Howes, B.L., Coupled nitrification-denitrification measured in situ in vegetated salt marsh sediments using a nitrogen-15 ammonium tracer. *Marine Ecology Progress Series* 2005, 299:123-135.

Hefting, M. M.; Bobbink, R.; de Caluwe, H., Nitrous oxide emission and denitrification in chronically nitrate-loaded riparian buffer zones. *Journal of Environmental Quality* 2003, *32* (4), 1194-1203.

Hirota, M.; Senga, Y.; Seike, Y.; Nohara, S.; Kunii, H., Fluxes of carbon dioxide, methane and nitrous oxide in two contrastive fringing zones of coastal lagoon, Lake Nakaumi, Japan. *Chemosphere* 2007, *68* (3), 597-603.

Hochstein, L. I.; Tomlinson, G.A., The enzymes associated with denitrification. *Annual Review of Microbiology 1988*, 42, 231-261.

Hopfensperger, K. N.; Gault, C. M.; Groffman, P. M., Influence of plant communities and soil properties on trace gas fluxes in riparian northern hardwood forests. *Forest Ecology and Management* 2009, *258* (9), 2076-2082.

Hou, L. J.; Liu, M.; Xu, S. Y.; Ou, D. N.; Yu, J.; Cheng, S. B.; Lin, X.; Yang, Y., The effects of semi-lunar spring and neap tidal change on nitrification, denitrification and N2O vertical distribution in the intertidal sediments of the Yangtze estuary, China. *Estuarine Coastal and Shelf Science* 2007, *73* (3-4), 607-616.

Huang, S. H.; Pant, H. K., Nitrogen transformation in wetlands and marshes. *Journal of Food Agriculture & Environment* 2009, *7* (3-4), 946-954.

Inubushi K., Otake S., Shibasaki N., Ali M., Itang A.M., and H. Tsuruta, Factors influencing methane emission from peat soils: Comparison of tropical and temperate wetlands. *Nutrient Cycling in Agroecosystems* 2005, 71, 93-99.

Islas-Lima, S.; Thalasso, F.; Gomez-Hernandez, J., Evidence of anoxic methane oxidation coupled to denitrification. Water Research 2004, 38, 13-16.

Jenkins, M. C.; Kemp, W. M., The coupling of nitrification and denitrification in 2 estuarine sediments. *Limnology and Oceanography* 1984, *29* (3), 609-619.

Jensen, H. B.; Jorgensen, K. S.; Sorensen, J., Diurnal-variation of nitrogen cycling in coastal, marine sediments. 2. Nitrous oxide emission. *Marine Biology* 1984, *83* (2), 177-183.

Jordan, T. E.; Andrews, M. P.; Szuch, R. P.; Whigham, D. F.; Weller, D. E.; Jacobs, A. D., Comparing functional assessments of wetlands to measurements of soil characteristics and nitrogen processing. *Wetlands* 2007, *27* (3), 479-497.

Juutinen, S.; Larmola, T.; Remus, R.; Mirus, E.; Merbach, W.; Silvola, J.; Augustin, JThe contribution of Phragmites australs slitter to methane

(CH4) emission in planted and non-planted fen microcosms. *Biology and Fertility of Soils* 2003, 38: 10-14.

Kankaala, P.; Ojala, A.; Kaki, T., Temporal and spatial variation in methane emissions from a flooded transgression shore of a boreal lake. *Biogeochemistry* 2004, *68* (3), 297-311.

Kaplan, W.; Valiela, I.; Teal, J.M., Denitrification in a salt marsh ecosystem. Limnology and Oceanography 1979, 24(4): 726-734.

Kaki, T.; Ojala, A.; Kankaala, P. Diel variation in methane emissions from stands of *Phragmites australis* (Cav.) Trin ex Steud. and *Typha latifolia* L. in a boreal lake. Aquatic Botany 2001, 71, 259-271.

Kim, J.; Verma, S. B.; Billesbach, D. P., Seasonal variation in methane emission from a temperate Phragmites-dominated marsh: effect of growth stage and plant-mediated transport. *Global Change Biology* 1999, *5* (4), 433-440.

King, G. M.; Garey, M. A., Ferric tron reduction by bacteria associated with the roots of freshwater and marine macrophytes. *Applied and Environmental Microbiology* 1999, *65* (10), 4393-4398.

King, J. Y.; Reeburgh, W. S.; Regli, S. K., Methane emission and transport by arctic sedges in Alaska: Results of a vegetation removal experiment. *Journal of Geophysical Research-Atmospheres* 1998, *103* (D22), 29083-29092.

Kirwan, M. L.; Blum, L. K., Enhanced decomposition offsets enhanced productivity and soil carbon accumulation in coastal wetlands responding to climate change. *Biogeosciences* 2011, *8* (4), 987-993.

Kool, D.M., Dolfing, J., Wrage N., Van Groenigen, J. W., Nitrifier denitrification as a distinct and significant source of nitrous oxide from soil. *Soil Biology & Biochemistry* 2011, 43, 174-178.

Konneke, M.; Bernhard, A. E.; de la Torre, J. R.; Walker, C. B.; Waterbury, J. B.; Stahl, D. A., Isolation of an autotrophic ammonia-oxidizing marine archaeon. *Nature* 2005, *437* (7058), 543-546.

Kristensen, E.; Flindt, M. R.; Ulomi, S.; Borges, A. V.; Abril, G.; Bouillon, S., Emission of $CO(2)$ and $CH(4)$ to the atmosphere by sediments and open waters in two Tanzanian mangrove forests. *Marine Ecology-Progress Series* 2008, *370*, 53-67.

Kristensen, E.; Kostka, J. E., Macrofaunal burrows and irrigation in marine sediment: microbiological and biogeochemical interactions. In Interactions between macro- and microorganisms in marine sediments; Kristensen, E.; Haese, R.R.; Kostka, J.E; Eds.; Coastal and Estuarine

Studies 60; American Geophysical Union: Washington D.C., 2005; pp. 125-158.

Kroeger, K. D.; Cole, M. L.; Valiela, I., Groundwater-transported dissolved organic nitrogen exports from coastal watersheds. *Limnology and Oceanography* 2006, *51* (5), 2248-2261.

Kroeger, K. D.; Swarzenski, P. W.; Greenwood, W. J.; Reich, C., Submarine groundwater discharge to Tampa Bay: Nutrient fluxes and biogeochemistry of the coastal aquifer. *Marine Chemistry* 2007, *104* (1-2), 85-97.

Laanbroek 2010 Laanbroek, H. J., Methane emission from natural wetlands: interplay between emergent macrophytes and soil microbial processes. A mini-review. *Annals of Botany* 2010, *105* (1), 141-153.

LaMontagne et al. 2003. LaMontagne, M. G.; Duran, R.; Valiela, I., Nitrous oxide sources and sinks in coastal aquifers and coupled estuarine receiving waters. *Science of the Total Environment* 2003, *309* (1-3), 139-149.

Langley, J.A., McKee, K.L., Cahoon, D.R., Cherry, J.A., Megonigal, J.P., 2009. Elevated CO2 stimulates marsh elevation gain, counterbalancing sea-level rise. Proceedings of the National Academy of Sciences of the United States of America 106 (15), 6182-6186.

Larsen, L.G.; Moseman, S.; Santoro, A.; Hopfensperger, K.; Burgin, A.J., Eco-DAS: A complex systems approach to predicting effects of sea level rise and N loading on N cycling in coastal wetland ecosystems. In: Proceedings of Ecological Dissertations in Aquatic Sciences, Kemp, P.; Ed.; Eco-DAS VIII; *American Society of Limnology and Oceanography*, 2010; 67-92. DOI: 10.4319/ecodas.2010.978-0-9845591-1-4.67

Law, C. S.; Rees, A. P.; Owens, N. J. P., Nitrous-oxide production by estuarine epiphyton. *Limnology and Oceanography* 1993, *38* (2), 435-441.

Lee, R. Y.; Joye, S. B.; Roberts, B. J.; Valiela, I., Release of N-2 and N2O from salt-marsh sediments subject to different land-derived nitrogen loads. *Biological Bulletin* 1997, *193* (2), 292-293.

Liikanen, A.; Silvennoinen, H.; Karvo, A.; Rantakokko, P.; Martikainen, P. J., Methane and nitrous oxide fluxes in two coastal wetlands in the northeastern Gulf of Bothnia, Baltic Sea. *Boreal Environment Research* 2009, *14* (3), 351-368.

Lindau, C. W.; Delaune, R. D., Dinitrogen and nitrous-oxide emission and entrapment in Spartina alterniflora salt marsh soils following addition of N-15 labeled ammonium and nitrate. *Estuarine Coastal and Shelf Science* 1991, *32* (2), 161-172.

Liu, D. Y.; Ding, W. X.; Jia, Z. J.; Cai, Z. C., Relation between methanogenic archaea and methane production potential in selected natural wetland ecosystems across China. *Biogeosciences* 2011, *8* (2), 329-338.

Liu, L. L.; Greaver, T. L., A review of nitrogen enrichment effects on three biogenic GHGs: the CO(2) sink may be largely offset by stimulated N(2)O and CH(4) emission. *Ecology Letters* 2009, *12* (10), 1103-1117.

Lomans, B. P.; Luderer, R.; Steenbakkers, P.; Pol, A.; van der Drift, A. P.; Vogels, G. D.; den Camp, H., Microbial populations involved in cycling of dimethyl sulfide and methanethiol in freshwater sediments. *Applied and Environmental Microbiology* 2001, *67* (3), 1044-1051.

Lovell, C.R, Belowground interactions among salt marsh plants and microorganisms. In *Interactions between macro- and microorganisms in marine sediments;* Kristensen, E.; Haese, R.R.; Kostka, J.E; Eds.; Coastal and Estuarine Studies 60; American Geophysical Union: Washington D.C., 2005; pp. 61-84.

Ma, W. K.; Bedard-Haughn, A.; Siciliano, S. D.; Farrell, R. E., Relationship between nitrifier and denitrifier community composition and abundance in predicting nitrous oxide emissions from ephemeral wetland soils. *Soil Biology & Biochemistry* 2008, *40* (5), 1114-1123.

Madigan, M. T.; Martinko, J. M., In *Brock Biology of Microorganisms;* Carlson, G.; Ed.; Pearson: Upper Saddle River, NJ,2006; 11th edition, pp.426-430.

Magenheimer, J. F.; Moore, T. R.; Chmura, G. L.; Daoust, R. J., Methane and carbon dioxide flux from a macrotidal salt marsh, Bay of Fundy, New Brunswick. *Estuaries* 1996, *19* (1), 139-145.

McKenney, D. J.; Drury, C. F.; Findlay, W. I.; Mutus, B.; McDonnell, T.; Gajda, C., Kinetics of denitrification by Pseudomonas fluorescens-oxygen effects. *Soil Biology & Biochemistry* 1994, *26* (7), 901-908.

Megonigal, J. P.; Faulkner, S. P.; Patrick, W. H., The microbial activity season in southeastern hydric soils. *Soil Science Society of America Journal* 1996, *60* (4), 1263-1266.

Mermillod-Blondin, F.; Lemoine, D.; Boisson, J. C.; Malet, E.; Montuelle, B., Relative influences of submersed macrophytes and bioturbating fauna on biogeochemical processes and microbial activities in freshwater sediments. *Freshwater Biology* 2008, *53* (10), 1969-1982.

Mitsch, W. J.; Nahlik, A.; Wolski, P.; Bernal, B.; Zhang, L.; Ramberg, L., Tropical wetlands: seasonal hydrologic pulsing, carbon sequestration, and methane emissions. *Wetlands Ecology and Management* 2010, *18* (5), 573-586.

Mitsch, W.J.; Gosselink, J.G., Wetlands; John Wiley & Sons, Inc.: Hoboken, NJ, 2001; Vol. 4.

Morris, J. T.; Whiting, G. J., Emission of gaseous carbon-dioxide from salt marsh sediments and its relation to other carbon losses. *Estuaries* 1986, *9* (1), 9-19.

Morris, J. T.; Whiting, G. J., Gas advection in sediments of a South Carolina salt marsh. *Marine Ecology-Progress Series* 1985, *27* (1-2), 187-194.

Moseman-Valtierra S.; Gonzalez, R.; Kroeger, K.; Tang, J.; Chun, W.; Crusius, J.; Bratton, J.; Green, A.; Shelton, J. Short-term nitrogen additions can shift a coastal wetland from a sink to a source of N2O. *Atmospheric Environment* 2011, 45: 4390-4397.

Moseman-Valtierra, S.; Kroeger, K.; Tang, J.; Deegan, L.; Valiela, I., Nitrous oxide fluxes from New England coastal marshes with a range of pulsed or chronic (8- and 31-year) nutrient additions. *In prep.*

Nahlik, A. M.; Mitsch, W. J., Methane Emissions From Created Riverine Wetlands. *Wetlands* 2010, *30* (4), 783-793.

Neubauer, S. C.; Givler, K.; Valentine, S. K.; Megonigal, J. P., Seasonal patterns and plant-mediated controls of subsurface wetland biogeochemistry. *Ecology* 2005, *86* (12), 3334-3344.

Odum, E. P., The status of three ecosystem-level hypotheses regarding salt marsh estuaries: tidal subsidy, outwelling and detritus based food chains. In *Estuarine Perspectives,* Kennedy, V. S.; Ed.; Academic: New York, NY, 1980, pp 485–95.

Oquist, M. G.; Nilsson, M.; Sorensson, F.; Kasimir-Klemedtsson, A.; Persson, T.; Weslien, P.; Klemedtsson, L., Nitrous oxide production in a forest soil at low temperatures - processes and environmental controls. *Fems Microbiology Ecology* 2004, *49* (3), 371-378.

Raghoebarsing, A. A.; Pol, A.; van de Pas-Schoonen, K. T.; Smoders, A. J. P.; Ettwig, K. F.; et al., A microbial consiturm couples anaerobic methane oxidation to denitrification. Nature 2006, 440, 918-921.

Rajkumar, A. N.; Barnes, J.; Ramesh, R.; Purvaja, R.; Upstill-Goddard, R. C., Methane and nitrous oxide fluxes in the polluted Adyar River and estuary, SE India. *Marine Pollution Bulletin* 2008, *56* (12), 2043-2051.

Rocha, A. V.; Goulden, M. L., Large interannual CO(2) and energy exchange variability in a freshwater marsh under consistent environmental conditions. *Journal of Geophysical Research-Biogeosciences* 2008, *113* (G4).

Ritchie, G.A.F.; Nicholas, D.J.D., Identification of the sources of nitrous oxide produced by oxidative and reductive processes in *Nitrosomonas europaea*. *Biochemical Journal* 1972, 129, 1181-1191.

Roobroeck, D.; Butterbach-Bahl, K.; Brueggemann, N.; Boeckx, P., Dinitrogen and nitrous oxide exchanges from an undrained monolith fen: short-term responses following nitrate addition. *European Journal of Soil Science* 2010, *61* (5), 662-670.

Roulet, N. T., Peatlands, carbon storage, greenhouse gases, and the Kyoto Protocol: Prospects and significance for Canada. *Wetlands* 2000, *20* (4), 605-615.

Samuelsson, M. O., Dissimilatory nitrate reduction to nitrite, nitrous oxide, and ammonium by *Pseudomonas putrefaciens*. *Applied and Environmental Microbiology* 1985, *50* (4), 812-815.

Schiller, C. L.; Hastie, D. R., Exchange of nitrous oxide within the Hudson Bay lowland. *Journal of Geophysical Research-Atmospheres* 1994, *99* (D1), 1573-1588.

Seitzinger and Kroeze 1998 Seitzinger, S. P.; Kroeze, C., Global distribution of nitrous oxide production and N inputs in freshwater and coastal marine ecosystems. *Global Biogeochemical Cycles* 1998, *12* (1), 93-113.

Seitzinger, S. P., Denitrification in freshwater and coastal marine ecosystems-ecological and geochemical significance. *Limnology and Oceanography* 1988, *33* (4), 702-724.

Seitzinger, S. P.; Nixon, S. W., Eutrophication and the rate of denitrification and N2O production in coastal marine sediments. *Limnology and Oceanography* 1985, *30* (6), 1332-1339.

Seitzinger et al. 1983 Seitzinger, S. P.; Pilson, M. E. Q.; Nixon, S. W., Nitrous oxide production in nearshore marine sediments. *Science* 1983, *222* (4629), 1244-1246.

Sha, C.; Mitsch, W. J.; Mander, U.; Lu, J. J.; Batson, J.; Zhang, L.; He, W. S., Methane emissions from freshwater riverine wetlands. *Ecological Engineering* 2011, *37* (1), 16-24.

Smith, C. J.; Delaune, R. D.; Patrick, W. H., Nitrous oxide emission from Gulf coast wetlands. *Geochimica Et Cosmochimica Acta* 1983, *47* (10), 1805-1814.

Smith, M. S.; Zimmerman, K., Nitrous oxide production by non-denitrifying soil nitrate reducers. *Soil Science Society of America Journal* 1981, *45* (5), 865-871.

Sommerfeld, R. A.; Mosier, A. R.; Musselman, R. C., CO2, CH4 and N2O flux through a Wyoming snowpack and implications for global budgets. *Nature* 1993, *361* (6408), 140-142.

Sorensen, J.; Tiedje, J. M.; Firestone, R. B., Inhibition by sulfide of nitric and nitrous-oxide reduction by denitrifying *Pseudomonas fluorescens*. *Applied and Environmental Microbiology* 1980, *39* (1), 105-108.

Steudler, P. A.; Bowden, R. D.; Melillo, J. M.; Aber, J. D., Influence of nitrogen fertilization on methane uptake in temperate forest soils. *Nature* 1989, *341* (6240), 314-316.

Stief et al. 2009. Stief, P.; Poulsen, M.; Nielsen, L. P.; Brix, H.; Schramm, A., Nitrous oxide emission by aquatic macrofauna. *Proceedings of the National Academy of Sciences of the United States of America* 2009, *106* (11), 4296-4300.

Sutton-Grier, A. E.; Keller, J. K.; Koch, R.; Gilmour, C.; Megonigal, J. P., Electron donors and acceptors influence anaerobic soil organic matter mineralization in tidal marshes. *Soil Biology & Biochemistry* 2011, *43* (7), 1576-1583.

Teal, J.M., Energy flow in the salt marsh ecosystems of Georgia. *Ecology* 1962, 43: 614-624.

Valentine D.W., Holland E.A., Schimel D.S., Ecosystem and physiological controls over methane production in northern wetlands. *Journal of Geophysical Research* 1994, 99(D1), 1563-1571.

Van der Nat, F. J.; Middelburg, J. J., Methane emission from tidal freshwater marshes. *Biogeochemistry* 2000, *49* (2), 103-121.

Vanderborght, J. P.; Billen, G., Vertical distribution of nitrate concentration in interstitial water of marine sediments with nitrification and denitrification. *Limnology and Oceanography* 1975, *20* (6), 953-961.

Venterea, R. T.; Rolston, D.E., Mechanisms and kinetics of nitric and nitrous oxide production during nitrification in agricultural soil. *Global Change Biology* 2000, 6, 303-316.

Wagner, D.; Pfeiffer, E. M., Two temperature optima of methane production in a typical soil of the Elbe river marshland. *Fems Microbiology Ecology* 1997, *22* (2), 145-153.

Wang, D. Q.; Chen, Z. L.; Sun, W. W.; Hu, B. B.; Xu, S. Y., Methane and nitrous oxide concentration and emission flux of Yangtze Delta plain river net. *Science in China Series B-Chemistry* 2009, *52* (5), 652-661.

Wang Y. et al. 2008 Wang, Y. H.; Inamori, R. H.; Kong, H. N.; Xu, K. Q.; Inamori, Y. H.; Kondo, T. S.; Zhang, J. X., Nitrous oxide emission from polyculture constructed wetlands: Effect of plant species. *Environmental Pollution* 2008, *152* (2), 351-360.

Ward, B. B.; Eveillard, D.; Kirshtein, J. D.; Nelson, J. D.; Voytek, M. A.; Jackson, G. A., Ammonia-oxidizing bacterial community composition in estuarine and oceanic environments assessed using a functional gene microarray. *Environmental Microbiology* 2007, *9* (10), 2522-2538.

Ward, B. B., Molecular approaches to marine microbial ecology and the marine nitrogen cycle. *Annual Review of Earth and Planetary Sciences* 2005, *33*, 301-333.

Weller, D.E.; Correll, D.L.; Jordan, T.E., Denitrification in riparian forests receiving agricultural discharges. In *Global Wetlands: Old and New;* Mitsch, W.J.; Ed; Elsevier Science, 1994: pp.117-131.

Weston, N. B.; Vile, M. A.; Neubauer, S. C.; Velinsky, D. J., Accelerated microbial organic matter mineralization following salt-water intrusion into tidal freshwater marsh soils. *Biogeochemistry* 2011, *102* (1-3), 135-151.

Wigand, C.; Brennan, P.; Stolt, M.; Holt, M.; Ryba, S., *Soil respiration rates in coastal marshes subject to increasing watershed nitrogen loads in southern New England*, USA. *Wetlands* 2009, *29* (3), 952-963.

Wrage, N.; Velthof, G. L.; van Beusichem, M. L.; Oenema, O., Role of nitrifier denitrification in the production of nitrous oxide. *Soil Biology & Biochemistry* 2001, 33 (12-13), 1723-1732.

Yu, J. B.; Liu, J. S.; Sun, Z. G.; Sun, W. D.; Wang, J. D.; Wang, G. P.; Chen, X. B., The fluxes and controlling factors of N(2)O and CH(4) emissions from freshwater marsh in Northeast China. *Science China-Earth Sciences* 2010, 53 (5), 700-709.

Yu, J. B.; Liu, J. S.; Wang, J. D.; Sun, W. D.; Patrick, W. H.; Meixner, F. X., Nitrous oxide emission from Deyeuxia angustifolia freshwater marsh in northeast China. *Environmental Management* 2007, *40* (4), 613-622.

Zhang, Y. H.; Ding, W. X.; Cai, Z. C.; Valerie, P.; Han, F. X., Response of methane emission to invasion of Spartina alterniflora and exogenous N deposition in the coastal salt marsh. *Atmospheric Environment* 2010, *44* (36), 4588-4594.

Zumft, W. G.; Korner, H., Enzyme diversity and mosaic gene organization in denitrification. *Antonie Van Leeuwenhoek International Journal of General and Molecular Microbiology* 1997, 71 (1-2), 43-58.

Reviewed by Dr. Kevin D. Kroeger of the US Geological Survey Coastal and Marine Science Center and Dr. Kristine N. Hopfensperger in the Department of Biological Sciences at Northern Kentucky University.

In: Marshes
Editors: D. C. Abreu et al.

ISBN 978-1-61942-715-0
© 2012 Nova Science Publishers, Inc.

Chapter 2

THE INTRODUCTION, IMPACTS, AND MANAGEMENT OF A LARGE, INVASIVE, AQUATIC RODENT IN THE UNITED STATES

Gary Witmer[1], Trevor R. Sheffels,[2] and Stephen R. Kendrot[3]

[1] USDA National Wildlife Research Center, Fort Collins, Colorado, US
[2] Portland State University, Portland, Oregon US
[3] USDA/APHIS Wildlife Services, Cambridge, Maryland US

INTRODUCTION

Marshes, both tidal and non-tidal, are productive and complex ecosystems. The water in these systems ranges from fresh, to brackish, to saline as one moves from inland to coastal areas. Marshes are an interface between upland and aquatic habitats, and many biotic and abiotic processes lead to increased species richness and diversity (Gedan et al., 2009). Marshes provide many ecological services, including recharge and discharge of ground water; water quality control; retention, removal, and transformation of nutrients; habitats for many floral and faunal species; biomass production and exports; flood control and storm buffering; and stabilization of sediments and slowing of erosion (Southwick Associates, 2004; Woodward et al., 2001). Marshes also provide for human activities such as hiking, wildlife viewing, hunting, trapping, fishing, etc. (Bounds and Carowan, 2000; Southwick Associates, 2004).

Marshes in North America, and elsewhere in many parts of the world, have been greatly affected by human activities, including dredging, filling, water diversions, flood control structures, contamination by pollutants, conversion to agricultural cropland and urban centers, introduction of invasive species, salinization, habitat fragmentation, and other factors (Bounds and Carowan, 2000; Takekawa et al., 2006; Pathikonda et al., 2008; McFalls et al., 2010). Sea level rise and hurricanes also affect marshes and species interactions (Pathikonda et al., 2008; Pyke et al., 2008). Additionally, many marshes have been invaded by exotic species, upsetting normal physical and ecological functions, species richness, and species interactions. Much has been studied and published about invasive plants invading marshes (e.g., Guntenspergen and Nordby, 2006; Pathikonda et al., 2008), but much less has been reported about invasive herbivore impacts in marshes.

Nutria, or coypu (*Myocastor coypus*), are semi-aquatic rodents native to southern South America. In the first half of the 20th century, nutria were widely promoted as a farmable fur bearer and introduced to more than 20 US states, beginning in California in 1899 (Carter and Leonard, 2002). Through a series of accidental and intentional releases, to establish fur resources or to control aquatic weeds, feral populations have since become established in 17 states and are considered an invasive species causing detrimental impacts to native habitats, agricultural resources, and water control structures. In the United States, nutria impacts have mainly occurred in the mid-Atlantic, Southeast, and Pacific Northwest regions of the country. The feeding activities of these herbivores can damage agricultural crops and aquatic vegetation, leading to altered aquatic ecosystems. Their burrowing habits can weaken water control structures, and they are a host for some infectious diseases.

Management of nutria and the damage they cause can be problematic for natural resource managers. Nutria are habitat generalists, prolific breeders, and are capable of long-distance dispersals – all characteristics of successful invaders. Eradication or local extirpation may be feasible and desirable in areas where risk of reinvasion can be minimized, but a number of challenging criteria must be met for eradication efforts to succeed. However, in contiguously occupied habitats, control through population suppression may be the only viable alternative for protecting high priority resources. Both management strategies are labor intensive and require specialized equipment to reach nutria populations in wetland environments with limited access. Control efforts can be further complicated where nutria are considered a valuable resource and regulated harvest occurs, such as in Louisiana. In this chapter, we will discuss nutria biology, ecology, introductions, impacts as an invasive species, and management and eradication efforts.

NUTRIA BIOLOGY, ECOLOGY, AND BEHAVIOR

Nutria are semi-aquatic rodents that have stout, highly arched bodies with a large head and a long rat-like tail sparsely covered with bristly hairs (Figure 1). Adults typically weigh between 5-7 kilograms, and males are slightly larger than females. The front feet have four non-webbed digits that are used for digging and feeding on vegetation. The hind feet have 5 digits and four are webbed, making nutria efficient swimmers. Other aquatic adaptations include eyes set near the top of the head and a valvular nose and mouth, allowing individuals to stay underwater for several minutes (LeBlanc, 1994). The fur consists of a dense reddish-brown to yellowish-brown outer coat containing long, coarse bristles (guard hairs). The under coat is dense and dark gray. The large, ever-growing incisors are distinctly orange colored. Nutria have conspicuous white whiskers and fur around their mouth, a distinguishing feature when compared to other aquatic mammals (e.g., muskrat, beaver). They have a hunched appearance when on land, but are agile enough to quickly retreat to the water when sensing danger using advanced auditory and olfactory senses.

Figure 1. A foraging nutria (*Myocastor coypus*).

The primary habitat for nutria is freshwater marshes, but populations are able to persist in a variety of slow-flowing aquatic systems, including lakes, ponds, swamps, drainage canals, rivers, and streams (LeBlanc, 1994). Home ranges are typically less than 10 ha, but much larger home ranges have been reported (Nolfo-Clements, 2009). Individuals generally stay within a few hundred meters of their burrows, but daily movements up to 3.2 km have been documented (Linscombe et al., 1981). Populations can become quite dense, reaching 25 nutria per ha. Nutria usually remain in their original home range area throughout their lives, however, they may disperse up to 80 km due to cold weather or drought conditions (Woods et al., 1992). Dispersal is typically through aquatic corridors, but nutria can also disperse across land when necessary.

Nutria form social groups and utilize a polygynous mating system. Groups consist of several adult females, a dominant male, and juveniles of both sexes. Female nutria are polyestrous and can reach sexual maturity within six months. They are non-seasonal breeders capable of producing 3 litters a year with an average of 4 to 5 kits per litter (Bounds et al., 2003). Gestation is approximately 130-132 days (LeBlanc 1994). The young are precocial and able to swim and consume vegetation within a few days of being born. Sub-adult males are often driven from the group by the dominant males (Gosling, 1977). Average lifespan is about 3 years with annual mortality rates of 53-74% (Chapman et al., 1978).

Nutria are primarily nocturnal, although they can be frequently seen during the day. Daytime feeding activity may increase during winter months to conserve energy (Gosling et al., 1980). Their main activities involve feeding, grooming, and sleeping. Nutria sometimes live in burrows which they make themselves or usurp from other animals. Generally, burrows have multiple entrances near the water line. Burrows may be up to 15 m in length and may be simple or somewhat complex (Nowak, 1999). Nutria also build elevated feeding and resting platforms out of aquatic vegetation. Runs or slides at the water's edge are created where nutria repeatedly exit the water to feed. These modifications can substantially impact vegetative communities (Evans, 1970; Kinler et al., 1987), as clearing of vegetation by nutria may alter plant succession and convert marsh ecosystems to more open-water environments.

Nutria are voracious consumers of vegetation and known to completely denude vegetation from areas where they feed before moving to another area (Mach, 2002). Nutria prefer the basal portion of plants and they can consume up to 25% of their body weight in vegetation daily (Hutchins et al., 2004). Other researchers have noted that nutria are also wasteful feeders with as much as 90% of damaged plant material not consumed when they forage on belowground roots and tubers (Taylor and Grace, 1995), which is common during the winter months. Nutria show preference for certain plant species, resulting in over-utilization of these species, but diet is also adjusted seasonally based on food availability (Borgnia et al., 2000). Nutria also feed occasionally on mussels and other invertebrates (LeBlanc, 1994; Hutchins et al., 2004).

NUTRIA IN THEIR NATIVE RANGE

Nutria, known as coypu outside of the US, are native to a large area of southern South America. Their range extends from southern Brazil and Peru down through Bolivia, Uruguay, Paraguay, Argentina, and Chile. Their range, biology, ecology, and history of introductions have been reviewed by Woods et al. (1992), Lever (1995), Nowak (1999), Carter and Leonard (2002), Long (2003), and Hutchins et al. (2004), and we draw from those sources for materials presented in this and the next section. Native nutria populations generally inhabit low elevation freshwater wetlands, marshes, and rivers. However, they have been found at 1,190 m elevations and in brackish and salt water systems in Chile (Woods et al., 1992). Few scientific studies of nutria in their native range were published in the past, but a relatively large volume of scientific literature has been published in recent years (e.g., Borgnia et al., 2000; Guichón and Cassini, 2005; Guichón et al., 2003a,b,c; Guichón and Cassini, 2005; Corriale et al., 2006; Martino et al., 2008; Gayo et al., 2011).

Much of the nutria research in their native range has been on social structure and life history. They may live in pairs, but often form colonies of 10 or more individuals consisting of related adult females, a dominant male, and juveniles of both sexes (Guichón et al., 2003a). Guichón et al. (2003a) also documented high group fidelity and reported interactions and cooperative behaviors such as nursing in groups, allo-grooming, and alarm calls within groups. In their native range, the main predators are jaguars (*Felis onca*), mountain lions (*F. concolor*), ocelots (*F. pardalis*), little spotted cats (*F. tigrinus*), and caimans (*Caiman* spp.) (Woods et al. 1992). Nutria are also affected by a large number of disease agents and parasites (Woods et al. 1992, Martino and Stanchi, 1994; Gayo et al., 2011). Martino et al. (2008) necropsied nutria from 4 areas of Argentina and found the most common mortality factors, in declining order, to be: trauma (predation or vehicle-killed), poisoning by various toxins, starvation, infectious diseases, and miscellaneous causes. As might be expected, mortality (12-55%) is lower in protected areas of Argentina (Guichón et al. 2003c).

In agro-ecosystems of Argentina, nutria feed preferentially on aquatic monocots (40-60% of the diet) (Borgnia et al., 2000). In contrast, terrestrial monocots comprised 30-35% of the diet and were consumed in proportion to their availability. Nutria consumed dicots (0-15% of the diet) significantly less than their availability. Borgnia et al. (2000) also reported that the most preferred monocots were *Eleocharis bonariensis* in the winter and spring and *Lemna* species in the summer and fall. It appears that the preference of nutria for aquatic vegetation versus terrestrial vegetation is not related to nutritional content of the plants, but probably because predation risk is lower when they feed in or near water (Guichón et al., 2003b). These authors also noted that less than 2% of the 6 crops grown in the area were consumed by nutria and that they were unlikely to cause significant crop damage if a narrow fringe of native vegetation along riparian systems was left as a buffer.

In their native range, nutria have historically been heavily exploited for their plush fur, as a source of food, and occasionally kept as pets to supply the fur, food, and pet trades (Guichón and Cassini, 2005). They are also considered a pest species, although research suggests otherwise. Grazing damage in urban areas has been documented (Corriale et al., 2006), but the social perception of nutria as an agricultural pest species is not supported by research (Guichón and Cassini, 1999). As a result of exploitation and pest control efforts, nutria densities are rather low in areas of Argentina (Guichón and Cassini, 2005) and other parts of South America. As a conservation measure, authorities began regulating harvests and established protected reserves in the 1990s where no harvesting is allowed (Nowak, 1999; Guichón et al., 2003c). Additionally, captive breeding farms have been established to provide a continuous supply of pelts and meat while relieving pressure on wild populations.

WORLDWIDE NUTRIA INTRODUCTIONS

Nutria have been introduced to many countries around the world, including Canada, Great Britain, Ireland, Norway, Finland, Belgium, Netherlands, Denmark, France, Germany, Austria, Switzerland, Bulgaria, Czech Republic, Slovakia, Poland, Romania, Italy, Greece, Yugoslavia, Russian Federation, Asia, Israel, Turkey, Thailand, China, South Korea, Japan, Kenya, Tanzania, Zambia, Zimbabwe, and Botswana. Background on these introductions was compiled by Lever (1985), Carter and Leonard (2002), and Long (2003). The introductions occurred between the years of 1882 (France) and 1967 (Switzerland) (Carter and Leonard, 2002). Most of the introductions were escapes or releases from captive populations being bred for their fur, although in some cases, nutria spread from initial introductions in neighboring countries. Nutria never became established or became extinct in several countries: Kenya, Zambia, Zimbabwe, Botswana, Thailand, Denmark, Norway, Finland, Ireland, Spain, and Sweden. Dry or cold conditions probably were responsible for most of these failures.

Although often considered a valuable resource, in many of the introductions feral nutria became a serious pest, damaging crops, marsh systems, and water control structures. These feral populations also pose a disease hazard (Gosling and Baker, 1989). Efforts to eliminate or greatly reduce feral nutria populations using trapping, shooting, and poisons have resulted in varying levels of success. Generally, an intensive and sustained trapping effort is needed to achieve success and often requires incentive payments to trappers to maintain a high level of trapping effort, especially when population densities decline. This approach resulted in the successful eradication of feral nutria in England in 1989 (Gosling, 1989; Gosling and Baker, 1989). Government intervention and support, along with substantial population biology research, were important aspects of the successful eradication (Sheal, 2003).

Outside of the United States and England, much of the recently published scientific literature on introduced nutria originates from Italy. Nutria became established in Italy between 1960 and 1970 after escaping from fur farms (Reggiani et al., 1995). These authors studied the population dynamics of nutria in a 37.5 ha plot within a nature preserve in central Italy. Based on mark-recapture methods, they estimated that the population size varied from 27-137 individuals between 1989 and 1991. The population trend was decreasing numbers in the winter and increasing numbers from summer to winter. They also noted that the population remained fairly stable through mild winters, but that reproductive activity and recruitment were generally high after colder winters. Density-dependent factors such as pregnancy failure and newborn losses were important in the population's dynamics. These findings were similar to those of Gosling et al. (1983) and provide evidence that sustained cold winters are a main limiting factor for nutria distribution in non-native habitats.

Prigioni et al. (2005a) studied the food habits of nutria in northwestern Italy and found that aquatic macrophytes provided the majority (81.8%) of the diet year round. Nutria fed mostly in the water, but also fed on terrestrial vegetation near water (especially young nutria). While they noted that only slight damage to vegetation occurred, they warned that some sensitive aquatic plants species could suffer long-term damage. These results, along with findings from England (Ellis, 1963) and the US (Wilsey et al., 1991), demonstrate that nutria in non-native environments are generalist herbivores and can utilize a variety of food resources depending on availability.

Panzacchi et al. (2007) estimated that between 1995 and 2000, nutria caused about 11,631,721 euros of damage in Italy and control activities cost about 2,614,408 euros. More than 220,000 nutria were removed through control programs during this time period. They projected that nutria range in Italy may expand 2.5-3.3 times and that economic losses may reach 9-12 million euros per year. While nutria can be successfully trapped with periodic trapping sessions, populations can quickly rebound (through births and immigration), hence long-term reductions have not resulted from trapping programs (Prigioni et al., 2005b; Panzacchi et al., 2007; Cocchi and Riga, 2008). This confirms what was learned in England: that only a very intensive and sustained trapping effort can reduce or eliminate introduced nutria populations. Panzacchi et al. (2007) also suggested that although the nutria eradication in England was very costly (5 million euros over 11 years), that approach may still have a more positive cost-benefit ratio in the long-term compared with the permanent control program in Italy (14 million euros spent over only 6 years).

A few other interesting findings have come from nutria studies in Europe. Meyer et al. (2005) noted that introduced nutria in urban areas of Germany are often diurnal (not nocturnal as in their native range), feeding on foods provided by humans. In France, Waterkeyn et al. (2010) studied the occurrence of freshwater invertebrates in the fur of introduced nutria. They retrieved more than 800 invertebrates representing 14 different taxa from the fur of 10 nutria. They concluded that in addition to vegetation and digging damage, nutria may alter invertebrate communities by introducing new species or genotypes to water bodies in which they did not originally occur.

NUTRIA INTRODUCTIONS IN THE UNITED STATES

The introduction, natural history, value, management, and impacts of the nutria in the United States have been described in detail (Evans, 1970; Willner, 1982; Kinler et al., 1987; Bounds et al., 2003). Nutria were first introduced into the United States in 1899 to establish a fur farm in California, but this initial introduction failed due to lack of reproductive success (Ashbrook, 1948). During the 1930s, nutria were imported for fur farms in Louisiana, Ohio, New Mexico, Washington, Michigan, Oregon, and Utah (Kinler et al., 1987). In addition, nutria were promoted as controllers of nuisance aquatic vegetation (such as water hyacinth, *Eichhornia crassipes*, and alligator weed, *Alternanthera philoxeroides*) and were rapidly introduced in the Southeast in the 1930s and 1940s (Evans, 1970). Since then, accidental and intentional releases have permitted nutria to become established in at least 15 states (Figure 2) (Willner, 1982), with the highest densities occurring along the Gulf Coast of Louisiana and Texas (LeBlanc 1994). The introductions of nutria have been summarized by Carter and Leonard (2002) and Long (2003). The main limiting factor for the spread of nutria in North America seems to be the severity of minimum winter temperatures (Sheffels and Sytsma, 2007).

IMPACTS BY INTRODUCED NUTRIA

Agriculture. Impacts by nutria to agriculture include foraging on crops, weakening irrigation structures by digging burrows, and potential disease transmission to livestock.

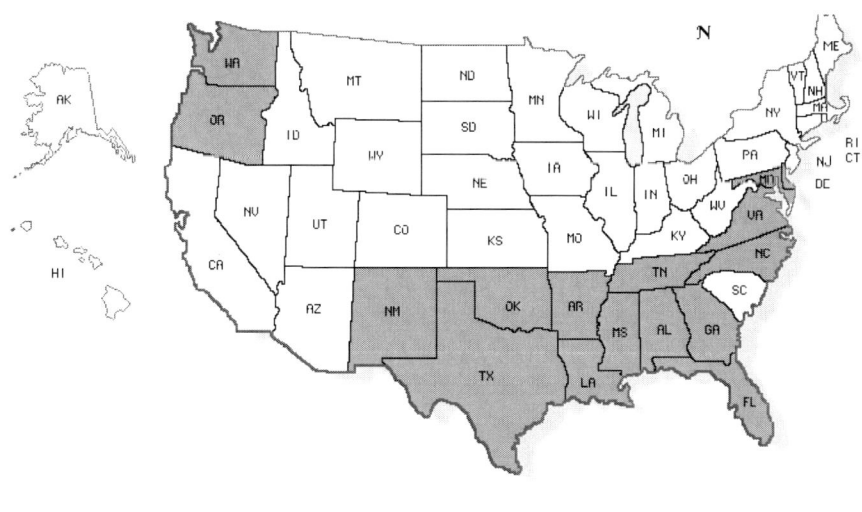

Figure 2. US states (shaded) with established nutria populations.

Crop damage is most prevalent in areas adjacent to aquatic habitats supporting nutria, and especially where nutria are abundant (Bounds et al., 2003). The primary crops damaged by nutria in the United States are sugarcane and rice, but others include corn, milo (grain sorghum), sugar and table beets, alfalfa, wheat, barley, oats, peanuts, and various melons and vegetables (LeBlanc, 1994). In Louisiana, nutria commonly undermine and break through water-retaining levees in flooded fields used for rice and crawfish production (LeBlanc, 1994). Nutria can be infected with pathogens (e.g., leptospirosis) and parasites transmissible to livestock, which is especially a concern in situations where livestock drink from water contaminated by nutria urine and feces (LeBlanc, 1994).

Erosion. In addition to compromising agricultural water control structures, nutria burrowing activity can weaken flood control levees that protect low-lying areas, as well as roadbeds and dikes (LeBlanc, 1994). Weakened banks can cave in under heavy weight, posing serious risks to heavy equipment operators. Erosion impacts are particularly costly in developed areas where infrastructure is compromised. Nutria burrowing can also result in substantial erosion of natural stream banks. This results in large amounts of sediment entering the stream system and subsequent water quality impacts (Sheffels and Sytsma, 2007), which are of particular concern in areas being managed to preserve sensitive aquatic species.

Disease Transmission. Numerous diseases have been identified in nutria (Pridham et al., 1966; Howerth et al., 1994; LeBlanc, 1994; Bounds et al., 2003). Transmission of diseases and parasites from nutria to humans is not well-documented, but could potentially involve toxoplasma, chlamydia, salmonella, and other diseases (Bounds et al., 2003). Diseases are common in captive populations where high densities of nutria are housed in close proximity and cleaning standards are low (Bounds et al., 2003). In turn, these conditions pose the greatest risk to human handlers who do not wear appropriate personal protective equipment such as gloves while handling animals, or masks while cleaning pens. Nutria parasites most often transmitted to humans are nematodes and blood flukes (*Strongyloides myopotami* and *Schistosoma mansoni*) that cause what is commonly known as "swimmer's itch" (LeBlanc, 1994).

Native Vegetation. Nutria in high densities also can be detrimental to coastal and inland marshes and other riverine and wetland areas. Nutria are recognized as at least a contributing factor to the decline of native Louisiana coastal marsh, declining vegetative biomass, and changing plant communities (Shaffer et al., 1992; Grace and Ford, 1996; Evers et al., 1998). Louisiana has lost about 22,000 acres of marsh to nutria vegetative damage and over 100,000 acres of marsh have been negatively impacted by nutria (Marx et al., 2004). In Maryland, nutria are considered a primary factor in the decline of the marsh in the Delmarva Peninsula due to their "eat out" of the vegetative root mat. The vegetative root mat is a floating marsh above a layer of fluid mud. Nutria will chew through the mat, which exposes the mud and leads to erosion caused by tidal currents and wave action. Erosion causes sinking of the marsh surface, which results in vegetation loss to flooding. The areas damaged by nutria can become permanent, open water ponds (Figure 3). Much of this marsh loss removes habitat for native wildlife species such as waterfowl, wading birds, and muskrats. Marsh damage by introduced nutria in the United States is considered in more detail in the case studies below.

Competition with Native Muskrats. Native muskrats (*Ondatra zibethicus*) are widespread in North America and have contributed substantially to the fur industry in the United States since the colonial times (Erb and Perry, 2003). Nutria and muskrats co-exist in numerous areas, but it is surmised that the much larger, exotic nutria can out-compete muskrats. This may have contributed to declines in muskrat populations observed in various parts of the United States (Evans, 1970; Lowery, 1974; Genesis Laboratories, Inc., 2002). Anecdotal evidence suggests nutria and muskrats may compete for food, resting platform sites, and den sites. Nutria have also been observed attacking muskrats confined in traps, suggesting nutria are a more dominant species (Lowery, 1974).

Figure 3. (Continued).

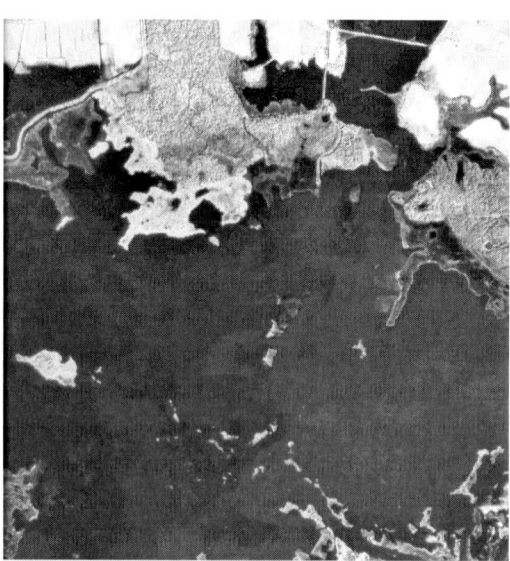

Figure 3. Nutria damage to marsh vegetation at the Blackwater National Wildlife Refuge, Maryland. The top photograph was taken in 1938; the bottom photograph was of the same area in 1989.

REGIONAL CASE STUDIES

Southeastern United States: Louisiana. Nutria were introduced to Louisiana in the 1930s for fur farming, a growing industry in many parts of the United States. As with other states, some animals escaped (especially during flooding or storm events) and some were intentionally released. They first became established in the western coastal marsh areas, but later spread eastward. Nutria are found in freshwater, brackish water, and salt water marshes, although most harvested nutria are taken from freshwater marshes (Jordan and Mouton, 2010). By the mid-1950s, muskrat numbers were declining, nutria populations were still expanding, and farmers began to report serious rice damage in southwestern Louisiana and sugarcane damage in southeastern Louisiana. By the late 1950s, it was estimated that 20 million nutria occupied coastal Louisiana (Genesis Laboratories, Inc., 2002). In 1958, Louisiana placed nutria on the unprotected species list and put a $0.25 bounty on each nutria harvested in several south Louisiana parishes. However, funds were never provided for the bounty.

The history of nutria markets, both values and harvests, has been nicely summarized by Jordan and Mouton (2010) and Genesis Laboratories, Inc. (2002). The Louisiana Department of Wildlife and Fisheries (LDWF) began working toward development of a nutria fur market, which began to grow slowly in the 1960s due to a demand in the German fur industry. In the 1950s, about a half million nutria per year were being harvested (Figure 4). Fur prices continued to rise, and the harvest grew steadily with annual harvests of over one million from 1961-1980. In 1962, the nutria harvest surpassed the muskrat harvest, becoming the backbone of the Louisiana fur industry.

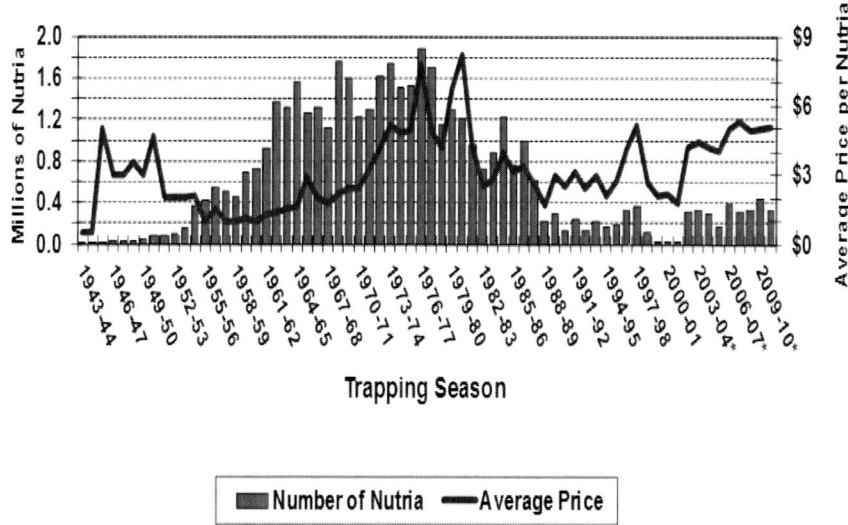

Figure 4. Nutria harvests and prices in Louisiana, 1943-2010 (courtesy of Edmond Mouton, Louisiana Department of Wildlife and Fisheries).

In 1965, the state returned nutria to the protected species list with regulated harvests. Between 1971 and 1981, the average annual value of harvested nutria to coastal trappers was $8.1 million. The peak nutria harvest occurred in 1976 with a value of $15.7 million to coastal trappers. After several years of declining fur value and nutria harvests, the Russian fur demand increased, resulting in increased fur value and nutria harvests in Louisiana. The increased harvests were still well below the annual harvests of the 1970s and early 1980s, however, and it was short-lived as the Russian economy collapsed. Nutria harvests plummeted and the 1999-2000 trapping season resulted in only 29,544 pelts taken.

As a result of the low harvests, nutria populations increased rapidly, as did damage complaints starting in 1987 and becoming frequent in the early 1990s. The LDWF began aerial surveys of nutria damage in southeastern Louisiana in the early 1990s. Between 1993 and 1996, the acres of damaged marshland increased from 45,000 acres to 80,000 acres. More extensive surveys began with funding from the Coastal Wetlands Planning, Protection and Restoration Act (CWPPRA), which revealed areas covering about 90,000 acres damaged by herbivory. By 1999, this figure had increased to nearly 105,000 acres.

The marsh vegetation damage in Louisiana has been studied since at least the 1950s, and it is a dynamic process with many factors. Carter et al. (1999) created an extensive model that demonstrated the relationships between nutria population dynamics, vegetation removal, and biomass and acreage of marsh vegetation were complex. Ford and Grace (1998) studied the effects of fire and herbivory and found both to substantially reduce plant biomass. Plots fenced to exclude herbivores, but also burned, had greater plant species richness.

Research on the specific role of nutria herbivory in marsh decline has intensified as concerns about declining marsh acreage have grown. Many of the studies have made use of exclosures to measure nutria herbivory impacts. Harris and Webert (1962) were among the first to study nutria herbivory in Louisiana and found that the most damaged marsh vegetation species was big cordgrass (*Spartina cynosuroides*). Fuller et al. (1985) noted that exclusion of nutria from islands may be necessary for the re-establishment of vegetation after severe flooding events. More recently, Wilsey et al. (1991) demonstrated that nutria diets were comprised of a variety of plant species, but that certain species dominated (i.e., were highly preferred even when at low coverage levels). They also noted that the nutria diet varied between seasons. Taylor and Grace (1995) reported that nutria reduced plant biomass by as much as 30%, but that plant species richness was unaffected. However, Evers et al. (1998) concluded that nutria herbivory affected both plant biomass and plant species composition. Johnson and Foote (2005) reported that nutria foraging greatly reduced annual above ground plant production and that nutria fed heavily on *Spartina patens*. Geho et al. (2007) also reported substantial reductions in plant biomass due to nutria foraging and noted that nutria fed heavily on *Taxodium distichum* and *Typhus domingensis*.

Methods to restore marsh vegetation damage caused directly by nutria in Louisiana have been studied as well. Conner and Toliver (1987) studied methods to protect the restoration efforts of baldcypress (*Taxodium distichum*) in Louisiana that were commonly thwarted by nutria foraging. They found that the use of plastic Vexar® tubing around the seedlings did not provide protection from nutria, but chicken wire barriers did provide adequate protection. Llewellyn and Shaffer (1993) suggested that *Justicia lanceolata* be used to restore marsh vegetation because the plant is not a preferred food of nutria. McFalls et al. (2010) found that fertilizer addition increased plant biomass, but was most effective when nutria populations were reduced or excluded.

Despite these impacts, nutria are still considered an important resource in Louisiana, providing both income and recreation for hunters and trappers. They also help provide a prey base for alligators, another valuable resource in the state (Joanen et al., 1997; Gabrey et al., 2009). Hence, Louisiana has not opted for the eradication approach to feral nutria populations that Maryland and some western states have pursued. Nutria densities still need to be reduced to protect coastal marshes, so LDWF has pursued two approaches to accomplish that goal.

The first approach was to market nutria as a healthy alternative for human consumption, providing recipes on-line (www.nutria.com/site14.php) and in brochures (Kinler, undated). Nutria have just 1.5 g fat per 100 g of meat, compared to turkey with 2.9 g and beef with 26.6 g. Nutria also have a high protein level of 22.1 g per 100 g, compared to turkey with 21.8 g and beef with 16.6 g (Kinler, undated; Saadoum et al., 2006). Unfortunately, not much of a market for nutria meat ever developed.

The second approach to reducing nutria densities involved implementing a nutria control incentive program in 2002 (Jordan and Mouton, 2010). Funding for a Coastwide Nutria Control Program (CNCP) has been provided by the Coastal Wetlands Planning, Protection and Restoration Act through the Natural Resources Conservation Service and the Office of Coastal Protection and Restoration. The goal of the CNCP is to significantly reduce damage to coastal wetlands caused by nutria by removing 400,000 nutria annually. The LDWF administers the program through the following activities:

- Conduct and review the registration of participants in the program;
- Establish collection stations across coastal Louisiana;
- Count valid nutria tails and present participants with a receipt or voucher;
- Deliver tails to an approved disposal facility and receive documentation that nutria will be properly disposed of and will not leave the facility, and;
- Process and maintain records regarding participants as well as the number and location where tails were collected.

An incentive payment to registered trappers and hunters started at $4.00 per tail and in 2003-2004 a total of 332,596 nutria tails were collected by 346 participants under the CNCP. Because the harvest began to decline after the first few years, the incentive payment was raised to $5.00 in the 2006-2007 trapping season (Jordan and Mouton, 2010). The 2009-2010 trapping season had 306 participants who harvested 445,963 nutria and received $2,229,815 in incentive payments (Jordan and Mouton, 2010). Hence, the program has been achieving its goal of harvesting about 400,000 nutria per year. A majority of nutria were killed with firearms (61%), while 39% were trapped.

The CNCP continues to conduct annual aerial vegetation surveys following nutria harvests to assess damaged marsh acreage. Damaged acreage ranged from 79,444 to 97,271 acres before implementation of the CNCP incentive payments. Since implementation of the CNCP in 2002, annual damaged acreage has declined steadily from 82,080 acres in 2003, down to 55,755 acres in 2006, and only 8,475 acres in 2010. Additionally, it has been shown that marsh habitat can recover in the absence of nutria or with lower population densities of nutria. The amount of conversion of marsh vegetation to open water has also declined as marshes recover.

Northeastern United States: Maryland. The emergent wetlands of Maryland's Chesapeake Bay at one time covered about 205,815 acres (Southwick Associates, 2004). The Blackwater National Wildlife Refuge (NWR) is comprised of over 25,000 acres on the Delmarva Peninsula, including about 13,000 acres of coastal marshland. The refuge was established to protect and manage habitat for migratory birds, threatened and endangered flora and fauna, and other native species. Preservation activities include 1) administering prescribed burns on parts of the 13,000 acres of marshlands to improve marsh and forest habitats, 2) managing 650 acres of croplands to diversify the wildlife habitat, 3) managing 27 freshwater impoundments totaling 850 acres to provide resting and feeding habitat for migrating birds, 4) managing forest habitats for the endangered Delmarva fox squirrel, 5) administering a trapping program to manage furbearer populations, 6) controlling invasive species to protect native species, and 7) conducting research to improve management decision-making. The refuge and surrounding area is used for commercial and recreational fishing, clam and shellfish harvest, furbearer trapping, wildlife viewing, and other outdoor recreational activities. It has been estimated that the refuge is visited by 500,000 people each year, generating at least $15 million for the local economy (Bounds and Carowan, 2000).

Nutria were introduced into the Delmarva Peninsula of Maryland in 1943 (although possibly as early as late 1930s) to bolster the fur industry (Willner et al., 1979). Initially, they were raised in captivity on fur farms, but eventually some nutria escaped and/or were purposefully released when captive-rearing proved unprofitable (Bounds and Mollett, 2000). They spread rapidly, and severe damage to some areas of marsh was noticed as early as 1970 (Willner et al., 1979). It was estimated that the Blackwater NWR had between 35,000 and 50,000 nutria, but only about 20% or less were harvested each year (Bounds and Mollett, 2000). Densities ranged from 2.7-16.0 nutria per ha (Willner et al., 1979). Damage was especially heavy in marsh areas dominated by Olney 3-square bulrush (*Scirpus olneyi*), which formed over 80% of the nutria diet (Willner et al., 1979).

Over 7,000 acres of the refuge's 13,000 acres of marshland has been severely damaged to date, resulting in extensive ecological and economic impacts. Nutria feed heavily on the roots and stems of marsh plants and relatively little on the leaves or on algae (Willner et al., 1979). When nutria excavate roots, the submerged root mat is disturbed and sediments are exposed and subjected to tidal erosion and conversion to open water (M. Haramis and R. Colona, USDI Geological Survey, unpubl. data). An economic assessment on the impacts of overabundant nutria populations in Chesapeake Bay was conducted for the Maryland Department of Natural Resources (Southwick Associates, 2004). The researchers reported that the current economic losses to Maryland's commercial and sport fisheries, hunting, and wildlife watching industries is about $2.8 million per year, but that could balloon to $132.6 million per year in 50 years. Additional environmental and social losses were estimated to currently be at $800,000 per year, but that could also balloon to $37 million per year in 50 years.

Initial programs to reduce nutria numbers were similar to methods employed in Louisiana. The programs involved trying to encourage human consumption of nutria and using a bounty program whereby people were paid $1.50 for each nutria tail (Bounds and Mollett, 2000). Neither of those programs succeeded in reducing the growing nutria population in Maryland.

In 1994, the Maryland Department of Natural Resources convened a nutria summit to address the problems caused by nutria. Dr. M. Gosling, the scientist who spearheaded the successful United Kingdom nutria eradication effort in the 1980s, was brought in to consult and advise the natural resource management agencies. In 1997, a partnership of federal, state, and private natural resource organizations was formed to create a management plan to reduce or eliminate nutria on the Maryland Eastern Shore (Bounds and

Carowan, 2000; Kendrot, 2004). A five year two-phased pilot project was developed, and funding was obtained to initiate the "Maryland Nutria Project" in 2000. The first two-year phase of this pilot project focused on research to describe the health, reproductive characteristics, behavior, and population size of nutria at 9 study sites within the federally-managed Blackwater National Wildlife Refuge (BNWR), state-owned Fishing Bay Wildlife Management Area (FBWMA), and privately held Tudor Farms, Inc. (TF). Led by principle investigators from the University of Maryland Eastern Shore Cooperative Fish and Wildlife Research Unit, graduate students and a staff of 12 technicians conducted mark-recapture population estimates, necropsies, and radio telemetry studies to describe nutria biology in the Chesapeake Bay.

Phase 2 of the pilot project was implemented in 2002 by the US Department of Agriculture's Wildlife Services (WS) program through an interagency agreement with the US Fish and Wildlife Service. WS initially tested two removal strategies, saturation versus perimeter trapping, on the 9 study sites utilized in the first phase of the pilot project. WS quickly determined that testing eradication strategies on relatively small (600 acre) study areas was confounded by immigration from neighboring populations, and that perimeter trapping would not put all animals at risk of capture. Accordingly, the phase 2 study site was expanded to include all of BNWR, FBWMA, TF and private wetlands among and between these properties.

Between 2003 and 2006, 15 wildlife specialists with WS applied a systematic trapping campaign across nearly 100,000 acres in southern Dorchester County, Maryland, removing 10,000 nutria in the process. Continual population monitoring in previously trapped areas indicated that nutria densities were driven to near-zero densities and could be maintained by early detection and removal of new invaders. Marsh damage assessments conducted by the US Geological Survey's Patuxent Wildlife Research Center demonstrated the recovery of marsh grasses in previously damaged areas (M. Haramis, USDI Geological Survey, unpubl. data). At this point, project management decided that landscape-level eradication was achievable and worthwhile. The project scope was expanded to include all of the Delmarva Peninsula and renamed the Chesapeake Bay Nutria Eradication Project (CBNEP).

Using an adaptive management process, the CBNEP team has developed a suite of detection and removal techniques that have been applied over the course of a eradication campaign comprised of five phases:

- The *Survey* phase utilized various detection methods to delimit the distribution of nutria within a watershed or collection of watersheds.
- The *Knock-Down* phase involved the application of systematic trapping to reduce nutria populations to near-zero densities within management units.
- During the *Mop-Up* phase staff focused on the early detection and rapid removal of aggregations of nutria that form within previously trapped areas when new invaders or individuals that avoided trapping coalesce.
- During the *Verification* phase staff repeatedly applied detection methods. Failure to detect nutria despite repeated and ongoing efforts indicated that eradication had been achieved.
- Continual monitoring at a lower intensity during the *Surveillance* phase was conducted to ensure that eradication is maintained.

While these phases were generally followed sequentially, phases may be skipped or revisited depending on the detection of nutria.

No single method of removal or detection is 100% effective and in order to assure that all nutria are put at risk, CBNEP staff relied on a diverse suite of detection and removal tools and techniques. Detection methods and devices included:

- Shoreline surveys conducted by staff traveling by boat or kayak at slow speeds along waterways looking for tracks, scat, and other sign of nutria.
- Ground surveys by foot conducted in areas not accessible by boat.
- Detector dogs used to detect nutria by scent in conjunction with visual sign searches by boat or on foot.
- Detection Platforms are standardized devices comprised of a two foot square plywood base bonded to Ethafoam® for flotation. A wooden rim on the top surface of the platform prevents natural vegetation or straw bedding and any nutria sign (scat) from washing or blowing off the platform. Arrays of platforms were placed along navigable waterways and were routinely inspected for sign of use (scat, muddy tracks, hair samples, etc.). Platforms were also be used as a removal technique by applying a trap once sign has been detected.
- Judas nutria involved the use of sterilized and radio-tagged animals to locate colonies of free ranging nutria.

Removal methods included:

- Body gripping/instant kill traps set in trails, haul-outs, on platforms, and on floating trap stabilizers.
- Foothold traps set on submersion cables that quickly drown captured nutria set along waterways on false beds, platforms, and haul-outs.
- Cage-traps and snares were sometimes used to capture nutria alive for research purposes or in areas where landowners were concerned about use of kill traps around hunting dogs or pets.
- Shooting was an effective means of hunting nutria, particularly in winter months when ice aids mobility and snow cover facilitates tracking.
- Detector dogs were highly effective at finding and removing nutria at low densities.

Detection surveys were replicated numerous times throughout the different seasons in order to reduce the risk of failing to detect nutria when they were present. Similarly, not all nutria were vulnerable to being captured in a single device or set type, therefore, integrating multiple methods insured that all nutria were eventually put at risk of capture.

The key to achieving eradication with these traditional harvest methods was the systematic and progressive manner in which intense trapping pressure was applied and sustained over the long-term. The CBNEP used Geographic Information Systems (GIS) to prioritize staff deployment and manage data, and Global Positioning System (GPS) navigation devices to track staff movements and collect positional data on sign and captures. Using salaried wildlife specialists, prolonged trapping pressure was applied long after commercial trappers getting paid a bounty would abandon an area for more profitable capture rates.

Since expanding its focus to the entire Delmarva Peninsula, by October 2011 the CBNEP had reduced nutria to near-zero densities across 150,000 acres of coastal wetlands along the Chesapeake Bay and its tributaries in 5 counties on Maryland's Eastern Shore: Talbot, Caroline, Dorchester, Wicomico, and Somerset. In October of 2011, staff initiated surveys to delimit nutria populations throughout the rest of the Delmarva Peninsula, detecting previously unknown populations in the Wicomico River. The CBNEP has set a goal of eradicating nutria from the entire Delmarva Peninsula by the end of 2015.

The benefits of nutria removal efforts in Delmarva Peninsula are already being observed. Marsh vegetation has improved dramatically in many areas with large increases in vegetation cover (Figure 5).

Figure 5. Marsh vegetation recovery in the Blackwater National Wildlife Refuge in Maryland after nutria removal. Nutria damaged area (top) and the same area after nutria removal (bottom).

Northwestern United States: Oregon and Washington. Nutria were introduced to Oregon and Washington in the 1930s and into the 1940s for fur farming (Larrison, 1943; Willner, 1982). Nutria were first brought to the Northwest in expectation that nutria farming would become a lucrative endeavor (Guenther, 1950; Kuhn and Peloquin, 1974; Larrison, 1976). However, inflated breeding stock prices, poor reproduction, large farming expenses, and little economic return for nutria pelts (~$1.00 per pelt during the 1950s) resulted in the collapse of an industry whose boom was short-lived (Evans, 1970; Kuhn and Peloquin, 1974; Willner, 1982; Kinler et al., 1987).

More than 600 nutria farms existed in Oregon from the 1930s to the 1950s (Kuhn and Peloquin, 1974), and a number of farms existed in Washington at this time (Larrison, 1943; Guenther, 1950). Flooding and storms damaged holding structures and allowed some nutria to escape from fur farms, however, farmers often released their stock when farming became uneconomical. By the 1940s, feral nutria had been captured by trappers on both sides of the Cascade Mountains in Oregon and Washington, but most nutria were found in the Puget Sound area, the Willamette Valley, along coastal Oregon rivers, and along the Columbia River (Larrison, 1943; Ingles, 1965; Mace, 1970; Kuhn and Peloquin, 1974; Johnson and Cassidy, 1997). Only the Yakima River drainage in south-central Washington supported substantial numbers east of the Cascade Mountains until consecutive severe winters in the late 1970s greatly diminished this population (G. Brady, Washington Department of Fish and Wildlife, pers. comm.). As early as 1943, Larrison (1943) suggested that the nutria in the northwestern states should be studied so that control measures could be implemented before their range expanded. Unfortunately, little study of the growing nutria populations occurred. Indeed, even to the present day, the need for more research on the nutria in the northwestern states is being advocated (Sheffels and Sytsma, 2007).

As the feral nutria populations expanded in Oregon and Washington, nutria were trapped mostly by accidental catch until the 1970s (Sheffels and Sytsma, 2007). Then a major increase in pelt prices in the late 1970s and early 1980s corresponded with large increases in the annual trapping take. Trapping in Oregon peaked in the 1977-78 trapping year when 16,272 nutria were taken (Sheffels and Sytsma, 2007). However, pelt prices decreased and subsequently so did the annual nutria take. This trend was seen in other states, such as Louisiana, as well (Jordan and Mouton, 2010). The records indicate fluctuating harvest levels of nutria, which may reflect fluctuating pelt prices (Verts and Carraway, 1998) rather than fluctuating population densities. Nutria harvest data also indicate a relatively stable population geographically, in that nutria are consistently captured in the same counties (i.e., nutria do not appear to be spreading to previously unoccupied counties in appreciable numbers).

Short-term population stability, however, does not mean that all habitats suitable for nutria have been colonized or that a range expansion will not occur in the future. For example, Davison and Bohannon (2005) reported a small nutria population in Skagit County, Washington, which is relatively close to the Canadian border. An effort began immediately to remove the animals with the use of traps. Monitoring efforts continue, but no nutria sightings have been confirmed in Skagit County in several years (J. Dayton, USDA Wildlife Services, pers. comm.). In Oregon, anecdotal information suggests populations are expanding throughout the western side of the state, and nutria sightings have been confirmed near the southern border (Sheffels and Sytsma, 2007). A regional nutria habitat suitability model is being developed to identify areas for potential future range expansion in both Oregon and Washington (Carter et al., in prep.).

Initially, the nutria was listed as an unclassified wildlife species according to both Oregon and Washington administrative rules. More recently, it is classified as a prohibited non-native species in both states (Sheffels and Sytsma, 2007), and nutria can be harvested in unlimited numbers at any time of the year. All body-gripping traps (e.g., snares) are illegal in Washington, but no such restriction exists in Oregon. The classification of nutria as a prohibited species requires that all trapped animals be destroyed (i.e., are not to be released back to the wild) to reduce negative ecological and economic impacts caused by the species.

Nutria feed on a variety of plant species in the Pacific Northwest. Wentz (1971) found that broadleaf arrowhead (*Saggittaria latifolia*) and smartweed (*Polygonum* spp.) were selected by nutria in the Willamette Valley, Oregon, and he concluded these species may be locally reduced or extirpated by foraging nutria. Wentz observed nutria feeding on 40 different species of plants, and 15 species accounted for over 80% of the foraging observations. Wentz (1971) also noted that nutria densities varied with water level. Densities were lower (0.26 nutria/acre) during winter, but were much more clustered (56 nutria/acre) in summer when many seasonal ponds and streams were dried up.

Impacts to native vegetation were studied more recently by Meyer (2006) in coastal habitats of Oregon. He used paired exclosures and found that nutria herbivory on native vegetation was considerable, but varied depending on plant species type and disturbance history (Meyer and Beatty, 2006). Nutria foraged more heavily on herbaceous dicots (forbs) compared to monocots (grasses), resulting in lower herbaceous above ground biomass. Interestingly, below ground biomass did not vary inside and outside the exclosures, which is very different from what was reported in Maryland (Willner et al., 1979). Plant diversity also did not vary inside and outside the exclosures, but the authors noted that the study was only conducted over a 2-year period, hence changes in diversity may not have had time to manifest themselves. Meyer (2006) did not find a significant difference in herbivory in plots that previously had all above ground plant biomass removed ("harvested plots") versus plots that did not have biomass removed, but the unharvested plots had somewhat higher amounts of above ground biomass. Overall, the measured impacts on Oregon vegetation were not as severe as those reported in Maryland and Louisiana. Meyer (2006) also documented considerable erosion of banks as a result of nutria burrowing into banks to make dens. He noted that this could result in deteriorated habitat for native fish species.

Nutria herbivory can also be very destructive to regional wetland and riparian habitat restoration projects. Herbivory at a single restoration project site resulting in damages totaling $400,000 has been documented (T. Esary, City of Vancouver, pers. comm). Sheffels and Sytsma (2009) studied the impact of nutria on a wetland vegetation replanting project in the Willamette Valley, Oregon, and the use of plastic mesh seedling protection tubes to mitigate herbivory damage. Black cottonwood (*Populus balsamifera*), red osier dogwood (*Cornus sericea*), and willow (*Salix* spp.) live stakes were installed and monitored over a 14-week period. Unprotected plantings only had a 12% survival rate over the monitoring period, while live stakes protected by the plastic tubing demonstrated a 100% survival rate. Nutria displayed a preference for black cottonwood over both dogwood and willow, as nearly 90% of the unprotected cottonwood plantings were removed within 10 days. While the protection tubing did eliminate nutria herbivory over the 14-week period, Sheffels and Sytsma (2009) noted that this damage mitigation method may not be as successful over a longer period. In contrast, a similar study in Louisiana reported that plastic mesh tubing was completely ineffective for mitigating herbivory damage, even in the short-term (Conner and Toliver, 1987).

Nutria also have the potential to impact native fauna both directly and indirectly. Apparent declines in muskrat numbers have been observed in areas where nutria are abundant on the Finley National Wildlife Refuge in western Oregon (H. Brunkal, U.S. Fish and Wildlife Service, pers. comm.). Alteration of the vegetative community would be expected to have a significant influence on native fauna, especially sensitive amphibians and species that have niches similar to the nutria (e.g., muskrat, some waterfowl). Unfortunately, little information is available on the direct or indirect impacts of nutria on other fauna in the Pacific Northwest.

Nutria activities also result in direct and indirect impacts to humans, particularly in developed areas. The largest category of damage caused by nutria in the northwestern states involves burrowing and associated erosion (Sheffels and Sytsma, 2007), compared to extensive marsh damage in Maryland and Louisiana. In addition to erosion in natural systems, nutria burrowing results in substantial damage to private property, roads, and earthen water control structures (e.g. dikes, levees, embankments). This can lead to dangerous situations, with several reports of heavy machinery rolling over due to cave-ins of weakened banks (G. Oman, Wahkiakum County Diking District, pers. comm). Economic impacts can also be sizable, even for private citizens. For example, homeowners living near stream or wetland systems can face costs of thousands of dollars to repair nutria erosion damage (J. Stevenson, USDA Wildlife Services, pers. comm.)

Herbivory damage to a variety of agricultural crops also occurs in both Oregon and Washington. Larrison (1943) warned of the potential of increased damage to vegetable production in the Puget Sound area as early as the 1940s. Kuhn and Peloquin (1974) reported historic nutria damage to agricultural crops in the Willamette Valley and estimated losses of thousands of dollars per year. The crop damage was common to severe by the 1960s with damage to seed, grain, forage, hay, and trees (Kuhn and Peloquin, 1974). Damage to regional agricultural crops such as alfalfa, wheat, corn, peas, and sugar beets is still common today, but comprehensive damage estimates are not available. In contrast, state agencies in California took action early on to prevent the spread of nutria, eliminated most populations, and passed protective regulations on the farming of nutria. As a result, nutria did not become an agricultural pest in California (Schitoskey et al., 1972).

The widespread presence of nutria in suburban areas in the northwestern states creates additional issues (Sheffels and Sytsma, 2007). For example, people feeding nutria in public parks is a common occurrence (Figure 6). This phenomenon can result in high density nutria populations at these locations, increasing the risk of disease transmission. Nutria are known to be reservoirs for a variety of wildlife diseases, some of which are potentially transmissible to people, pets, and livestock (Howerth et al., 1994). Additionally, the potentially aggressive behavior of nutria poses a hazard to children and pets that approach them too closely (J. Tabor, Washington Department of Fish and Wildlife, pers. comm.) (Figure 7). Finally, private property damage issues are widespread. In addition to the erosion damage already discussed, private citizens often submit complaints of damage to gardens and lawns resulting from nutria feeding (J. Stevenson, USDA Wildlife Services, pers. comm.).

Figure 6. Managing nutria in urban/suburban areas can be particularly problematic. Here, people are feeding carrots to nutria along an urban wetland trail in Gresham, Oregon.

Figure 7. Close encounters with feral nutria can result in bites and disease transfer.

Personnel with the USDA Wildlife Services and state wildlife officers respond to nutria damage complaints. Although a number of damage prevention and control methods exist for nutria, commercial trapping appears to be the most common method used in Oregon and Washington. Some trappers have benefited from the introduction of nutria, although the monetary benefits now appear limited as nutria pelts are no longer highly valued for fur (Verts and Carraway, 1998). Low pelt prices offer little incentive to most trappers and consequently, commercial trapping may be limited as a management tool for nutria populations. Conversely, control of pest nutria can be a source of income for some trappers and pest control professionals. The development of new trapping methods with potentially higher efficiency, such as multiple capture traps (Witmer et al., 2008), are currently being researched (Sheffels et al., in prep.).

Unlike the coordinated control programs in Louisiana and Maryland, no organized nutria control program exists in the Pacific Northwest. Trapping and localized control efforts have been used to manage nutria populations since they were first introduced, and these techniques will likely continue to provide for nutria management in the near future. Trapping records indicate a relatively stable nutria population in the Pacific Northwest. However, nutria breed throughout the year in the northwestern states (Kuhn and Peloquin, 1974; Peloquin, 1969), and this prolific reproductive capability suggests rapid population growth is possible, especially if the current practice of localized nutria control and management continues.

Until new information indicates that regional nutria impacts are particularly severe to certain species, ecological communities, or geographic areas, it is unlikely that current management methods will be greatly altered or replaced. Lobbying efforts to ban trapping or outcries for nutria eradication could alter the status quo, but these scenarios do not appear to be immediate issues in Oregon or Washington. With the exception of research by Peloquin (1969) on growth and reproduction, Wentz (1971) on nutria density and impacts to marsh vegetation, Sheffels and Sytsma (2009) on herbivory damage mitigation, and Sheffels et al. (in prep) on alternative trapping methods, little study of the nutria has been conducted in the Pacific Northwest. Future research should focus on how the nutria's alteration of aquatic environments and its physical presence (i.e., potential competition and disease transmission) could impact sensitive fauna and vegetative communities. This research may also prompt additional work on alternative management techniques for nutria, particularly in suburban areas where current management options are limited.

NUTRIA MANAGEMENT AND RESEARCH NEEDS

Management plans to control nutria populations and their damage typically involve population reduction or eradication (Schitoskey et al., 1972; Gosling and Baker, 1989; Carter and Leonard, 2002). In the past, commercial trapping may have kept nutria populations at lower densities, especially when fur prices were high. However, with the decline in fur prices and reduced trapping effort, other methods to reduce populations and damage must be implemented. The tools used to accomplish reduction or eradication of nutria need to be assessed based on management objectives and approaches. The tools and methods of wildlife management vary by state, and even county, so it is important to make sure that federal, state, and county laws and regulations are being followed.

An analysis of methods to reduce the nutria population and marsh damage in Louisiana was conducted by Genesis Laboratories, Inc., and it serves as a good basis for establishing a management program (Genesis Laboratories, Inc., 2002; Mach, 2002). The potential methods that they identified in declining order of effectiveness were:

- Incentive payment plan;
- Chemical control;
- Incentive-bonus program;
- Trapping;
- Hunting;
- Induced infertility, and;
- Chemical repellents.

They noted that the last two methods are not available for nutria control at this time. The only mammalian infertility control material registered for use in the United States is GonaCon™, but it is only for use as an injectable drug for white-tailed deer (Gionfriddo et al., 2009). No nutria repellents are registered, and no effective repellent products have even been identified through research (LeBlanc, 1994). The incentive payment program, the number one recommendation of Genesis Laboratories, Inc., is the approach that the LDWF implemented as described in the Louisiana case study previously covered.

Rodent management often involves the use of several methods in an Integrated Pest Management (IPM) approach to maximize effectiveness and to minimize hazards to non-target animals (Witmer, 2007). Some aspects of nutria management options are considered below. Importantly, we discuss recent research and some research needs. Research needs that have been identified include improvement of nutria management and especially monitoring techniques, lures and attractants, toxicants, and multiple capture systems (Bounds et al., 2003; Sheffels and Sytsma, 2007). Additionally, landscape-level population and management modeling may also provide useful techniques to future management (Carter et al., 1999). Finally, we hope that more benefit-cost analyses (e.g., Panzacchi et al., 2007) will be conducted to assure an economic benefit to nutria management or eradication programs.

Monitoring Techniques. Detecting and reducing or eliminating low-density populations of nutria is a major challenge in the effort to completely remove nutria from an area. Low population densities occur when an invasive species is first introduced into an area and again after management efforts to reduce or eliminate the species are implemented. The investment of resources and effort by resource managers can be negated by residual nutria that go undetected and are left to quickly repopulate an area, so methods to detect the few remaining individuals are important. For example, Wildlife Services' use of Labrador retrievers at Blackwater NWR has facilitated their efforts to remove any remaining nutria that personnel may have missed (Kendrot, 2004). Retrievers are effective at detecting nutria on air currents both in open water and mud situations. With the help of retrievers, personnel can remove individual nutria from an area immediately rather than making repeated visits to the site when using traps.

Adequate marking and monitoring methods are also essential for the study of free-ranging nutria. Fichet-Calvet (1999) found that rhodamine B fluorescence remained in nutria guard hairs for at least 255 days, hence could be useful in various nutria population, food habits, and habitat use studies. Radio telemetry has commonly been used in nutria studies, but various problems result from using this method of marking and locating individuals such as radio-transmitter failure or removal and possibly increased predation risk (Nolfo and Hammond, 2006; Nolfo-Clements, 2009). Nolfo and Hammond (2006) found that implanted radio-transmitters alleviated some of these problems. Similarly, Meyer (2006) found that injected passive integrative transponders (PIT tags) were an effective nutria marking method and did not result in the problems found with ear tags and radio-transmitters. Haramis and White (2011) developed a beaded collar to which radio-transmitters could be attached. These devices were lighter and caused less friction than traditional radio-transmitter collars. Similarly, Merino et al. (2007) developed a tail-mounted radio-transmitter for nutria which avoided some of the problems that neck collars cause. Finckbeiner (2005) developed a method to recognize individual nutria from their whisker pattern. Finally, Callahan et al. (2005) identified a suite of microsatellite DNA markers that can be used to study population dynamics, migration, and breeding structure in nutria populations.

Lures/Attractants. Lures and attractants are useful in nutria control for attracting nutria to sites where a treatment is presented (e.g., trap, rodenticide bait station, monitoring device). Attractants can increase the number of nutria visiting bait stations and reduce time required for bait stations to be operational, thereby reducing non-target exposure. Most rodent species have a keen sense of smell and respond to various odors (Mason et al., 1994). When presented with visual, auditory, and odor cues, nutria responded best to odors; thus olfactory cues appear to have the greatest potential for developing future attractants (Nolte et al., 2004). In other olfactory trials, nutria were most attracted to synthetic semiochemicals such as fur extract from female nutria and nutria anal gland secretions (Finckbeiner, 2005; Lee et al., 2007; Jojola et al., 2009). Additionally, nutria are more attracted to fertilized marsh plants when offered with non-fertilized marsh plants (Witmer et al., 2008; Jojola et al., 2009). Conversely, while nutria emit audio calls, recorded calls tended to be avoided and nutria are indifferent toward live conspecifics as cues (Nolte et al., 2004). The assessment of other potential olfactory attractants for nutria should continue to increase the effectiveness of management techniques.

Trapping. As previously discussed, trapping is an important nutria management tool with cage, leg-hold, and kill traps all being used (LeBlanc, 1994). However, Chapman et al. (1978) noted that leg-hold traps caused more injuries and deaths to nutria than cage traps. Some researchers have found that the placement of traps on floating platforms reduces non-target animal captures and increases trapping success (Baker and Clarke, 1988; Welch, 2005). Another study found baited rafts to be less effective when placed in coastal marsh, but the researchers noted that nutria had access to other food sources available in late spring when the study took place (Nolte et al., 2004). They suggested employing baited rafts during the winter when native forage is less abundant. In Germany, Meyer (2006) was able to capture adequate numbers of nutria for field studies using a dip net. However, that was in an urban setting where the nutria were acclimated to the presence of humans. Multiple-capture traps (Figure 8) would enable several nutria to be captured within a single trap, thereby reducing the effort of maintaining numerous traps and checking them frequently. Traps with one-way doors are ideal for multiple-capture systems in that captured live nutria may serve as a lure for other nutria in the area. Witmer et al. (2008) developed and tested a nutria multiple-capture live trap. The traps were effective in catching nutria when baited with fertilized marsh plants or food items such as corn, carrots, and grains. Researchers or trappers can visit these traps periodically (as per state regulations) to mark and release nutria, to remove and translocate the nutria (where regulations allow), or to euthanize the nutria. Additional research on the efficacy of this multiple-capture trap design is being conducted (Sheffels et al., in prep).

Toxicants. Zinc phosphide is the only toxicant currently registered for controlling nutria in the United States (LeBlanc, 1994), but other rodenticides have the potential to be effective control materials for nutria (Genesis Laboratories, Inc., 2002; Mach, 2002). Schitoskey et al. (1972) recommended toxicants, such as zinc phosphide, for large-scale nutria control. Placing zinc phosphide-treated bait on rafts has been an effective method to reduce nutria populations on canals and other open waterways and to reduce exposure to non-target animals to the toxic baits (LeBlanc, 1994). There is a growing concern in the United States and several other countries about primary (consumption of the toxic bait) and secondary (consumption of poisoned nutria) exposure of non-target animals to rodenticides and especially anticoagulant rodenticides. Evans and Ward (1967) found that dogs and mink (*Mustela vison*) could be poisoned by feeding them nutria that had been poisoned with anticoagulants and recommended that these compounds not be used to control nutria in coastal areas of the United States. Conversely, Witmer et al. (2010) determined that the risk to alligators from consuming poisoned nutria was low.

Figure 8. Nutria within a multiple-capture live trap in Louisiana.

CONCLUSION

Our review demonstrates the significant impact that a large, invasive, aquatic herbivore can have on marsh ecosystems and other valuable resources. Introduced nutria are a challenge to control and even more difficult to eradicate from a sizable area. However, with an effective strategy and sufficient resources and effort, they can be removed from large areas. Alternatively, intensive management of populations can maintain nutria densities at levels whereby damage to marshes and other resources can be kept at environmentally and economically acceptable levels. Improving the tools available to managers would enhance the effectiveness and efficiency of nutria control. For example, Labrador retrievers are more commonly being used to detect nutria at low densities. Effective attractants will most likely be biologically-based or food-based olfactory cues and would serve to enhance other means of control such as single-animal and multiple-capture traps and rodenticide baits. Zinc phosphide is currently the only registered toxicant for nutria, and research has been conducted to improve its effectiveness while reducing potential hazards. Other toxicants could be developed and tested on nutria, along with different types of delivery systems. Substantial progress has been made on methods to mark, monitor, and identify individual nutria for field studies and control efforts. We now know that marsh ecosystems can recover after nutria population reduction or elimination. Hopefully, sufficient resources will be made available and effort put forth to accomplish the task of population reduction or elimination in the United States and other countries where nutria have been introduced.

REFERENCES

Ashbrook, F. G. (1948). Nutrias grow in United States. *Journal of Wildlife Management* 12, 87-95.

Baker, S. J. and Clarke, C. N. (1988). Cage trapping coypus (Myocastor coypus) on baited rafts. *Journal of Applied Ecology* 25, 41-48.

Borgnia, M., Galante, M. L., and Cassini, M. H. (2000). Diet of the coypu (nutria, Myocastor coypus) in agro-systems of Argentinean pampas. *Journal of Wildlife Management* 64(2), 354-361.

Bounds, D. B. and Carowan, Jr., G. A. (2000). Nutria: a nonnative nemesis. *Transactions of the North American Wildlife and Natural Resources Conference* 65, 405-413.

Bounds, D.B. and Mollett, T.A. (2000). Can nutria be eradicated in Maryland? In T.P. Salmon and A.C. Crabb (Eds.), *Proceedings of the 19th Vertebrate Pest Conference.* (Pg. 121-126), Davis, California: University of California.

Bounds, D. L., Sherfy, M. H., and Mollett, T. A. (2003). Nutria. In G. A. Feldhamer, B. C. Thompson, and J. A. Chapman (Eds.), *Wild mammals of North America: biology, management, and conservation.* (Pp. 1119-1147), Baltimore, Maryland: John Hopkins University Press.

Callahan, C. R., Henderson, A. P., Eackles, M. S., and King, T. L. (2005). Microsatellite DNA markers for the study of population structure and dynamics in nutria (Myocastor coypus). *Molecular Ecology Notes* 5(1), 124-126.

Carter, J., Foote, A. L., and Johnson-Randall, L. A. (1999). Modeling the effect of nutria (Myocastor coypus) on wetland loss. *Wetlands* 19(1), 209-219.

Carter, J. and Leonard, B. P. (2002). A review of the literature on the worldwide distribution, spread of, and efforts to eradicate the coypu (Myocastor coypus). *Wildlife Society Bulletin* 30, 162-175.

Chapman, J. A., Willner, G. R., Dixon, K. R., and Pursley, D. (1978). Differential survival rates among leg-trapped and live-trapped nutria. *Journal of Wildlife Management* 42(4), 926-928.

Cocchi, R. and Riga, F. (2008). Control of a coypu Myocastor coypus population in northern Italy and management implications. *Italian Journal of Zoology* 75(1), 37-42.

Conner, W. H. and Toliver, J. R. (1987). The problem of planting Louisiana swamplands when nutria (Myocastor coypu) are present. In N. R. Holler (Ed.), *Proceedings of the 3rd Eastern Wildlife Damage Control Conference.* (Pp. 42-49), Gulf Shores, Alabama: 3rd Eastern Wildlife Damage Control Conference (Oct 18-21, 1987).

Corriale, M. J., Arias, S. M., Bó, R. F., and Porini, G. (2006). Habitat-use patterns of the coypu Myocastor coypus in an urban wetland of its original distribution. *Acta Theriologica* 51(3), 295-302.

Davison, M. and Bohannon, J. (2005). Nutria (Myocastor coypus) in Skagit County, WA: background, trapping results, and recommendations. Washington Department of Fish and Wildlife.

Ellis, E. A. (1963). Some effects of selective feeding by the coypu (Myocastor coypus) on the vegetation of Broadland. *Transactions of the Norfolk and Norwich Naturalists' Society* 20, 32-35.

Erb, J. and Perry, Jr., H. R. (2003). Muskrats. In G. A. Feldhamer, B. C. Thompson, and J. A. Chapman (Eds.), *Wild mammals of North America: biology, management, and conservation.* (Pp. 311-348), Baltimore, Maryland: John Hopkins University Press.

Evans, J. (1970). About nutria and their control. Resource Publ. No. 86. Washington, D.C.: Fish and Wildlife Service, U.S. *Department of Interior.* 65 pp.

Evans, J. and Ward, A. L. (1967). Secondary poisoning associated with anticoagulant-killed nutria. *Journal of the American Veterinary Medical Association* 151(7), 856-861.

Evers, D. E., Sasser, C. E., Gosselink, J. G., Fuller, D. A. and Visser, J. M. (1998). The impact of vertebrate herbivores on wetland vegetation in Atchafalaya Bay, Louisiana. *Estuaries* 21(1), 1-13.

Fichet-Calvet, E. (1999). Persistence of a systematic labeling in fur and guard hairs by ingestion of rhodamine B in Myocastor coypus (Rodentia). *Mammalia* 63(2), 241-244.

Finckbeiner, S. M. (2005). Partial characterization of coypu scent gland compounds and a new technique for computer-aided photographic identification of individual coypu. Master's thesis. Ithaca, New York: *Cornell University.* 109 pp.

Ford, M. A. and Grace, J. B. (1998). The interactive effects of fire and herbivory on a coastal marsh in Louisiana. *Wetlands* 18(1), 1-8.

Fuller, D. A., Sasser, C. E., Johnson, W. B., and Gosselink, J. G. (1985). The effects of herbivory on vegetation on islands in Atchafalaya Bay, Louisiana. *Wetlands* 4, 105-114.

Gabrey, S. W., Kinler, N., and Elsey, R. M. (2009). Impacts of nutria removal on food habits of American alligators in Louisiana. *Southeastern Naturalist* 8(2), 347-354.

Gayo, V., Cuervo, P., Rosadilla, D., Birriel, S., Dell'Oca, L., Trelles, A., Cuore, U., and Mera y Sierra, R. (2011). Natural fasciola hepatica infection in nutria (Myocastor coypus) in Uruguay. *Journal of Zoo and Wildlife Medicine* 42(2), 354-356.

Geho, E. M., Campbell, D., and Keddy, P. A. (2007). Quantifying ecological filters: the relative impact of herbivory, neighbours, and sediment on an oligohaline marsh. *Oikos* 116, 1006-1016.

Genesis Laboratories, Inc. (2002). Nutria (Myocastor coypus) in Louisiana. Wellington, Colorado: *Genesis Laboratories*, Inc. 155 pp.

Gionfriddo, J. P., Eisemann, J. D., Sullivan, K. J., Sealey, R. S., Miller, L. A., Fagerstone, K.A., Engeman, R. M. and Yoder, C. A. (2009). Field test of a single-injection gonadotrophin-releasing hormone immunocontraceptive vaccine in female white-tailed deer. *Wildlife Research*, 36, 177-184.

Gosling, L.M. (1977). Coypu. In G. B. Corbet and H. N. Southern (Eds.), *The Handbook of British mammals*. Second Edition. (Pp. 256-265), Oxford: Blackwell Scientific Press.

Gosling, M. (1989). Extinction to order. *New Science* 121(1654), 44-49.

Gosling, L. M. and Baker, S. J. (1989). The eradication of muskrats and coypus from Britain. *Biological Journal of the Linnean Society* 38, 39-51.

Gosling, L. M., Guyon, G. E., and Wright, K. M. (1980). Diurnal activity of feral coypus (Myocastor coypus) during the cold winter of 1978-9. *Journal of Zoology* (London) 192,143-146.

Grace, J. B. and Ford, M. A. (1996). The potential impact of herbivores on the susceptibility of the marsh plant Sagittaria lancifolia to saltwater intrusion in coastal wetlands. *Estuaries* 19, 13-20.

Guenther, S. E. (1950). Nutria. Game Bulletin 2:5. Olympia, Washington: Washington State Game Department.

Guichón, M. L., Benítez, V. B., Abba, A., Borgnia, M., and Cassini, M. H. (2003b). Foraging behavior of coypus Myocastor coypus: why do coypus consume aquatic plants? *Acta Oecologica* 24, 241-246.

Guichón, M. L., Borgnia, M., Fernández Righi, C., Cassini, G. H., and Cassini, M. H. (2003a). Social behavior and group formation in the coypu (Myocastor coypus) in the Argentinean pamas. *Journal of Mammalogy* 84(1), 254-262.

Guichón, M. L. and Cassini, M. H. (1999). Local determinants of coypu distribution along the Luján River, eastcentral Argentina. *Journal of Wildlife Management* 63(3), 895-900.

Guichón, M. L. and Cassini, M. H. (2005). Population parameters of indigenous populations of Myocastor coypus: the effect of hunting pressure. *Acta Theriologica* 50 (1), 125-132.

Guichón, M. L., Doncaster, C. P., and Cassini, M. H. (2003c). Population structure of coypus (Myocastor coypus) in their region of origin and comparison with introduced populations. *Journal of Zoology*, London 261, 265-272.

Guntenspergen, G. R. and Nordby, J. C. (2006). The impact of invasive plants on tidal-marsh vertebrate species: common reed and smooth cordgrass as case studies. *Studies in Avian Biology*, 32, 229-237.

Haramis, G. M. and White, T. S. (2011). A beaded collar for dual micro GPS/VHF transmitter attachment to nutria. *Mammalia* 75(1), 79-82.

Harris, V. T. and Webert, F. (1962). Nutria feeding activity and its effect on marsh vegetation in southwestern Louisiana. Special Scientific Report: Wildlife No. 64. Washington: *USDI Fish and Wildlife Service*. 53 pp.

Howerth, E. W., Reeves, A. J., McElveen, M. R., and Austin, F. W. (1994). Survey for selected diseases in nutria (Myocastor coypus) from Louisiana. *Journal of Wildlife Diseases* 30(3), 450-453.

Hutchins, M., Kleiman, D. G., Geist, V., and McDade, M. C. (Eds.). (2004). Grzimek's Animal Life Encyclopedia, Second Edition, Volume 16, Mammals V. Farmington Hills, Michigan: *Gale, Inc*. 670 pp.

Ingles, L. G. (1965). *Mammals of the Pacific States*: California, Oregon, Washington. Stanford, California: Stanford University Press. 507 pp.

Joanen, T., McNease, L., Elsey, R., and Staton, M. (1997). The commercial consumptive use of the American Alligator (Alligator mississippiensis) in Louisiana: its effect on conservation. In C. H. Freese (Ed.), Harvesting Wild Species – *Implications for Biodiversity*. (Pp. 465-506), Baltimore, Maryland: Johns Hopkins University Press.

Johnson Randall, L. A. and Foote, A. L. (2005). Effects of managed impoundments and herbivory on wetland plant production and stand structure. *Wetlands* 25(1), 38-50.

Johnson, R. E. and Cassidy, K. M. (1997). Terrestrial mammals of Washington State: location data and predicted distributions. Washington State Gap Analysis - Final Report, Volume 3. Seattle, Washington: *Washington Cooperative Fish and Wildlife Research Unit, University of Washington*. 304 pp.

Jojola, S. M., Witmer, G. W., and Burke, P. W. (2009). Evaluation of attractants to improve trapping success of nutria on Louisiana coastal marsh. *Journal of Wildlife Management* 73(8), 1414-1419.

Jordan, J. and Mouton, E. (2010). Nutria harvest and distribution 2009-2010 and a survey of nutria herbivory damage in coastal Louisiana in 2010. Coastal and Nongame Resources, Louisiana Department of Wildlife and Fisheries. Coastwide Nutria Control Program CWPPRA Project (LA-03b).

Kendrot, S. (2004). Eradication strategies for nutria in Chesapeake and Delaware Bay Wetlands: annual report September 1, 2002-August 31,

2003. Nutria Project, U.S. Department of Agriculture/Wildlife Services, Annapolis, Maryland, USA. 12 pp.

Kendrot, S. (2011). Restoration through eradication: protecting Chesapeake Bay marshlands from invasive nutria (Myocastor coypus). In D. Veitch, M. Clout, and D. Towns (Eds.), *Island Invasions: Eradication and Management.* (Pp. 313-319), Gland, Switzerland: IUCN.

Kinler, N. (Undated). Louisiana Nutria. *Menu*. New Iberia, Louisiana. 4 pp.

Kinler, N. W., Linscombe, G., and Ramsey, P. R. (1987). Nutria. In M. Novak, J. A. Baker, M. E. Obbard, and B. Malloch (Eds.), *Wild furbearer management and conservation in North America*. (Pp. 327-342), Ontario, Canada: Ministry of Natural Resources.

Kuhn, L. W. and Peloquin, E. P. (1974). Oregon's nutria problem. In W. V. Johnson, R. E. Marsh, and A. Chin (Eds.), *Proceedings of the 6th Vertebrate Pest Conference* (Pp. 101-105), Davis, California: University of California.

Larrison, E. J. (1943). Feral coypus in the Pacific Northwest. *The Murrelet* 24, 3-9.

Larrison, E. J. (1976). Mammals of the Northwest: Washington, Oregon, Idaho, and British Columbia. Seattle, Washington: *Seattle Audubon Society*. 256 pp.

LeBlanc, D. J. (1994). Nutria. In S. E. Hygnstrom, R. M. Timm and G. E. Larson (Eds.), Prevention and Control of Wildlife Damage. (Pp. B-71 - B-80), Lincoln, Nebraska: Cooperative Extension Division, University of Nebraska.

Lee, H., Finckbeiner, S., Yu, J. S., Wiemer, D. F., Eisner, T., and Attygalle, A. B. (2007). Characterization of (E,E)-farnesol and its fatty acid esters from anal scent glands of nutria (Myocastor coypus) by gas chromatography – mass spectrometry and gas chromatography – infrared spectrometry. *Journal of Chromatography* A 1165, 136-143.

Lever, C. (1985). *Naturalized mammals of the world*. New York, New York: Longman Inc. 487 pp.

Linscombe, G. (2001). 2000-2001 Annual report. Louisiana Fur and Alligator Advisory Council, Louisiana Department of Wildlife and Fisheries, New Iberia, Louisiana.

Linscombe, G., N. Kinler, N. W., and Wright, V. (1981). Nutria population density and vegetative changes in brackish marsh in coastal Louisiana. In J. A. Chapman and D. Pursley (Eds.), *Proceedings of the Worldwide Furbearer Conference* (Pp. 129-141).

Llewellyn, D. W. and Shaffer, G. P. (1993). Marsh restoration in the presence of intense herbivory: the role of Justicia lanceolata (Chapm.) small. *Wetlands* 13(3), 176-184.

Long, J. L. (2003). *Introduced mammals of the world*. Collingwood, Australia: CSIRO Publishing. 590 pp.

Lowery, G. H. (1974). *The mammals of Louisiana*. Baton Rouge, Louisiana, Louisiana State University. 565 pp.

Mace, R. U. (1970). Oregon's furbearing animals. Wildl. Bull. No. 6. Portland, Oregon: *Oregon State Game Commission*. 82 pp.

Mach, J. J. (2002). Nutria control in Louisiana. In R. M. Timm and R. H. Schmidt (Eds.), *Proceedings of the 20th Vertebrate Pest Conference*. (Pp. 32-39), Davis, California: University of California.

Martino, P., Sassaroli, J. C., Calvo, J., Zapata, J., and Gimeno, E. (2008). A mortality survey of free range nutria (Myocastor coypus). *European Journal of Wildlife Research* 54(2), 293-297.

Martino, P. and Stanchi, N. (1994). Epizootic pneumonia in nutria. *Journal of Veterinary Medicine, Series* B. 41, 561-566.

Marx, J., Mouton, E., and Linscombe, G. (2004). Nutria harvest distribution 2003-2004 and a survey of nutria herbivory damage in coastal Louisiana in 2004. Baton Rouge, Louisiana: Fur and Refuge Division, Louisiana Department of Wildlife and Fisheries/Coastwide Nutria Control Program, *CWPPRA Project* (LA-03b). 45pp.

Mason, J. R., Epple, G., and Nolte, D. L. (1994). Semiochemicals and improvements in rodent control. In B. G. Galef, P. Valsecchi, and M. Mainard (Eds.), Ontogeny and social transmission of food preferences in mammals: *basic and applied research*. (Pp. 327-346), Reading, United Kingdom: Harwood Academic.

McFalls, T. B., Keddy, P. A., Campbell, D., and Shaffer, G. (2010). Hurricanes, floods, levees, and nutria: vegetation responses to interacting disturbance and fertility regimes with implications for coastal wetland restoration. *Journal of Coastal Research* 26(5), 901-911.

Merino, S., Carter, J., and Thibodeaux, G. (2007). Testing tail-mounted transmitters with Myocastor coypus (nutria). *Southeastern Naturalist* 6(1), 159-164.

Meyer, A. (2006). The impacts of nutria on vegetation and erosion in Oregon. Master's Thesis. Binghamton, New York: *State University of New York at Binghamton*. 60 pp.

Meyer, A. M. and Beatty, S. W. (2006). The impacts of nutria on vegetation in Oregon. In R. M. Timm and J. M. O'Brien (Eds.), *Proceedings of the*

22nd Vertebrate Pest Conference. (Pp. 187-191), Davis, California: University of California.

Meyer, J. (2006). Field methods for studying nutria. *Wildlife Society Bulletin* 34(3), 850-852.

Meyer, J., Klemann, N., and Halle, S. (2005). Diurnal activity patterns of coypu in an urban habitat. *Acta Theriologica* 50(2), 207-211.

Nolfo-Clements, L. E. (2009). Nutria survivorship, movement patterns, and home ranges. *Southeastern Naturalist* 8(3), 399-410.

Nolfo, L. E. and Hammond, E. E. (2006). A novel method for capturing and implanting radiotransmitters in nutria. *Wildlife Society Bulletin* 34(1), 104-110.

Nolte, D. L., Barras, A. E., Adams, S. E., Linscombe, R. G., and LeBlanc D. J. (2004). Assessing potential for using zinc phosphide bait to control nutria on Louisiana coastal marsh. In R. M. Timm and W. P. Gorenzel (Eds.), *Proceedings of the 21st Vertebrate Pest Conference.* (Pp. 150-157), Davis, California: University of California.

Nowak, R. M. (Ed.). 1999. *Walker's Mammals of the World*, Sixth Edition, Volume II. Baltimore, Maryland: John Hopkins University Press. 1936 pp.

Panzacchi, M., Bertolino, S., Cocchi, R., and Genovesi, P. (2007). Population control of coypu Myocastor coypus in Italy compared to eradication in UK: a cost-benefit analysis. *Wildlife Biology* 13, 159-171.

Pathikonda, S., Ackleh, A. S., Hasenstein, K. H., and Mopper, S. (2008). Invasion, disturbance, and competition: modeling the fate of coastal plant populations. *Conservation Biology* 23(1), 164-173.

Peloquin, E. P. (1969). Growth and reproduction of the feral nutria Myocotor coypus (Molina) near Corvallis, Oregon. M. S. Thesis. Corvallis, Oregon: *Oregon State University*. 55 pp.

Pridham, T. J., Budd, J., and Karstad, L. H. A. (1966). Common diseases of fur bearing animals II. Diseases of chinchillas, nutria, and rabbits. *Canadian Veterinary Journal* 7(4), 84-87.

Prigioni, C., Balestrieri, A., and Remonti, L. (2005a). Food habits of the coypu, Myocastor coypus, and its impact on aquatic vegetation in a freshwater habitat of NW Italy. *Folia Zoology* 54(3), 269-277.

Prigioni, C., Remonti, L., and Balestrieri, A. (2005b). Control of the coypu (Myocastor coypus) by cage-trapping in the cultivated plain of northern Italy. *Hystrix Italian Journal of Mammalogy* 16(2), 159-167.

Pyke, C. R., Thomas, R., Porter, R. D., Hellmann, J. J., Dukes, J. S., Lodge, D. M., and Chavarria, G. (2008). Current practices and future opportunities for policy on climate change and invasive species. *Conservation Biology* 22(3), 585-592.

Reggiani, G., Boitani, L., and De Stefano, R. (1995). Population dynamics and regulation in the coypu Myocastor coypus in central Italy. *Ecography* 18, 138-146.

Saadoun, A., Cabrera, M. C., and Castellucio, P. (2006). Fatty acids, cholesterol and protein content of nutria (Myocastor coypus) meat from an intensive production system in Uruguay. *Meat Science* 72, 778-784.

Schitoskey, Jr., F., Evans, J., and LaVoie, G. K. (1972). Status and control of nutria in California. *In R. E. Marsh* (Ed.), *Proceedings of the 5th Vertebrate Pest Conference.* (Pp. 15-17), Davis, California: University of California.

Shaffer, G. P., Sasser, C. E., Gosselink, J. G., and Reják̇nek, M. (1992). Vegetation dynamics in the emerging Atchafalaya Delta, Louisiana, USA. *Journal of Ecology* 80, 677-687.

Sheal, J. (2003). Government and the management of an alien pest species: a British perspective. *Landscape Research* 28(1), 101-111.

Sheffels, T. and Sytsma, M. (2007). Report on nutria management and research in the Pacific Northwest. Unpublished Report. Portland, Oregon: Portland State University. 49 pp.

Sheffels, T. and Sytsma, M. (2009). Nutria herbivory at Delta Ponds Wetland Complex in Eugene, OR. Unpublished Report. Portland, Oregon: Portland State University. 13 pp.

Southwick Associates. (2004). Potential economic losses associated with uncontrolled nutria populations in Maryland's portion of the Chesapeake Bay. Ferandina Beach, Florida: Southwick Associates. 17 pp.

Takekawa, J. Y., Woo, I., Spautz, H., Nur, N., Grenier, L., Malamud-Roam, K., Nordby, J. C., Cohen, A. N., Malmud-Roam, F. and Wainwright-De La Cruz, S.E. (2006). Environmental threats to tidal marsh vertebrates of the San Francisco Bay estuary. *Studies in Avian Biology* 32, 176-197.

Taylor, K. L. and Grace, J. B. (1995). The effects of vertebrate herbivory on plant community structure in the coastal marshes of the Pearl River, Louisiana, USA. *Wetlands* 15(1), 68-73.

Verts, B. J. and Carraway, L. (1998). *Land mammals of Oregon.* Berkeley, California: University of California Press. 668 pp.

Waterkeyn, A., Pineau, O., Grillas, P., and Brendonck, L. (2010). Invertebrate dispersal by aquatic mammals: a case study with nutria Myocastor coypus (Rodentia, Mammalia) in Southern France. *Hydrobiologia* 654(1), 267-271.

Welch, B. (2005). Floating colony traps for muskrats. *American Trapper* 45, 34-36.

Wentz, W. A. (1971). The impact of nutria (Myocastor coypus) on marsh vegetation in the Willamette Valley, Oregon. M. S. Thesis. Corvallis, Oregon: Oregon State University. 41 pp.

Willner, G. R., Chapman, J. A., and Pursley, D. (1979). Reproduction, physiological responses, food habits, and abundance of nutria on Maryland marshes. *Wildlife Monographs* 65, 1-43.

Willner, G. R. (1982). Nutria. In J. A. Chapman and G. A. Feldhamer (Eds.), *Wild mammals of North America: biology, management, and economics.* (Pp. 1059-1076), Baltimore, Maryland: Johns Hopkins University Press.

Wilsey, B. J., Chabreck, R. H., and Linscombe, R. G. (1991). Variation in nutria diets in selected freshwater forested wetlands of Louisiana. *Wetlands* 11(2), 263-278.

Witmer, G. W. (2007). The ecology of vertebrate pests and integrated pest management (IPM). M. Kogan and P. Jepson (Eds.). *Perspectives in Ecological Theory and Integrated Pest Management.* (Pp. 393-410), Cambridge, United Kingdom: Cambridge University Press.

Witmer, G. W., Burke, P. W., Jojola, S., and Nolte, D. L. (2008). A live trap model and field trial of a nutria (Rodentia) multiple capture trap. *Mammalia* 72, 352-354.

Witmer, G. W., Eisemann, J. D., Primus, T. M., O'Hare, J. R., Perry, K. R., Elsey, R. M., and Trosclair III, P. L. (2010). Assessing potential risk to alligators, Alligator mississippiensis, from nutria control with zinc phosphide rodenticide baits. *Bulletin of Environmental Contamination and Toxicology* 84, 698-702.

Woods, C. A., Contreras, L., Willner-Chapman, G., and Whidden, H. P. (1992). Myocastor coypus. *Mammalian Species* 398, 1-8.

Woodward, R. T., and Wui, Y. S. (2001). *Ecological Economics*, 37, 257-270.

In: Marshes
Editors: D. C. Abreu et al.

ISBN 978-1-61942-715-0
© 2012 Nova Science Publishers, Inc.

Chapter 3

THE MESOCOSM MARSH ECOLOGY OF TWO SOUTHWESTERN SPANISH ESTUARIES: APPLICATIONS

M. L. González-Regalado[1], F. Ruiz[*,1], J. Borrego[2], M. Abad[1], E. X. García,[3] and A. Toscano[1]

[1]Departamento de Geodinámica y Paleontología,
Universidad de Huelva, Avda. Tres de Marzo, Huelva, Spain
[2]Departamento de Geología, Universidad de Huelva,
Avda. Tres de Marzo, Huelva, Spain
[3]Departamento de Botánica y Zoología,
Universidad de Guadalajara, México

ABSTRACT

This paper analyzes the foraminiferal and ostracod assemblages of marsh environments in two estuaries of southwestern Spain. High and low marsh deposits may be differentiated according to the percentages of some foraminiferal species (*Jadammina macrescens*, *Trochammina inflata*), the presence/absence of other foraminifers (mainly miliolids) or the presence/absence of ostracods. These features and some variations observed in different estuarine environments (fluvial, middle, marine) are directly applicable in the detection of (palaeo-)eustatic changes, salinity variations or hydrodynamic gradients.

1. INTRODUCTION

Marshes are one of the most important environments of recent estuarine systems. They present a very high biological diversity, with a remarkable contribution to the human food resources of littoral areas. In addition, their importance as archives of recent environmental changes is largely recongnised (e.g. Fatela et al., 2009).

Both foraminifera and ostracoda are included between the most interesting mesocosm groups of these environments. They are applied to evaluate the present-day sea level rise (e.g. Rossi et al., 2011), changes derived from heavy metal pollution (e.g. Ruiz et al., 2004) or the detection of tsunami-induced deposits (Horton et al., 2011).

This chapter reviews the foraminiferal and ostracod faunas collected until now in fluvial to salt marshes of two southwestern Spanish estuaries. Data are mainly extracted from Morales (1993), Ruiz et al. (1996), Ruiz et al. (2000), and González-Regalado et al. (2001). A wide comparison was made with: a) some environmental parameters (salinity, grain size, organic carbon); and b) the mesocosm assemblages of both groups in other estuarine marshes located worldwide. Finally, some possible applications are proposed.

2. STUDY AREA

The southwestern Spanish littoral is transversed by the Guadiana, Piedras, Odiel, Tinto and Guadalquivir rivers, which form different estuaries on a clastic Plio-Pleistocene substrate (Figure 1). The Guadiana river is the main sediment source of this zone, with a mean annual discharge of 144.4 m^3s^{-1} (Ojeda, 1988). Near the mouth, this estuary presents the so-called Carreras subsystem, an area characterized by marsh deposits protected by sandy spits and separated by distributary channels.

The Piedras River is a short stream with very restricted fluvial supply (144.4 m^3s^{-1}) due to the presence of an important dam located upstream (Borrego and Pendón, 1989). Its mouth is occupied by a bar-built estuary protected by an elongated spit.

Interaction between both fresh and marine waters delimits three sectors in each estuary (see Figure 1 for location and Table 1 for salinity ranges): a): (a) Fluvial Estuary, dominated by riverine transport and sedimentation processes; (b) Middle Estuary, well mixed during spring tides and partially stratified during neap tides; and (c) Marine Estuary, a tide-dominated zone. This distinction is clear in the Guadiana Estuary, whereas these sectors are more diffuse in the Piedras Estuary.

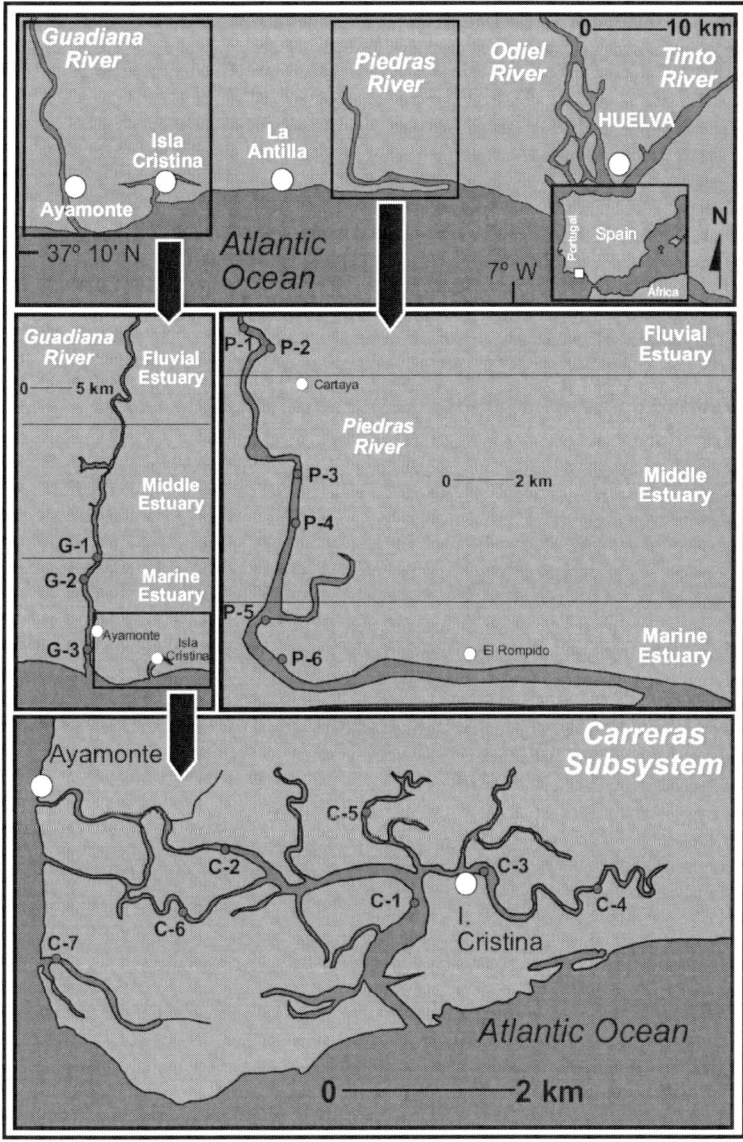

Figure 1. Geographical setting of the Guadiana and Piedras estuaries, with location of the samples studied.

The tidal regime is mesotidal and semidiurnal, with a mean range of 2 m and different critical tide levels (Figure 2: modified from Borrego et al., 1993). Low marsh environments are located between the Mean Neap High Water level (MNHW) and the Mean High Water Level (MHW) and present alternating conditions of exposure and submersion that allow the colonization by halophytes (mainly *Spartina*, *Salicornia* and *Sarcocornia*). These deposits are overlain by similar high marsh sediments (Figure 2: MHW-MSHW), more oxidized due to the increasing aerial exposure.

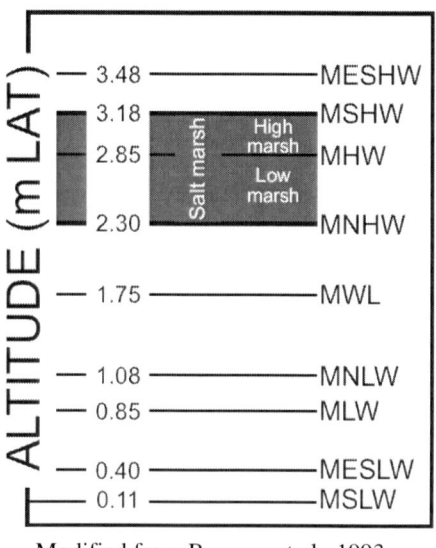

Modified from Borrego et al., 1993.

Figure 2. Critical tidal levels in the Huelva estuaries. LAT: Low Astronomical Tide; MESLW: Mean Esquinox Spring Low Water; MSLW; Mean Sprin Low Water, MLW: Mean Low Water; MWL: Mean Water Level; MNHW: Mean Neap High Water; MHW: Mean High Water; MSHW: Mean Spring High Water; MESHW: Mean Equinox Spring High Water.

These marshes are characterized by silty sediments in most cases, although fluvial bars may have attached incipient sandy marsh bodies (Table 1: samples P1 or P2). Heavy metal contents are low o moderate (Cr: 42-125 mg kg^{-1}; Cu: 9-88 mg kg^{-1}; Zn: 57-232 mg kg^{-1}; Pb: 17-86 mg kg^{-1}), owing to the presence of millenial mining activities in the drainage basins of both rivers during the last 4000-5000 years (Davis et al., 2000).

Table 1. Multidisciplinary analysis of samples

SAMPLES	ENVIRONMENT	SALINITY (o/oo)		GRAIN SIZE				C (%) organic	HEAVY METALS (mg kg^{-1})				
		Low tide	High tide	Sand (%)	Silt (%)	Clay (%)	Floc (%)		Cr	Cu	Zn	Pb	
G1	Low marsh	0.4	8	24.9	70.1	5	20.5	20.5	101	49	167	39	
G2	Low marsh	11	22	2.5	94.3	3.2	53.8	22.6		nd			
G3	Low marsh	30	36	79.1	17.5	3.4	13.8	9.9	42	9	74	17	
C1	High marsh	33.7	36	9.2	86.2	4.4	43.8	23.3	90	64	208	46	
C2	High marsh	28	35	1	95.5	3.5	57.5	23.2	100	73	232	60	
C3	High marsh	33.6	35.6	3.8	85.6	10.6	67.5	26.8		nd			
C4	Low marsh	28	33	1.6	88.4	10	65.1	27.5	125	32	164	86	
C5	High marsh	28	33	0.9	91.6	7.5	74	18.8		nd			
C6	High marsh	25	35	1.5	94.4	4.1	43.2	19.4	109	47	159	42	
C7	Low marsh	30	36	38.7	52.1	9.2	33.8	11.6		nd			
P1	High marsh	24.4	32.8	97.5	1.5	1	2.1	1.1	103	42	57	34	
P2	High marsh	26	33.5	92.1	6.9	1	3.4	nd		nd			
P3	Low marsh	28	34	12.8	85	2.2	29.4	nd		nd			
P4	High marsh	30	35	3.6	92.7	3.7	38	nd		nd			
P5	High marsh	33.6	35.3	5.9	81.2	12.8	66	1.3	110	88	180	50	
P6	Low marsh	34	35.4	3.9	90.8	5.3	29.7	1.1	120	68	148		

3. METHODOLOGY

Sixteen samples (50 g dry weight sediment per sample) were obtained from low and high marshes of these estuaries. All samples were washed through a 63-μm sieve and then dried in an oven at 70°C. If possible, a minimum of 100 foraminifers (F) and 100 ostracod valves and carapaces (O) were picked from each sample, with a later recalculation to yield the total number of both groups in the whole sample. In addition, the percentages of each species were obtained.

4. RESULTS AND DISCUSSION

4.1. Foraminifera

Up to 800 specimens were determined belonging to ten species. Two of them (*Trochammina inflata*: 49.5%; *Jadammina macrescens*: 34.3%) represent up to 80% of the foraminiferal fauna, characterized by very low densities (0-3.2 individuals/gram) and diversities (0-7 species per sample). No foraminifers were found in the fluvial marshes of the Piedras Estuary (Table 2: samples P1 and P2).

Trochammina inflata is the dominant species in low marsh samples with foraminifers (0-97.7%; mean: 57.2%), with *Jadammina macrescens* as secondary species (0-34%; mean: 18.1%). In the Guadiana Estuary, miliolids (*Quinqueloculina oblonga*, *Quinqueloculina seminulum*) were found exclusively in this environment (0-10.6%).

Transition to high marsh is delimited by higher percentages of *Jadammina macrescens* (0-73%; mean: 35.7 %) and a decrease of *Trochammina inflata* (0-53%; mean: 28.7%). These two species constitute up to 99% of the high marsh foraminifers in the Piedras Estuary, whereas *Ammonia tepida* present a remarkable presence (8.5-36.4%; mean 21.3%) in the Carreras subsystem.

Table 2. Foraminifera. Distribution, density and diversity

SPECIES \ SAMPLES	G1 N	G1 %	G2 N	G2 %	G3 N	G3 %	C1 N	C1 %	C2 N	C2 %	C3 N	C3 %	C4 N	C4 %	C5 N	C5 %	C6 N	C6 %	C7 N	C7 %	P1 N	P1 %	P2 N	P2 %	P3 N	P3 %	P4 N	P4 %	P5 N	P5 %	P6 N	P6 %
Ammonia tepida					9	16.1	6	8.5	11	23.9	11	16.4			4	36.4			4	19					13	54.2						
Astrononion stelligerum					6	10.7			2	13.4	6	9	5	10.6					14	66.7									1	33.3		
Cribroelphidium vadescens					12	21.4																										
Elphidium williamsoni					5	8.9					6	9							1	4.8												
Eponides antillarum																													1	33.3		
Haynesina germanica											4	6																				
Jadammina macrescens			35	34.3	7	12.5	32	45.1	43	46.3	21	31.3	13	27.7	5	45.5	71	46.7							4	16.7	35	73			17	17
Quinqueloculina oblonga	1	2.3																														
Quinqueloculina seminulum					5	8.9							5	10.6					2	9.5												
Trochammina inflata	43	97.7	67	65.7	12	21.4	33	46.5	23	41.8	19	28.4	24	51.1	2	18.2	81	53.3							7	24.1	13	27	1	33.3	83	83
INDIVIDUALS	44		102		56		71		79		67		47		11		152		21						24		48		3		100	
SPECIES	2		2		37		3		4		6		4		3		2		4						3		2		3		2	
ENVIRONMENT	LM		LM		LM		HM		HM		HM		LM		HM		HM		LM		HM		HM		LM		HM		HM		LM	

N: number of specimens/50 g
LM: low marsh
HM: high marsh

Table 3. Ostracoda. Distribution, density and diversity

SPECIES \ SAMPLES	G1 N	G1 %	G2 N	G2 %	G3 N	G3 %	C1 N	C1 %	C2 N	C2 %	C3 N	C3 %	C4 N	C4 %	C5 N	C5 %	C6 N	C6 %	C7 N	C7 %	P1 N	P1 %	P2 N	P2 %	P3 N	P3 %	P4 N	P4 %	P5 N	P5 %	P6 N	P6 %
Cyprinotus salinus																			1	3.6												
Cytherois fischeri			2	100	2	50													20	71.4												
Leptocythere castanea																																
Leptocythere pellucida													1	100																		
Leptocythere porcellanea																			6	21.4									4	80	1	33.3
Loxoconcha elliptica					2	50																									1	33.3
Loxoconcha rhomboidea																			1	3.6									1	20	1	33.3
INDIVIDUALS			2		4								1						28										5		3	
SPECIES			1		2								1						4										2		3	
ENVIRONMENT	LM		LM		LM		HM		HM		HM		LM		HM		HM		LM		HM		HM		LM		HM		HM		LM	

N: number of specimens/50 g;

LM: low marsh;

HM: high marsh.

4.2. Ostracoda

These microcrustaceans are scarce in these environments. The taxonomical analysis of forty-three valves and carapaces allows us to differentiate seven species, with a relatively random distribution (Table 3). The higher diversities (4 species) and densities (< 6 individuals/10 gram dry weight sediment) were observed in low marshes of the marine estuaries, close to the main channels of both rivers (samples G3, C7 and P6). High marsh is usually devoid of ostracods.

Two genera (*Leptocythere*, *Loxoconcha*) are the most representative of , although isolated samples contain numerous valves of *Cytherois fischeri* (e.g. sample C7).

4.3. Applications

These results may have different applications:

Sea Level

A rapid or sea level rise would cause the replacement of high marsh assemblages (mainly *Jadammina macrescens* -F-) by low marsh species (*Trochammina inflata* -F-, *Loxoconcha* -O-, *Leptocythere* -O-), with increasing both total densities and diversities of these mesocosm groups. These changes have been observed in recent marshes and sediment cores worldwide (see Leorri et al., 2010 for a review). In addition, some marine species (e.g. miliolids -F-) will be found in the innermost zones of estuaries, which evolve to coastal bays. This colonization has been inferred during the maximum of the Flandrian transgressión (~ ca. 6500 yr BP) in other estuaries of southwestern Spain (Pozo et al., 2010). On the contrary, a sea level fall will imply an inverse evolution.

Hydrodynamic Gradient

The presence of *Loxoconcha elliptica* (O) is usually linked to the main estuarine channels, with high hydrodynamic gradients (Carbonel, 1980). The presence of this species will indicate a proximity to these channels in Pleistocene-Holocene marsh deposits. On the contrary, *Ammonia tepida* -F- seems to prefer more quiet environments, e.g., the Carreras subsystem.

Salinity/Estuarine Environment

Both diversity and density are lower in the fluvial/middle estuary, an area with moderate to high salinity variations due to mixing processes. Some of the species (*Trochammina inflata*, *Jadammina macrescens*) show positive correlations with salinity in some European estuaries (e.g. Horton and Murray, 2007). Consequently, these parameters may be used to reconstruct palaeogeographical changes or past salinity trends (e.g. Ruiz et al., 2005).

Conclusion

Both foraminiferal and ostracod assemblages of marsh deposits show both low densities and diversities in the Guadiana and Piedras estuaries. Low marsh is characterized by high percentages of *Trochammina inflata* (F), moderate contents of *Jadammina macrescens* (F) and scarce ostracod faunas (mainly Loxoconchidae and Leptocytheridae -O-). Transition to high marsh can be detected by increasing percentages of *Jadammina macrescens* (F) and the almost disappearance of ostracods. In addition, the presence of some calcareous forms (e.g., miliolids) permits to delimitate the marine estuaries, whereas other species (*Loxoconcha elliptica* -O-, *Ammonia tepida* -F-) would provide information on hydrodynamic gradients. These changes can be applied to the study of eustatic variations.

Acknowledgments

This work was funded by a Spanish DGYCIT Project (CGL2010-15810), an Excellent Project of the Andalusia Board funded by FEDER (SEJ-4770) and two Research Groups of the Andalusia Board (RNM-238 and RNM-276).

References

Borrego, J., Pendón, J. G. (1989). Caracterización del ciclo mareal en la desembocadura del río Piedras (Huelva). *Com. XII Cong. Nac. Sed.*, 1, 97-100.

Borrego, J., Morales, J. A., Pendón, J. G. (1993). Holocene filling of a estuarine lagoon along the mesotidal coast of Huelva: the Piedras River mouth, Southwestern Spain. *J. Coast. Res.*, 9, 242-254.

Carbonel, P. (1980). Les Ostracodes et leur intérêt dans la définition des écosystmèmes estuariens et de la plate-forme continental. Essais d'application à des domains anciens. *Mém. Inst. Géol. Bassin d'Aquitaine*, 11, 1-350.

Davis, R. A., Welty, A. T., Borrego, J., Morales, J. A., Pendón, J. G., Ryan, J. G. (2000). Rio Tinto Estuary (Spain): 5000 years of pollution. *Environ. Poll.*, 39, 1107-1117.

González-Regalado, M. L., Ruiz, F., Baceta, J. I., González-Regalado, E., Muñoz, J. M. (2001). Total benthic foraminifera assemblages in the southwestern Spanish estuaries. *Geobios*, 34, 39-51.

Fatela, F., Moreno, J., Moreno, F., Araujo, M. F., Valente, T., Antunes, C., Taborda, R., Andrade, C., Drago, T. (2009). Environmental constraints of foraminiferal assemblages distribution across a brackish tidal marsh (Caminha, NW Portugal). *Mar. Micropal.*, 70, 70-89.

Horton, B. J., Murray, J. W. (2007). The role of elevation and salinity as primary controls on living foraminiferal distributions: Cowpen Marsh, Tees Estuary, UK. *Mar. Micropal.*, 63, 169-186.

Horton, B. P., Sawai, Y., Hawkes, A. D., Witter, R. C. (2011). Sedimentology and paleontology of a tsunami deposit accompanying the great Chilean earthquake of February 2010. *Mar. Micropal.*, 79, 132-138.

Leorri, E., Gehrels, W. R., Horton, B. P., Fatela, F., Cearreta, A. (2010). Distribution of foraminifera in salt marshes along the Atlantic coast of Sw Europe: tools to reconstruct past sea-level variations. *Quat. Int.*, 221, 104-115.

Morales, J. A. (1993). Sedimentología del estuario del río Guadiana (SO España-Portugal). *Ph.D. Thesis,* University of Seville, 300 pp.

Ojeda, J. (1988). Aplicaciones de la teledetección espacial a la dinámica litoral (Huelva). Geomorfología y Ordenación del Territorio. *Ph.D. Thesis* (unpublished), University of Seville, 411 p.

Pozo, M., Ruiz, F., Carretero, M. I., Rodríguez Vidal, J., Cáceres, L. M., Abad, M., González-Regalado, M. L. (2010). Mineralogical assemblages, geochemistry and fossil associations of Pleistocene-Holocene complex siliciclastic deposits from the Southwestern Donana National Park (SW Spain): A palaeoenvironmental approach. *Sed. Geol.*, 225, 1-18.

Rossi, V., Horton, B. P., Reide, D., Leorri, E., Perez-Belmonte, L., Douglas, B. C. (2011). The application of foraminifera to reconstruct the rate of 20th century sea level rise, Morbihan Golfe, Brittany, France. *Quat. Int.*, 75, 24-35.

Ruiz, F., González-Regalado, M. L., Morales, J. A. (1996). Distribución y ecología de los foraminíferos y ostrácodos actuales del estuario mesomareal del río Guadiana. *Geobios*, 29, 513-528.

Ruiz, F., González-Regalado, M. L., Baceta, J. I., Muñoz, J. M. (2000). Comparative ecological analysis of the ostracod faunas from low- and high-polluted southwestern Spanish estuaries: a multivariate approach. *Mar. Micropal.*, 40, 345-376.

Ruiz, F., González-Regalado, M. L., Borrego, J., Abad, M., Pendón, J. G. (2004). Ostracoda and foraminifera as short-term tracers of environmental changes in very polluted areas: the Odiel Estuary (SW Spain). *Environ. Poll.*, 129, 49-61.

Ruiz, F., González-Regalado, M. L., Pendón, J. G., Abad, M., Olías, M., Muñoz, J. M. (2005). Correlation between foraminifera and sedimentary environments in recent estuaries of southwestern Spain: Applications to Holocene reconstructions. *Quat. Int.*, 140-141, 21-36.

In: Marshes
Editors: D. C. Abreu et al.

ISBN 978-1-61942-715-0
© 2012 Nova Science Publishers, Inc.

Chapter 4

FACTORS CONDITIONING THE VEGETATION IN THE SALT MARSHES OF THE ATLANTIC COAST OF THE IBERIAN PENINSULA*

José M. Sánchez
Departamento de Bioloxía Vexetal e Ciencia do Solo,
Universidade de Vigo, Vigo, Spain

ABSTRACT

The zonation of saltmarsh vegetation is a universal phenomenon related to apparently simple physical and chemical gradients. Nonetheless, the relationship between these factors and the vegetation is seldom a direct one, but mediated through a number of other correlated variables. Of these ultimate variables, we have documented that elevation, salinity and redox potential are correlated with the vegetation gradient. Some possible factors have been considered are anoxia due to waterlogging (inundation of vegetated parts of the saltmarsh), direct toxic effect of salts (salinity), or the formation of potentially toxic ions (at low redox potential values).

Interacting with those simple physical factors, there are some other factors that arise by the action of the biota itself. Therefore a number of biotic interactions contribute to the final result of plant distribution in salt marshes. Among them (many times, above them) the anthropogenic influence is conditioning the salt marsh vegetation through a number of different kinds of impacts.

---

* A version of this chapter also appears in *Biogeochemistry and Pedogenetic Process in Saltmarsh and Mangrove Systems*, edited by Xose Luis Otero Perez and Felipe Macias Vazquez, published by Nova Science Publishers, Inc. It was submitted for appropriate modifications in an effort to encourage wider dissemination of research.

1. INTRODUCTION

Saltmarsh vegetation is a clear example of a relatively simple communities that is strongly related to marked physical and chemical gradients (see for example Adam 1990, Lefor et al. 1987, Sánchez et al. 1996, 1998, Sanderson et al. 2001, Caçador et al. 2007, and references therein). An example of which can be seen in the idealized schematic representation of the vegetation in Figure 1. Vegetation zonation in intertidal habitats is a universal phenomenon (see for example Adam 1990) that broadly reflects the distance to the shore line through proximate variables such as substrate salinity (Rozema et al. 1985a, 1985b, Callaway et al. 1990) or flooding time (Huiskes 1990). At a local scale, simple disposition can be obscured by factors such as topography (Sánchez et al. 1996), hydraulic conductivity (Ursino et al. 2004), local climate (Huiskes 1990), and biotic interactions (see Ungar 1998 and references therein), that interact with those proximate variables.

We have studied in detail the relationship between plant communities and the main physical and chemical factors discussed on Ortigueira saltmarshes, at the nord Atlantic coast of the Iberian Peninsula.

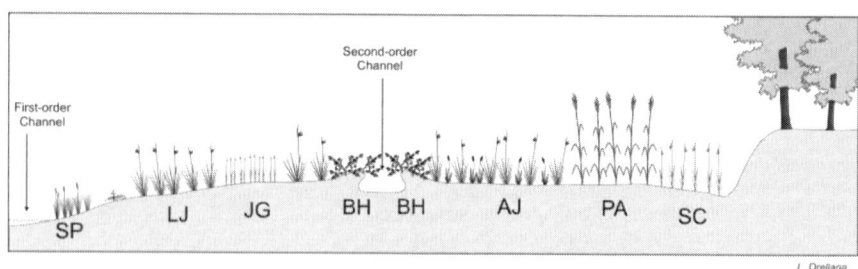

Figure 1. A schematic profile of an idealized salt marsh of NW Iberia representing the plant communities considered in this study.
SP. Spartina maritma community (Spartinetum maritimae),
LJ. Juncus maritimus community (Junco maritimae-Caricetum extensae);
JG. Juncus gerardi community (Junco maritimae-Caricetum extensae juncetosum gerardii);
BH. Halimione portulacoides community (Obionetum portulacoidis);
AJ. Agrostio stolonierae-Juncetum maritimae;
PA. Junco maritimae-Phragmitetum australis;
SC. Scirpetum compacti.

2. RESULTS AND DISCUSSION

2.1. Micro-topography

Although elevation above mean sea level is not a factor directly affecting the physiology of saltmarsh plants, there are a number of physical and chemical factors conditioned by elevation, and therefore by the number and intensity of tidal floods. These relationships are hardly simple, and interactions are many. Just as an example, elevation itself can be modified by the plants, specifically those that enhance sediment entrapment (see Bertness and Shumway 1993, Morris et al. 2002, Morris 2006). Nonetheless, at a broad scale vegetation does reflect the elevation gradient.

In Galician saltmarshes we have found an evident relationship between vegetation zonation and altitude. Such relationship have been extensively described in the literature (from Johnson and York 1915 and Hayon and Pelt 1969 to date), since in tidal environments slight elevation differences will have significant effect on flooding.

In a study conducted in Ortigueira saltmarshes (43°40'N,7°50'W) we have found that both species and plant communities follow a clear zonation pattern related to the elevation of the soil. Plant data were obtained along 14 different transects perpendicular to the tidal gradient, in $0.25m^2$ quadrats were plant species composition and cover were recorded (a total of 1417 quadrats). Vegetation was analyzed with two different approaches: first, the species composition and cover from the quadrats (whose area is representative of this vegetation type) was used to perform a cluster analysis of the individual quadrats; second, the vegetation of the area was also analyzed according to the conventional Zurich-Montpellier methodology (see Izco and Sánchez 1996 for a thorough description of the vegetation). Elevation was measured for each quadrat, and each point measured was also attributed to a syntaxon (syntaxa analysis). Of the 1417 quadrats 1080 could be readily assigned to a syntaxa. The maximum elevation range for all transects (difference between the maximum and minimum elevation) was 243cm.

Considering the specie's presence/absence, a clear elevation pattern can be seen (Figure 2). The species rank curve of mean elevation occurrence is sigmoid, which reflects lower species richness in the lower parts of the marsh and a higher diversity in the upper salt marsh.

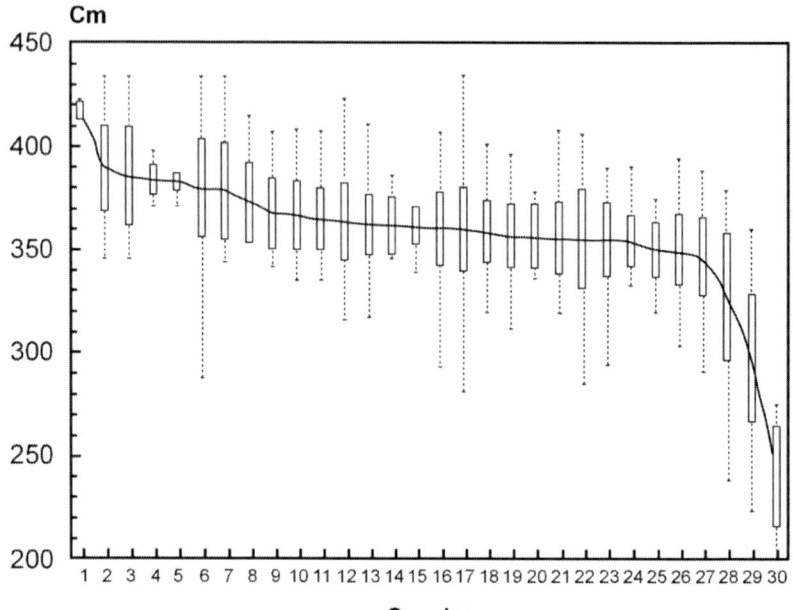

1 **Eleocharis uniglumis**	2 **Limonium binervosum** REDUCE SPACE BETWEEN LINES
3 Paspalum vaginatum	4 Apium. graveoiens
5 Scirpus lacustris	6 Festuca litoralis
7 Agrostis stolonifera	8 Frankenia laevis
9 Carex extensa	10 Glaux mantima
11 Samolus valerandi	12 Juncus gerardi
13 Armeria maritima	14 Scipus maritimus
15 Centaurium puchelum	16 Plantago maritima
17 Juncus maritimus	18 Aster tripolium
19 Puccinellia maritima	20 Inula crithmoides
21 Suaeda maritima	22 Halimione portulacoides
23 Limonium narbonense	24 Sarcocornia perennis
25 Salicornia ramosissima	26 Spergularia media
27 Trigochin maritima	28 Bostrychia scorpioides
29 Spartina maritima	30 Zostera noltii

Figure 2. Elevation range of species occurrence along a saltmarsh transects. Species are ordered according to decreasing mean height. Vertical bars represent standard deviation and dotted lines the complete range. Elevation values are referred to the zero of the Spanish nautical charts.

Table 1. Summarized species composition of the 21 groups obtained by clustering

Cluster	1	2	3	4	5	6	7	8	9	10	11	12	13	14	15	16	17	18	19	20	21
Quadrats per clusters	9	59	6	33	14	34	53	14	405	45	28	43	6	107	6	5	7	11	118	6	264
Lychnis flos-cuculi	III	.	.	.	.	.	.	.	.	.	.	.	.	.	.	.	.	.	.	.	.
Galium palustris	III	.	.	.	.	.	.	.	.	.	.	.	.	.	.	.	.	.	.	.	.
Juncus obtusifolius	II	.	.	.	.	.	.	.	.	.	.	.	.	.	.	.	.	.	.	.	.
Parapholis strigosa	.	r	.	.	.	.	.	.	.	.	.	.	.	.	.	.	.	.	.	.	.
Eleocharis uniglumis	V	.	.	.	.	.	r	.	.	.	.	.	.	.	.	.	.	.	.	.	.
Festuca arundinacea	V	.	.	.	.	.	r	.	.	.	.	.	.	.	.	.	.	.	.	.	.
Hypochaeris radicata	III	.	.	.	.	.	II	.	.	.	.	.	.	.	.	.	.	.	.	.	.
Limonium binervosum	.	V	V	IV	.	III	.	.	.	.	.	I	.	r	.	.	.	.	.	.	+
Festuca litoralis	.	.	V	V	.	V	r	.	.	r	.	.	.	r	.	.	.	.	.	.	.
Agrostis stolonifera	V	r	+	V	V	I	V	IV	r	+	III	.	I	.	.	.	.	.	.	.	.
Paspalum vaginatum	II	III	IV	VI	I	r	III	I	.	.	V	I	.	.	.	.	.	.	.	.	.
Apium graveolens	.	.	.	.	IV	.	r	.	.	.	.	.	.	.	.	.	.	.	.	.	.
Scirpus lacustris	.	.	.	.	V	.	II	.	.	.	V	.	.	.	.	.	.	.	.	.	.
Juncus gerardi	IV	.	.	I	II	r	IV	V	I	II	V	.	I	.	.	.	.	.	.	.	.
Armeria maritima	.	V	II	II	.	IV	.	I	IV	+	.	II	V	.	.	.	.	.	.	.	.
Glaux maritima	.	I	r	.	V	II	IV	V	V	+	IV	.	.	.	.	.	.	.	.	.	.
Carex extensa	.	V	II	II	V	V	I	V	I	I	I	.	I	.	.	.	.	.	.	.	.
Samolus valerandi	.	.	.	III	.	I	+	V	I	I	r	.	.	r	.	.	.	.	.	.	.

Table 1. (Continued)

Species																			
Scirpus maritimus	.	.	.	.	V	.	r	.	.	.	.	.	.	.	I	.	.	.	.
Frankenia laevis	.	II	.	.	.	.	.	.	.	.	.	r	.	.	.	.	.	.	r
Centaurium pulchellum	.	.	.	.	.	+	.	.	.	.	I	.	.	.	.	.	.	.	.
Plantago maritima	.	r	.	III	.	.	.	+	.	.	II	V	.	I	+	III	+	.	.
Juncus maritimus	II	.	V	V	V	.	.	V	V	V	III	III	V	V	V	.	+	.	r
Aster tripolium	.	V	r	r	.	r	r	+	.	.	r	I	.	.	.	.	.	.	r
Puccinellia maritima	.	II	V	V	.	r	.	r	.	.	III	V	.	.	.	I	.	.	+
Inula crithmoides	.	.	.	r	.	.	.	.	.	.	r	.	.	r	.	.	.	.	.
Suaeda maritima	.	II	.	.	.	.	.	.	.	.	III	I	.	.	.	.	.	r	.
Phragmites australis	.	.	.	.	.	.	.	+	.	.	.	.	V	.	.	.	.	.	.
Halimione portulacoides	.	II	II	I	+	.	.	II	.	.	r	r	.	+	.	IV	r	II	r
Limonium narbonense	.	.	I	r	.	II	.	II	.	V	.	I	I	.	+	III	III	.	.
Salicornia ramosissina	.	+	V	.	.	.	.	r	.	.	III	r	.	+	.	.	r	.	r
Spergularia media	.	r	V	.	.	.	.	r	.	I	III	V	I	.	.	.	III	.	r
Triglochin maritima	.	.	II	.	III	.	V	II	III	V	II	+	V	V	IV	V	V	.	.
Bostrychia scorpioides	.	I	r	.	.	+	.	I	+	II	r	IV	.	r	.	+	V	IV	r
Sarcoconia perennis	.	.	.	.	.	.	.	.	.	.	V	r	.	.	.	.	.	.	.
Spartina maritima	.	.	.	.	.	.	.	.	r	.	r	+	.	+	.	.	V	V	+
Zostera noltii	.	.	.	.	.	.	.	.	.	.	.	.	.	.	.	.	V	V	V

Reduce size of this table until it fit in one page.

Roman numerals indicate percentage frequency of species in cluster quadrats: V:>81%; IV:61-80%; III:41-60%; II:21-40%; I:11-20%; +:6-10%; r:<6%.

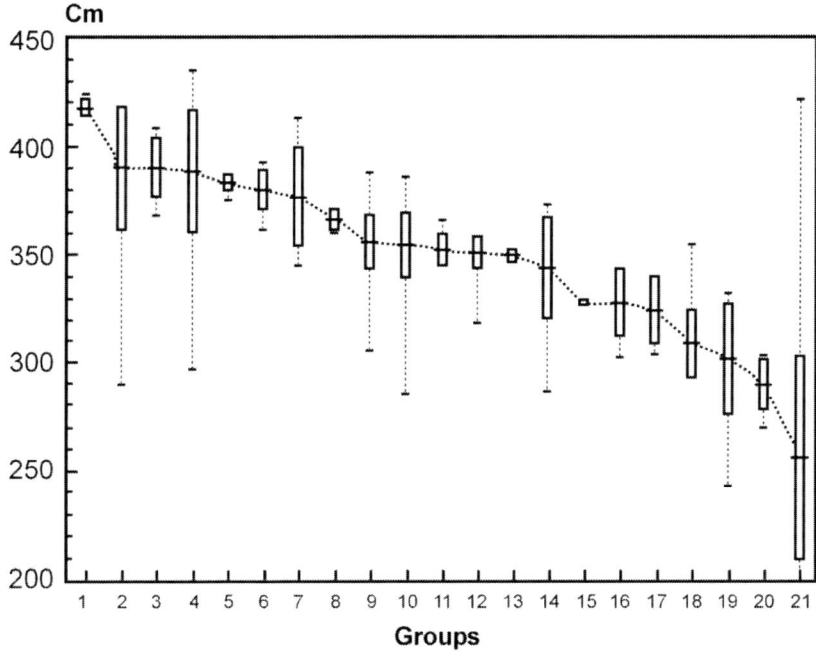

Figure 3. Sequence of 21 quadrat clusters ordered as to mean altitude range. Vertical bars represent standard deviations; dotted lines the groups' complete range. Group numbers as in Table 1.

The lowest level is occupied by *Zostera noltii* and this zone is clearly separated from the next higher level, which is occupied by *Spartina maritima*. These two levels constitute the tidal flat and the low marsh, and are also abruptly separated from the mid-altitude level, which is largely occupied by communities dominated by *Juncus maritimus*. The occurrence of between–species differences in mean altitude of occurrence are much less pronounced in this elevation range (Figure 2). At the higher levels of the profile, such differences again become marked.

The first vegetation analysis using clustering resulted in 21 groups (Table 1). The ranking plot of mean elevation occurrence of the groups is also sigmoid (Figure 3). Between-group differences are most notable at the extremes of the elevation gradient, as in the species plot (Figure 2). However, the slope of the central part of the curve is steeper for the clusters (Figure 3).

Despite the 21 groups of the cluster analysis, the syntaxa identified using the Braun-Blanquet approach was only 11. This inconsistency must be attributed to subtle differences in species composition that arise with the

cluster analysis, but are too small for the descriptive aims of the phytosociological interpretation. The syntaxa sequence (partly shown in Figure 4A) is similar to the species' with a lower steep gradient, and small differences at the middle section. The groups from the cluster analysis seem to be more sensitive to elevation than species or relevés; keeping in mind that species are recorded as present/absent, thus the smooth gradient of the middle section of the plot in Figure 2 is indicating that occasional presences of those mid-marsh species are frequent. On the other hand, groups from the clustering are more reliable as altitude indicators since they include both species composition
and cover.

The principal topographic features of the typical saltmarsh profile (e.g. Long and Mason 1983; Pethick 1984) are the 'steps' separating the tidal flat and the low, middle and upper marshes. In the present study, these steps were located at ca. 260, 350 and 400 cm above mapped zero, respectively.

The upper tidal flat and low saltmarsh are typically occupied by single species, such as *Zostera noltii* or *Spartina maritima*, while the middle saltmarsh is occupied by a relatively wide range of species. The upper marsh is characterized by mesohalophytes, of which *Eleocharis uniglumis* is a good example. The transition from middle to upper saltmarsh is apparent in Figures 2 and 3. However, the upper levels of some transect crossed areas of freshwater input, typically just upstream of areas occupied by *Phragmites australis* stands; here the transition between middle and upper marsh was less well defined.

Our data indicate that the altitudinal ranges of the tidal flat and low saltmarsh species *Zostera noltii* and *Spartina maritime*, as the communities in which they are included, are wider than those of other saltmarsh species. Other authors have reported similar findings. For example, Adams (1963) and Lefor et al. (1987) found that *Spartina alterniflora* occurs over elevation ranges of ca. 90 and 50 cm respectively. Such wide ranges may be attributed to the absence of competitors in the high-stress tidal flat environment. A number of studies on saltmarsh vegetation have suggested that intensity of competition increases with elevation; physiological tolerance is considered the limiting factor at lower levels, while competitive ability became more important at higher levels (Rand 2000; La Peyre et al. 2001). Hutchings and Russell (1989) found that seed production and seedling loss were greatest at higher levels, while Rand (2000) reported a lower seed germination rate at lower levels (higher stress), but more seeding mortality (higher competition) at higher levels.

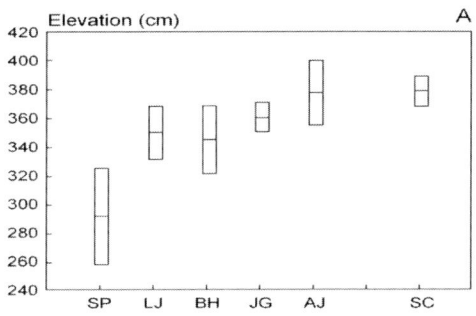
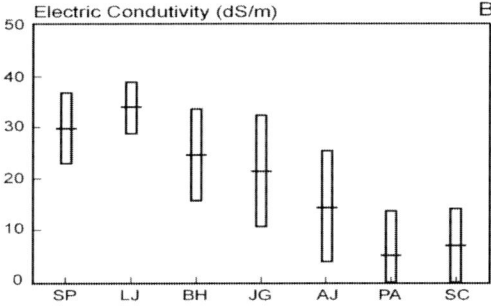
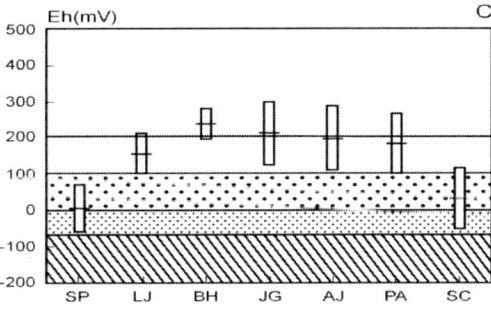

Plant community

Figure 4. A) Mean (±sd, standard desviation) elevation of the main plant communities studied arranged broadly according to their distance from the sea shore. (Plant communities as in figure 1 for all sub-figures). B) Mean salinity values of the plant communities studied arranged broadly according to their distance to sea shore. C) Mean (±sd) redox potential values of the plant communities studied arranged broadly according to their distance to sea shore.

In our study area, another species occurring over a wide elevation range is *Halimione portulacoides* (Figure 2). The wide elevation range of this species has been pointed out previously by Gehu-Frank and Gehu (1985) and Russell et all. (1985). According to Beeftink (1966) this species occurs on well aerated substrates ranging from euhaline to polyhaline.

Juncus maritimus is the dominant species throughout the middle marsh, particularly at higher elevation. This species was present in almost all quadrats at these levels, generally with high cover and sometimes forming monospecific stands. In plots where *Juncus maritumus* is present, other species have typically low cover values, unless mowing has opened the way for their expansion.

The possibility of predicting the saltmarsh vegetation type on the basis of elevation for a given biogeographical region was suggested as early as 1915 by Johnson and York. The result of our study partly supports this suggestion, since the differences between most plant communities were statistically significant. However, other factors may also have a significant effect (Chapman 1940), either physical or biotic (see below).

2.2. Factors Conditioned by the Topography

Once proven that, even though indirect, there is a relationship between elevation and vegetation, we studied a number of proximate physical and chemical factors conditioned by the distance to mean high water (namely electrical conductividy of groundwater, soil redox potential, water-table depth, and high tide flooding depth) and their relationship with the vegetation innthe coast of northwest Spain (Sánchez et al. 1998).

In our study we considered communities of perennial species occupying large areas of the marsh as the sampling units, with their distributions previously found to be related to elevation (Sánchez et al. 1996). Annual communities were excluded since a) their ephemeral character could lead to misinterpretations by reflecting ephemeral environmental conditions, and b) our study was extended over a longer period of time than the average living period of such communities.

One sampling point was selected in each plant community at one of two locations. Communities were determined according to the Zurich-Montpellier phytosociological method since, as previously stated, saltmarsh vegetation is clearly zoned and the boundaries between communities are clear. Variables were recorded at each sampling point at 29 day intervals over the period from

March 1992 to April 1993 inclusive, at low or high tide (see below) on the day of the newmoon spring tide. For monitoring of watertable depth and electrical conductivity of groundwater (both measured at low tide), a borehole as specified by Soil Survey Staff guidelines (7 cm in diameter and 100 cm deep, lined with a PVC tube rising to a sufficient height above the sediment to prevent submersion at high tide; Soil Survey Staff 1975, cited in Faulkner et al. 1989) as especified by Soil Survey Staff guidelines was dug at each sampling point. Watertable depth (cm below ground level, expressed as a negative value) and electrical conductivity (i.e., a measure of salinity) were determined within 15 min either side of the low tide as predicted by the Spanish Navy tide tables (IHM 1992 1993). Flooding depth (cm above ground level) was determined within 15 min either side of the high tide. Additionally, soil redox potential was determined at all sites on all sampling days, within 2 h either side of the low tide.

The results of a stepwise discriminant analysis showed that electrical conductivity and redox potential were the variables explaining the majority of the variation among groups (plant communities). Conductivity loaded heavily on the first discriminant function, while redox potential loaded mostly on the second; both functions explained almost 50% of the total variance of each function. Neither watertable depth nor flooding depth were effective predictors of the plant community. Flooding depth was clearly different in the *Spartina maritima* community, but did not discriminate among the other communities (Table 2). Mean watertable depth was highest (close to zero) in the *Spartina maritima* and *Scirpus maritimus* communities, and lowest (mean -17 cm) in the *Obionetum portulacoidis* community (Table 2). As expected, watertable depth was negatively correlated with redox potential (Spearman's correlation $r_s = -0.62$).

Flooding depth and water table depth are not directly correlated since there are various other soil factors conditioning the water table, for example the distance to the nearest channel (Sanderson et al., 2001; and specially Ursino et al., 2004).

Our results indicate that groundwater salinity and redox potential seem to be the two key factors conditioning the vegetation zonation in the saltmashes of the Atlantic Iberian Peninsula, and are in accordance with previous reports (see for example Armstrong et al. 1985; Brandyopadhayay et al., 1993; Caçador et al., 2007). In fact it seems to be the case that in most saltmarshes, except where a too harsh climatic environment is conditioning the zonation of the vegetation in the upper marsh (eg. in desertic areas, see Bornean et al., 2008).

Table 2. Watertable depth (cm below ground level) and high tide flooding depth (cm above ground level) for each of the syntaxa

Plant community	Water table depth	Flooding depth
SP	-0.2± 0.8	52.9±40.9
LJ	-5.9±12.1	18.9±34.9
BH	-17.1± 7.6	8.7±32.5
JG	-14.9±19.4	-1.1±32.9
AJ	-10.7±13.4	3.7±27.9
SC	-2.8±4.1 8	4±18.2
PA	-17.2± 6.2	-6.8±25.3

Values shown are mean ± standard deviation. If the high tide did not reach a site, flooding depth was recorded as watertable depth (i.e., a negative value).

The two other variables considered (watertable depth and hightide flooding depth) are not effective predictors of vegetation type. Watertable depth follows a complex pattern, even though its determinant (tidal periodicity) is relatively simple (Ursino et al., 2004). This complex pattern is even harder to track due to the difficulties involved in accurately measuring this variable (see Faulkner et al.,1989). Waterlogging regime is almost certainly a key factor affecting vegetation zonation because of its effect on redox potential. Flooding depth only discriminated the *Spartina maritima* community. This was in accordance with previous studies which have likewise shown that this variable is scarcely correlated with vegetation zonation in upper estuarine sites (see Adam, 1990). Therefore, these two variables will be not considered further, and the behaviour of the vegetation in relation with the two main conditioners, especially redox potential will be analyzed in the next sections.

Salinity

Electrical conductivity declined from the lower to the higher altitude parts of the marsh (Figure 4B). This indicates the existence of a gradient perpendicular to the coastline and broadly coincident with vegetation zonation along the topographic profile (Sánchez et al., 1996). Note, however, that mean salinity was highest not at the lowest SP sites but at the mid-saltmarsh LJ sites; this is discussed below.

Tolerance to NaCl appears to be the most important factor correlated with distribution of saltmarsh vegetation, as has been extensively pointed out in the literature (e.g. Armstrong et al., 1985, Rozema et al., 1985a or

Brandyopadhayay et al., 1993). Our data are in accordance with this finding, since electrical conductivity of groundwater was the variable loading most heavily on the first function in the discriminant analysis. Mean conductivity values declined with increasing distance from the sea and increasing elevation, in clear accordance with the principal pattern of vegetation zonation (Figure 4B). However, mean conductivity was highest in the middle marsh (the LJ community in our study area), probably as a result of evapotranspiration (see Kadlec, 1982; Ursino et al., 2004). It is well known that groundwater salinity is determined by tidal influences at low levels in the profile, but that climatic influence become increasingly important with increasing elevation (de Leeuw et al., 1990; 1991; Andreu et al., 1994).

Redox Potential

Redox potential were consistently less than 300 mV, indicating anaerobic conditions (see Faulkner and Patrick, 1992). However, both analysis of variance and discriminant analysis indicated significant differences among commuinities. In the *Spartina maritima* and *Scirpus maritimus* communities (SP and SC), redox potential values were very low and indeed in many cases negative (Figure 4C), indicating strongly reducing conditions. In the communities where *Juncus maritimus* is strongly present (LJ, JG, AJ and PA, see Figure 1), mean redox potential values were in the 100–200 mV range, while the highest values (mean >200 mV) were those recorded in the BH community (Figure 4C).

Redox potential was the second most important factor conditioning vegetation, with a loading similar to that of conductivity in the discriminant analysis. Under anaerobic conditions, saltmarsh microorganisms use any of various inorganic ions as terminal electron acceptors in the process of mineralization of organic matter. Depending on soil redox potential, the electron acceptors used (from high redox potential to low) are NO_3^-, Mn^{4+}, Fe^{3+} or SO_4^{2-}, these being reduced to NH_4^+, Mn^{2+}, Fe^{2+} and S^{2-} respectively (Patrick and Jugsujinda, 1992; Huerta-Díaz and Reimer in this book). The latter three ions (Mn^{2+}, Fe^{2+} and S^{2-}) are generally considered to be phytotoxic (see, for example, Ingold and Havill, 1984; Rozema et al., 1985b; Koch and Mendelssohn, 1989; Singer and Havill, 1993), and may be growth limiting. The reduction of Mn^{4+} to Mn^{2+}, Fe^{3+} to Fe^{2+}, and SO_4^{2-} to S^{2-} occur at redox potential values below about 200, 100, and 0mV respectively (according to Patrick and Jugsujinda, 1992; for Mn and Fe, and to Ingold and Havill, 1984, for S). The Eh values recorded in this study showed marked coincidence with these values (see Figure 4C), suggesting that the observed vegetation zonation may be at least partially due to manganese, iron and/or sulphur toxicity.

The community dominated by *Halimione portulacoides* (BH) is occupying the most strongly oxidizing soils: mean Eh for this community was more than 200mV (Figure 4), which is the point below which reduction of Mn^{4+} occurs. Although manganese toxicity has been ruled out as a factor affecting the distribution of this species by Singer and Havill (1993), there may be a sublethal effect of manganese on *Halimione* that decreases its competitive ability. Redox potential at sites occupied by this species (Figure 4C) are probably not low enough to cause Fe^{2+} or S^{2-} toxicity. This community also has the deepest watertable depth (Table 2). These results are in accordance with those of previous studies that have found *H. portulacoides* to be limited to well aerated areas of saltmarshes and to be a poor competitor in flooded soils (Beeftink, 1977; Armstrong et al., 1985). This species occurs mainly along the edges of the channels, where the higher hydraulic conductivity permits rapid drainage and thus favours aeration (see Jordan, 1985; Price et al., 1988)

In the communities with high cover values of *Juncus maritimus* (LJ, AJ, JG) or *Phragmites australis* (PA), redox potential values were significantly lower than in the BH community. In areas of the saltmarsh not adjacent to channels, evapotranspiration is the main cause of water loss from the soil (Dacey and Howes, 1984; Huiskes 1990; Ursino et al., 2004). As a result, watertable depth at such sites declines much more slowly than at sites on the side of the channel side sites, and most rapidly during the summer (Howes and Goehriger, 1994). In all of these communities, redox potential values were generally within the range at which Mn^{2+} exists stably, and indeed the species of these communities have been reported to tolerate this ion (Singer and Havill, 1993). However, our data suggest that these communities are rarely present at sites where redox potential is such that iron exists as Fe^{2+} (Figure 4C). This result appears to contradict those of other authors (Rozema et al. 1985b; Snowden and Wheeler, 1993), who have reported that these communities may be Fe^{2+} tolerant. Note that the three *Juncus* communities studied (LJ, AJ, and JG) could be discriminated by conductivity but not by redox potential (discriminant analysis results not shown).

The most strongly reducing conditions were recorded in the communities dominated by *Spartina maritima* (SP) and *Scirpus maritimus* (SC), as expected given the heavy waterlogging to which these communities are subjected to (Table 2). Redox potential values were well within the range at which iron exists as Fe^{2+}, and in many cases within the range at which sulphur exists as

S^{2-} (Figure 4C). The tolerance of species of the genus *Spartina* to Fe^{2+} and Mn^{2+} toxicity has been well documented (Adams, 1963; Rozema et al., 1985b), as has the resistance of *Scirpus maritimus* to Fe^{2+} (Clevering and van der Putten, 1995). That redox potential values were in many cases within the S^{2-} range is of interest, since this ion is generally phytotoxic and is widely considered to be one of the major constraints on the distribution of macrophytes in coastal ecosystems (see, for example, Ingold and Havill 1984; Mendelssohn and Mckee, 1988; Koch et al., 1990). Although we did not determine sulphide levels the characteristic 'bad eggs' smell of H_2S was noted at SP and SC sites.

Previous studies have likewise found *Spartina maritima* to occur at sites with strong reducing conditions (Castellanos et al., 1994), and similar results have been obtained for other species of this genus, such as *S. anglica* (Armstrong et al., 1985) and *S. alterniflora* (Bertness, 1991; Hackney et al., 1996). Under such conditions, *Spartina* species appear to avoid competition with other macrophytes which cannot tolerate sulphide. As a result, any increase in redox potential – due for example to sediment entrapment and thus increased altitude and reduction of tidal flooding – facilitates the invasion by other species and the subsequent displacement of *Spartina* (Bertnes, 1991b; Castellanos et al., 1994; Adams and Bate, 1995, Sánchez et al., 2001).

Greenhouse experiments performed by Koch and Mendelssohn (1989) have indicated that sulphide becomes toxic to *S. alterniflora* at concentrations above 1 mM, corresponding to redox potential values of -70 mV or lower (Koch et al., 1990). This result is in accordance with our findings in the present study, since redox potential at SP sites was rarely below this threshold (Figure 4C). At such low redox potential values of sulphide appears to be toxic to *Spartina* species because it inhibits alcohol dehydrogenase, an essential enzyme in the anaerobic respiration pathway used by the plant under anoxic conditions (Koch et al., 1990; Pezeshki et al., 1993); this leads to a reduced uptake of nitrogen, reduced energy availability and reduced growth (Koch and Mendelssohn, 1989; Koch et al., 1990; Bandyopadhayay et al., 1993).

Scirpus maritimus, like other species of the same genus (see Hackney et al., 1996), is also likewise able to withstand high sulphide levels. The lower values of Eh closely matched that at the *Spartina maritima* sites suggesting that the threshold level for sulphide toxicity is similar. Despite the similar distributions of the *Scirpus maritimus* and *Spartina maritima* communities with respect to redox potential, the latter was dependant on higher salinity values (Figure 4B); this is in accordance with a higher tolerance to salty soils of the species of the *Spartina* genus (see e.g. Broome et al., 1995).

2.3. Biotic Determinants

Although saltmarsh vegetation is often viewed as the result of only a few physical and chemical factors, especially in the lower elevation levels, these factors are interacting with a number of biotic factors. Biotic factors in saltmarshes have recieved less attention than abiotic ones, partly because the obvious importance of stress-tolerance in the lower marsh, but also because the relative importance of biotic factors is cryptic and they are hard to deal with. Most of the biotic factors are reviewed in an excellent article by Ungar (1998), and the most important are summarized here:

- Competition. Competition between saltmarsh plants, mainly light, has been proved. It is an especially limiting factor for the establishment of plants, emerging shoots and seedlings (Scholten et al., 1987; Morris, 2006). It is widely accepted that tolerance to harsh environmental conditions is the main factor for plants growing in the lower limits of saltmarshes, while competition is the main factor in the upper marsh (Pennings and Callaway, 1992). Many plant species are limited at their lower limit by tolerance, and by competition at the upper limit (Ungar 1998, and references therein). Some rhizomatous species are able to avoid competition by expanding to unvegetated areas where they can survive by physiological integration (Huckle et al., 2000).
- Facilitation. Some plant or animal species modify their environmental conditions in such a way that the environment becomes appropriate for other plant species to grow there (Bertness and Shumway, 1993), leading to substantial changes in the community and ultimately to the replacement of plant species. Some shrubs do reduce salt concentration and increase the moisture content of the soil they inhabit, as proven by Callaway (1994) for *Arthrocnemum subterminale*. Some crabs modify the drainage pattern and the redox potential of the soil by digging holes in the sediment (Bertness, 1985). Some species of the low marsh, mainly of the genus *Spartina*, are efficient sediment trappers; therefore they modify the saltmarsh topography enabling the colonization of less-tolerant species (Sánchez et al., 2001).
- Allelopathy. Although allelopathic studies are frecuent in desert communities, they are few and inconclusive in salmarshes, mainly because of the difficulty to discriminate allelopathy from competition or chemical inhibition.

- Chemical inhibition. Many saltmarsh plants have the ability to accumulate inorganic compounds (mainly salts) in their tissues, so when the dead parts are abscised the salinity of the soil around increase. This has been proven in salt deserts and Mediterranean marshes (Fireman and Hayward, 1952; Vivrette and Muller, 1977). Hovewer, again, there are no conclusive data from Atlantic saltmarshes, where tidal flooding may soften this effect.
- Herbivory and mowing. There has been some instances which have documented the increase of diversity in monospecific stands after they were cleared by grazers or mowed. The main effect is the installation of species from the low marsh in the cleared upper marsh, since light becomes available and soil salinity rises in the cleared areas (Bakker and Ruyter, 1981; Bakker, 1985; Kiehl et al., 1996; Tessier et al., 2003). On the other hand, too much pressure from grazers may result in the replacement of vegetated areas by bare mud in the lower marsh, or by cleared areas that become hipersaline (salt pans) in the mid and high marhs. This process is quicker in warmer climate zones where evapotranspiration is higher. A lot of salt marsh plants, especially shrubs, are sensitive to trampling, which may accelerate the formation of pans.
- Parasitism. Some saltmarsh plant species have been documented to be more sensitive than others to infestation by parasites, therefore being replaced by species which are more tolerants. Parasitism has been found more frequently in high marsh than in low (more flooded and saltier) saltmarshes (Pennings and Callaway, 1996).

2.4. The Human Factor

Although salt marshes are often viewed as pristine natural zones, free from human influence, such a view is naïve. Upon the natural causes conditioning the zonation of salt marsh vegetation, human intervention has modified salt marshes in North America and Japan, but specially Europe (Adam, 1990). According to Adam (2002), today's saltmarshes are the product of centuries of human modification. Even in the case that the human interference might cease, the possibility of restoration of the original conditions are few, since stochastic recruitment events and a number of other factors interact to control the species distribution (Seabloom et al. 2001). The main ways in which humans alter saltmarshes are thoroughly reviewed by Adam (2002), and summarized here:

- *Traditional uses, mainly linked to agriculture.* Grazing and haymaking were common in European saltmarshes, though rare today. Even crops were grown in the upper (less saline) saltmarshes. Sometimes management implied aggressive techniques such as fire to promote some game species or to attempt to control invasive plant species. Less aggressive practices such as plant gathering for direct human consumption (e.g. *Salicornia* spp.) or for floral arrangements (e.g. *Limonium* spp., personal observation) continue today in European saltmarshes.
- *Agricultural land claim.* Practiced in Europe since Roman times (Allen, 1992), mainly by building dikes to preclude sea inundation into saltmarshes. This is potentially reversible, and may contribute to the forming of new habitats of conservation value.
- *Residential and industrial land claim.* This implies land filling, and therefore, the impact on saltmarshes is irreversible.
- *Water table modification.* Either by water extraction, which can cause subsidence, or on the contrary, the water table can raise in some areas when agricultural uses next to saltmarshes require irrigation (Álvarez Rogel et al., 2007)
- *Salt production.* Salt production in evaporative ponds was once extended throughout Europe, but currently is affecting mainly to hot arid coasts.
- *Aquaculture.* The expansion of the aquaculture is rapidly growing in many coastal areas. This practice is having dramatic effects on the mangroves of South-East Asia and South America. Salt marshes are being affected to a lesser extent at the moment.
- *Dumping places.* A lot of saltmarshes have been used as dump sites, either for domestic or industrial refuse. Many filled saltmarshes are now being used as sporting facilities or even construction grounds, but most of them were not controlled at all when established, so they remain potential sources of toxic leachates. Although many of these actions occur on the small scale, and therefore are tolerated, the accumulation of such small impacts becomes a large one in many saltmarshes.

- *Insect control.* Many marshes, coastal and continental, have been filled to prevent the spread of diseases, such as malaria, by depriving their insect vectors (mosquitoes) of breeding areas. Other less aggressive techniques for insect fighting include hydrological alterations such as dike construction and flooding of the marsh during the breeding period of the insects, or construction of ditches to promote drainage.
- *Tidal energy.* Tidally powered mills have been used in Atlantic Europe since the Middle Ages and up to the mid-20th century. These mills involved the temporal embankment of small mudflat and saltmarsh areas. There are still some well preserved tidal mills on the Galician coast with a great cultural value of their own. Dikes are also used to enclose whole estuaries for the generation of hydroelectric energy, as has been tried in the last century mainly in France. Large environmental impacts are obviously linked to major alterations of the flooding regime as well as the construction work itself.
- *Tidal barriers to protect populated areas.* The paradigmatic case is the Dutch's Delta Plan, built after the 1953 floodings. Such interventions prevent sea flooding, turning former estuaries into brackish lakes.
- *Pollution.* A number of possible sources of pollution have been described to effect saltmarshes, either directly or indirectly by polluting coastal waters nearby. Agricultural, urban, and industrial pollutants have stained salmarshes all over the world, adding nutrients, organic pollutants or heavy metals among others. Nutrients surplus from agriculture has promoted eutrofication in some areas. Although heavy metals are thought to be immobilized in biologically unavailable reduced forms, frequent disturbance and oxidation of the sediment (either by natural or artifical causes) may release them into biologically available forms. Oil spills deserve special mention, since in many instances aggressive cleaning techniques have done more harm that the spill itself, and "natural clean-up" may be the best course of action (Baker et al., 1994) despite the political and social pressures for a quick response in such episodes.
- *Introduced invasive species.* Most saltmarshes of the world have experienced the invasion of exotic species due mainly to two factors: sea currents that can act as a long-distance dispersion vectors for drifting plant propagules, and mainly due to human action. Since the 19th century a number of invasive species have arrived to saltmarshes

in ships' ballasts. Some examples may be the arrival of *Cotula coronopifolia* to Eurpe and California from the southern hemisphere, or *Juncus acutus* to Australia from the Mediterranean. Special attention should be given to the species of the genus *Spartina*, which includes a number of seriously invasive species. Some of theses especies originated by hybridization between as distant species as the American *S. alterniflora* and the European *S. maritima* (the hybrid *S. anglica*), a good example of long distance dispersion on one hand and the aggressive invasive behaviour of the hybrid on the other. In many instances *S. anglica* has been deliberately planted to stabilize the substrate in tidal flats, but in others the invasion began accidentally; S. *patens*, now invading European saltmarshes, is thought to have arrived as packing material in ships boxes and crates, and then discarded on coastal dumping places so that surviving rhizomes accidentally rooted (SanLeón et al., 1998).

In conclusion, our results seem to indicate that (a) although not a factor in itself, elevation (microtopography) is highly correlated with plant zonation in saltmarshes by conditioning other proximate factors which act directly on the plants. Topography reflects the extent on which floodings are effecting plant communities. (b) tolerance to salinity is a key factor for plant distribution in saltmarshes; and (c) soil redox potential is another key factor, weighting about the same as salinity, effecting plant zonation in the saltmarshes of northwest Spain. As for elevation, redox potential is not a factor in itself, but it will condition the form in which some chemical compounds will be found in the soil, either soluble and therefore available for the plant and toxic, or insoluble and not harmful.

Biotic interactions increase their importance as factors as the saltmarsh become stabilized and environmental conditions are more bearable. Above all the factors determining the distribution of salt marsh plants in (ideal) undisturbed conditions, the human actions are the first of the conditioners since there are hardly any undisturbed saltmarsh left. As Seabloom et al. (2001) have said, "the distribution of species in dynamic environments will reflect a continually shifting balance between current environmental conditions and historical recruitment events". Therefore anthropogenic impacts, either in the past or on-going, are behind the configuration of most saltmarshes of the world.

REFERENCES

Adam P. 1990. *Saltmarsh ecology.* Cambridge University Press, Cambridge, 461 pp.

Adam P. 2002. Saltmarshes in a time of change. *Environmental Conservation*, 29, 39-61.

Adams D.A. 1963. Factors influencing vascular plant zonation in North Carolina saltmarshes. *Ecology*, 44, 445–456.

Adams J.B. and Bate G.C. 1995. Ecological implications of tolerance of salinity and inundation by Spartina maritima. *Aquat. Bot.* 52, 183–191.

Allen J.R.L. 1992. Tidally influenced marshes in the Severn Estuary, southwest Britiain. In: Saltmarshes. Morphodynamics, Conservation and Engineering Significance (eds. J.R.L. Allen and K. Pye) Cambridge, UK: Cambridge University Press, pp. 123–147.

Álvarez Rogel J., Jiménez-Cárceles F.J., Roca M.J. and Ortiz R. 2007. Changes in soils and vegetation in a Mediterranean coastal salt marsh impacted by human activities. *Estuarine, Coastal and Shelf Science*, 73, 510-526

Andreu L., Moreno F., Jarvis N.J. and Vachaud G. 1994. Application of the model MACRO to water movement and salt leaching in drained and irrigated marsh soils, Marismas, Spain. Agric. *Water Manag.* 25, 71–88.

Armstrong W., Wright E.J., Lythe S. and Gaynard T.J. 1985 Plant zonation and the springneap tidal cycle on soil aeration in a Humber salt marsh. *J. Ecol.* 7, 323–339.

Baker J.M., Adam P. and Gilfilan E. 1994. Biological impacts of oil pollution: saltmarshes. International Petroleum Industry Environmental Conservation Association, London, UK.

Bakker J.P. and Ruyter C. 1981. Effects of five years of grazing on a salt-marsh vegetation. *Vegetatio*, 44, 81-100.

Bakker J.P. 1985. The impact of grazing on plant communities, plant populations and soil conditions on salt marshes. *Vegetatio*, 62, 391-398.

Bandyopadhayay B.K., Pezeshki S.R., DeLaune R.D. and Lindau C.W. 1993. Influence of soil oxidationreduction potential and salinity on nutrition, 15N uptake, and growth of Spartina patens. *Wetlands*, 13, 10–15.

Beeftink W.G. 1977. The coastal marshes of western and northern Europe. Anecological and phytosociological approach. pp. 109–155. In: V. J. Chapman (ed.), Ecosystems of the world 1: Wet coastal ecosystems. Elsevier, Amsterdam.

Beeftink W.G. 1966. Vegetation and habitat of the salt marshes and beach plains in the south-western part of the Netherlands. Wentia 15, 83-108.

Bertness M.D. and Shumway S.W. 1993. Competition and facilitation in marsh plants. *Am. Nat.* 142, 718-724.

Bertness M.D. 1985. Fiddler crab regulation of *Spartina alterniflora* production on a New England salt marsh. *Ecology*, 66, 1042-1055.

Bertness M.D. 1991. Zonation of *Spartina patens* and *Spartina alterniflora* in a New England salt marsh. *Ecology*, 72, 138–148.

Bornean T.G., Adams J.B. and Bate G.C. 2008. Environmental factors controlling the vegetation zonation patterns and distribution of vegetation types in the Olifants Estuary, South Africa. *S. African J. Bot.* 74, 685-695

Broome S.W., Mendelssohn I.A. and McKee K.L. 1995. Relative growth of *Spartina patens* (Ait.) Muhl. and Scirpus olneyi Gray occurring in a mixed stand as affected by salinity and flooding depth. *Wetlands*, 15, 20–30.

Caçador I., Tiberio S., Cabral H.N. 2007. Species zonation in Corroios salt marsh in the Tagus estuary (Portugal and its dynamics in the past fifty years. *Hydrobiologia*, 587, 205-211

Callaway R. 1994. Facilitative and interfering effects of *Arthrocnemum subterminale* on winter annuals. *Ecology*, 75, 681-686.

Callaway R.M., Jones S., Ferren W.R. and Parikh A. 1990. Ecology of a mediterraneanclimate estuarine wetland at Carpinteria, California, plant distribution and soil salinity in the upper marsh. *Can. J. Bot.* 68, 1139–1146.

Castellanos E.M., Figueroa M.E. and Davy A.J. 1994. Nucleation and facilitation in saltmarsh succession: interactions between Spartina maritima and *Arthrocnemum perenne*. *J. Ecol.* 82, 239– 248.

Chapman V.J. 1940. Studies in salt marsh ecology: section VI and VII. Comparisons with marshes on the east coast of North America. *J. Ecol.* 28, 118-151.

Clevering O.A. and van der Putten W.H. 1995. Effects of detritus accumulation on the growth of *Scirpus maritimus* under greenhouse conditions. *Can. J. Bot.* 73, 852–861.

Dacey J.W.H. and Howes B.L. 1984. Water uptake by roots controls water table movement and sediment oxidation in short *Spartina* marsh. *Science*, 224, 487–489.

de Leeuw J., Olff H., Bakker J.P. 1990. Year to year variation in peak aboveground biomass of six saltmarsh angiosperm communities as related to rainfall deficit and inundation frequency. *Aquat. Bot.* 36, 139–151.

de Leeuw J., van den Dool A., de Munck W., Nieuwenhuize J., Beeftink W.G. 1991. Factors influencing the soil salinity regime along an intertidal gradient. *Estuarine Coastal Shelf Sci.* 32, 87–97.

Faulker S.P. and Patrick W.H. 1992. Redox and diagnostic soils indicators in bottomland hardwood forest. *Soil Sci. Soc. Am. J.* 56, 856–865.

Faulkner S.P., Patrick W.H. and Gambrell R.P. 1989. Field techniques for measuring wetland soil parameters. *Soil Sci. Soc. Am. J.* 53, 883–890.

Fireman M. and Hayward H.E. 1952. Indicator significance of some shrubs in the Escalante Desert, Utah. *Bot. Gaz.* 114, 143-155.

Géhu-Frank J. and Géhu J.M. 1985. Incidence de la microtopographie sur la végétation des prés salés. L'exemple de la Baie de La Canche. *Coll. Phytosociol.* 13, 807-810.

Hackney C.T., Brady S., Stemmy L., Boris M., Dennis C., Hancock T., O'Bryon M., Tilton C. and Barbee E. 1996. Does intertidal vegetation indicate specific soil and hydrologic conditions. *Wetlands*, 16, 89–94.

Hayon J.C. and Pelt J.M. 1969. Influence de la topographie et de la microtopographie sur la repartition des halophytes dans les stations salées de Lorraine. Bull. Soc. Bot. Nord France 22, 159-167.

Howes B.L. and Goehringer D.D. 1994. Porewater drainage and dissolved organic carbon and nutrient losses through the intertidal creekbanks of a New England salt marsh. *Mar. Ecol. Prog. Ser.* 114, 289–301.

Huckle J.M., Potter J.A. and Marrs R.H. 2000. Influence of environmental factors on the growth and interactions between salt marsh plants: effects of salinity, sediment and waterlogging. *J. Ecol.* 88, 492-505

Huiskes A.H.L. 1990. Possible effects of sea level changes on saltmarsh vegetation. In Expected effects of climatic change on marine coastal ecosystems (eds.: J. J. Beukema et al.), Kluwer Academic Publishers, Dordrecht, pp. 167–172

Hutichings M.C. and Russell P.J. 1989 The seed regeneration dynamics of an emergent salt-marsh. *J. Ecol.* 77, 615-637.

IHM (Instituto Hidrográfico de la Marina) 1992. Anuario de Mareas. Servicio de Publicaciones de la Armada, Cádiz.

IHM (Instituto Hidrográfico de la Marina) 1993. Anuario de Mareas. Servicio de Publicaciones de la Armada, Cádiz.

Ingold A. and Havill D.C. 1984. The influence of sulphide on the distribution of higher plants in salt marshes. *J. Ecol.* 72, 1043– 1054.

Izco J. and Sánchez J.M. 1996. Los medios halófilos de la ría de Ortigueira (A Coruña, España): vegetación de dunas y marismas. *Thalassas*, 12, 63–100.

Johnson D.S. and York H.H. 1915. The relation of plants to tide-levels. Carnegie Inst. Washington DC.

Jordan T.E. 1985. Nutrient chemistry and hydrology of interstitial water in brackish tidal marshes of Chesapeake Bay. *Estuarine Coastal Shelf Sci.* 21, 45–55.

Kadlec J.A. 1982. Mechanisms affecting salinity of Great Salt Lake marshes. *Am. Midl. Nat.* 107, 82–94.

Kiehl K.L., Eischeid L., Gettner S., and Walter J. 1996. Impact of different sheep grazing intensities on salt marsh vegetation in northern Germany. *J. Veg. Sci.* 7, 99-106.

Koch M.S. and Mendelssohn I.A. 1989. Sulphide as a soil phytotoxin: differential responses in two marsh species. *J. Ecol.* 77, 565–578.

Koch M.S., Mendelssohn I.A. and Mckee K.L. 1990. Mechanism for the hydrogen sulfideinduced growth limitation in wetland macrophytes. *Limnol. Oceanogr.*, 35, 399–408.

La Peyre M.K.G., Grace J.B., Hahn E., Mendelssoh, I.A. 2001. The importante of competition in regulating plant species abundante along a salinity gradient. *Ecology*, 82, 62-69.

Lefor M.W., Kennard W.C. and Civco D.L. 1987. Relationships of saltmarsh plant distributions to tidal levels in Connecticut. *Environ. Mgmt.* 1, 61–68.

Long, S.P. and Mason, C:F. 1996. Saltmarsh ecology. Blackie, Glasgow. 160 p.

Mendelssohn I.A. and McKee K.L. 1988. *Spartina alterniflora* dieback in Louisiana: timecourse investigation of soil waterlogging effects. *J. Ecol.* 76, 509–521.

Morris J.T., Sundareshwar P.V., Nietch C.T., Kjerfve B., Cahoon D.R. 2002. Responses of coastal wetlands to rising sea level. *Ecology*, 83, 2869-2877.

Morris J.T. 2006. Competition among marsh macrophytes by means of geomorphological displacement in the intertidal zone. *Estuarine Coastal Shelf Sci.* 69, 395-402.

Patrick W.H. and Jugsujinda A. 1992. Sequential reduction and oxidation of inorganic nitrogen, manganese and iron in flooded soils. *Soil Sci. Soc. Am. J.* 56, 1071–1073.

Pennings S.C. and Callaway R.M. 1992. Salt marsh plant zonation: the relative importance of competition and physical factors. *Ecology*, 73, 681–690.

Pennings S.C. and Callaway R.M. 1996. Impact of a parasitic plant on the structure and dynamics of salt marsh vegetation. *Ecology*, 77, 1410-1419.

Pethick, J. 1984. An introduction to coastal geomorphology. Edward Arnold, London.

Pezeshki S.R., Pardue J.H. and DeLaune R.D. 1993. The influence of soil oxygen deficiency on alcohol dehydrogenase activity, root porosity, ethylene production and photosynthesis in Spartina patens. *Environ. Exp. Bot.* 33, 565–573.

Price J., Ewing K., Woo M.K. and Kershaw K.A. 1988. Vegetation patterns in James Bay coastal marshes. II. Effects of hydrology on salinity and vegetation. *Can. J. Bot.* 66, 2586–2594.

Rand T.A. (2000) Seed dispsersal, habitat suitability and the distribution of halophytes across a salt marsh tidal gradient. *J. Ecol.* 88, 608-621.

Rozema J., Bijwaard P., Prast G. and Broekman R. 1985a. Ecophysiological adaptations of coastal halophytes from foredunes and salt marshes. *Vegetatio*, 62, 499–521.

Rozema J., Luppes E. and Broeckman R. 1985b. Differential response of saltmarsh species to variation of iron and manganese. *Vegetatio*, 62, 293–301.

Russell P.J., Flowers T.J. and Hutchings M.J. 1985. Comparison of niche breadths and overlaps of halophytes on salt marshes of differing diversity. *Vegetatio*, 61, 171-178.

Sánchez J.M., Izco J. and Medrano M. 1996. Relationships between vegetation zonation and altitude in a saltmarsh system in northwest Spain. *J. Veg. Sci.* 7, 695–702.

Sánchez J.M., Otero X.L. and Izco J. 1998. Relationships between vegetation and environmental characteristics in a salt-marsh on the coast of Northwest Spain. *Plant Ecol.* 136, 1-8.

Sánchez J.M., SanLeón D. and Izco J. 2001. Primary colonisation of mudflat estuaries by *Spartina maritima* (Curtis) Fernald in Northwest Spain: vegetation structure and sedimet accretion. *Aquat. Bot.* 69, 15-25.

Sanderson E.W., Foin T.C., Ustin S.L. 2001. A simple empirical model of salt marsh plant spatial distributions with respect to a tidal channel network. *Ecol. Mod.* 139, 293-307.

SanLeón D., Izco J. and Sánchez J.M. 1998. *Spartina patens* as a weed in Galician saltmarshes (NW Iberian Peninsula). *Hydrobiologia*, 415, 213-222.

Scholten M., Blaauw A., Stroetenga M. and Rozema J. 1987. The impact of competitive interactions on the growth and distribution of plant species in salt marshes. In Vegetation between land and sea (eds. AHL Huiskes et al.), Dr. Junk, Dordrecht, pp. 270–281

Seabloom E.W., Moloney K.A., and van der Valk A.G. 2001. Constraints on the establishment of plants along a fluctuating water-depth gradient. *Ecology*, 82, 2216-2232.

Singer C. E. and Havill D.C. 1993. Resistence to divalent manganese of saltmarsh plants. *J. Ecol.* 81, 797–806.

Snowden R.E.D. and Wheeler B.D. 1993. Iron toxicity to fen plant species. *J. Ecol.* 81, 35–46.

Tessier M., Vivier J.P., Ouin A., Gloaguen J.C., Lefeuvre J.C. 2003. Vegetation dynamics and plant species interactions under grazed and ungrazed conditionas in a western European salt marsh. *Acta Oecol.* 24, 103-111.

Ungar I.A. 1998. Are biotic factors significant in ingluencing the distribution of halophytes in saline habitats?. *Bot. Rev.* 64, 176-199.

Ursino N., Silvestgri S. and Marani M. 2004. Subsurface flow and vegetation patterns in tidal environments. *Water Resour. Res.* 40, W01514, doi:10.1029/2003WR002180

Vivrette N.J. and Mulle, C.H. 1977. Mechanism of invasion and dominance of coastal grassland by Mesembryanthemum crystallinum. *Ecol. Monog.* 47, 301-318.

In: Marshes
Editors: D. C. Abreu et al.

ISBN 978-1-61942-715-0
© 2012 Nova Science Publishers, Inc.

Chapter 5

NUTRIENT CYCLING IN SALT MARSHES: AN ECOSYSTEM SERVICE TO REDUCE EUTROPHICATION[*]

A. I. Lillebø[1,#], A. I. Sousa[1,2], M. R. Flindt[3], M. E. Pereira[1], A. C. Duarte[1], M. A. Pardal,[4] and I. Caçador[2]

[1]CESAM-Centre for Environment and Marine Studies,
Department of Chemistry - University of Aveiro,
Campus Universitário de Santiago, Aveiro, Portugal
[2]CO – Centre of Oceanography, Faculty of Sciences,
University of Lisbon, Campo Grande, Lisbon, Portugal
[3]Centre of Environmental Technology, Institute of Biology, University of Southern Denmark, Campusvej Odense M, Denmark
[4]CEF – Centre for Functional Ecology, Department of Life Sciences, University of Coimbra, Apartado, Coimbra, Portugal

---

[*] A version of this chapter also appears in *Eutrophication: Ecological Effects, Sources, Prevention and Reversal*, edited by Carolann D. Webber, published by Nova Science Publishers, Inc. It was submitted for appropriate modifications in an effort to encourage wider dissemination of research.
Corresponding authors: lillebo@ua.pt

ABSTRACT

Salt marshes are classified as sensitive habitat under the Habitats Directive (92/43/EEC), which aims to promote the maintenance of biodiversity. Worldwide, the reduction of salt marsh areas, as a result of anthropogenic disturbance is of major concern, and several studies on the ecology of estuaries have emphasized the negative consequences of its disappearance. In addition, as a result of increasing global population and increasing human activities, salt marshes, estuaries and other coastal waters have been subjected to increasing nutrient loadings with anthropogenic origin. This chapter aims to draw attention to the sequestration capacity of salt marshes for the excess of nutrients, and to evaluate the ecological services provided by salt marsh halophytes by regulating the biogeochemical cycles of nitrogen (N) and phosphorus (P). In this context, two case studies will be presented and discussed: By comparing young and mature marshes colonised by *Saprtina maritima*, we will evaluate their behaviour as sink or source of nutrients; By comparing two halophytes with distinct life cycles (*Spartina maritima* and *Scirpus maritimus*), we will evaluate species-specific N and P cycling and sequestration in salt marshes. This chapter will thus emphasise that salt marsh halophytes have a crucial role on nutrient cycling and sequestration, providing ecological services that contribute to maintain the ecosystem health.

Keywords: Salt marshes, Nitrogen, Phosphorus, Eutrophication, Ecosystem services

INTRODUCTION

Salt marshes are complex ecotones, located between land and coastal water environments, classified as sensitive habitat under the European Habitats Directive. This Directive aims "*to promote the maintenance of biodiversity, taking account of economic, social, cultural and regional requirements*", and, "*whereas the preservation, protection and improvement of the quality of the environment, including the conservation of natural habitats and of wild fauna and flora, are an essential objective of general interest*" (92/43/EEC). In addition, the reduction of salt marsh areas worldwide, as a result of anthropogenic disturbance, namely through habitat disruption and fragmentation, pollution, climate change, namely storm events, and coastal development, is of major concern, and several studies on the ecology of estuaries have emphasized the negative consequences of its disappearance (e.g. Valiela et al., 2000, Boorman, 2003, Lefeuvre et al. 2003, Best et al., 2007, Simas and Ferreira, 2007, Jin et al., 2007, Green et al., 2009). As a result of an increasing global human population, salt marshes, estuaries and other coastal waters have been subjected to increasing nutrient loadings with anthropogenic origin. This nutrient enrichment may compromise the ability of these habitats to maintain their high productivity and integrity. In fact, Deegan (2002) reviewed the effects of nutrient enrichment on salt marshes, namely the support of nekton community by salt marshes, and concluded that through combined negative effects, it favoured habitat fragmentation due to alteration of food webs characteristics within the ecosystem.

Major natural supplies of nutrients to estuarine water column include external sources, like diffusive runoff, freshwater discharge from rivers or anthropogenic point sources, and endogenous processes, such as salt marsh production, benthic sediment mineralization and sediment interstitial waters. However, in estuaries near dense populated regions the nutrient supply is augmented by domestic and industrial waste waters, urban drainage and agricultural effluents (*e.g.* Tappin, 2002, Hauxwell and Valiela, 2004). This is a common process within systems all over the world (*e.g.* Bricker et al., 1999, Hauxwell and Valiela, 2004, Lillebø et al., 2005, Dugdale et al., 2007), which represent the worldwide main agent of change for coastal ecosystems (Crouzet et al., 1999), and is named as *Cultural Eutrophication*. Eutrophication can be defined as *"the enrichment of water by nutrients, especially compounds of nitrogen and/or phosphorus causing an accelerate growth of algae and higher forms of plant life to produce and undesirable disturbance to the balance of organisms present in the water and to the quality of the water concerned"* (UWWT Directive 91/271/EEC) (Crouzet et al., 1999).

The nitrogen (N) and phosphorus (P) budgets in estuaries depend on their own characteristics, such as hydrodynamic and physicochemical factors (including water column and sediment properties), and on biological factors. Rivers may supply much of the N and P to estuaries of both pristine and human impacted catchments (Berner and Berner, 1996, Tappin, 2002, Lillebø et al., 2005). In pristine catchments it is mainly a function of the mechanical and chemical weathering of soil minerals, together with biogeochemical cycles, whilst in impacted systems, agriculture seem to be the main contributor to river concentrations (Tappin, 2002).

Salt marshes occur in low-energy environments, and are usually restricted to relatively sheltered areas, characterised mainly in five physiographic situations: in estuaries, in saline lagoons, behind barrier islands, at the heads of sea lochs, and on beach plains; allowing in all cases the accumulation of fine sediments (Best et al., 2007). The development of salt marsh vegetation is dependent on the presence of intertidal mudflats and other supplies of sediment, being naturally dynamic systems (Boorman, 2003). Salt marshes halophytes communities are spatially distributed according to the marsh's topography, which determines the frequencies and durations of tidal submersion, the physical and chemical characteristics of the sediment and the interspecific competition conditions (Lefeuvre et al., 2003). Salt marsh ecosystem shows a clear zonation according to the frequency of inundation, being the halophyte species adapted to regular immersion by the tides. These halophytes may act as sediment traps, playing an important role in the settling of suspended matter (e.g. Boorman, 2003). In addition, halophytes have similar nutrient requirements to non-saline-tolerant species and like these species they need a well-developed root- system for anchoring (Amos et al. 2004) and efficient uptake of nutrients (Boorman, 2003). The root-sediment interaction is complex and covers a wide range of biogeochemical processes. Several authors have reported chemical changes in the rhizosphere of several plants, including the redox potential (Eh), organic matter contents, and oxygen and nutrient profiles (e.g. Caçador et al., 1993, 1996, Lillebø et al., 2006, 2007a). Nitrogen content in plants tissue is directly related to the N availability in each ecosystem and strongly influences the net primary production, since N is usually a limiting nutrient in these systems. However, both N and P requirements for their healthy growth seems critical, and a slight shortage of either element will lead to the the other one become the limiting factor (Boorman, 1999 in Boorman, 2003). Salt marsh plants have been characterised as efficient sinks for nitrogen (N) and/or phosphorus (P), buffering the effects of nutrient inputs. So, the biomass production contributes to the removal of dissolved inorganic nutrients from the system, and their cycling in estuarine systems (e.g. Ibañez et al. 1999; Simas and Ferreira, 2007, Sousa et al. 2008). In natural intertidal salt marshes, plant diversity tend to decrease from low marsh towards high marsh (from a community dominated by 4 or 5 species to one dominated by 2 species) while primary production follows an opposite pattern (Lefeuvre et al. 2003). Thus, salt marshes are commonly characterized by a relatively small number of highly productive halophyte species (Lefeuvre et al. 2003), which during high tide are important nursery sites for juvenile fish and crustaceans (*e.g.* Jin et al., 2007, Green et al., 2009) with economical value.

Following the definition by the Ecological Society of America (http://www.esa.org/), Ecosystem Services are *"the processes by which the environment produces resources that we often take for granted*", namely they provide *services* that: "*mitigate drought and floods; cycle and move nutrients; maintain biodiversity*"; among others. Or, as defined by Costanza et al. (1997) ecosystem services "*represent the benefits human populations derive, directly or indirectly, from ecosystem functions*". The high value of the multiple services provided by wetlands, including tidal marshes, has already been estimated (Costanza et al., 1997), highlighting the need to preserve these ecosystems' health. In addition, the use of the biological elements such as salt marshes to assess the ecological quality status of transitional and coastal waters has received considerable attention, especially as part of the management requisites for the implementation of the Water Framework Directive (2000/60/EC) (Best et al., 2007, Simas and Ferreira, 2007).

This chapter aims to draw attention to the sequestration capacity of salt marshes for the excess of nutrients, and to evaluate the ecological services provided by salt marsh halophytes by regulating the biogeochemical cycles of nitrogen (N) and phosphorus (P).

SALT MARSHES AS A SINK OR SOURCE OF NUTRIENTS: CASE STUDY OF YOUNG AND MATURE MARSHES COLONISED BY *SPARTINA MARITIMA*

Nutrient cycling in the coastal ecosystems is a crucial role performed by salt marshes acting as transformers of nutrients (either functioning as sinks and/or sources) (Ibañez et al., 2000, Boorman, 2003, Caçador et al., 2004, 2007, Lillebø et al., 2004, Sousa et al., 2008). Their functioning, as sinks and/or source, seems to depend on several factors such as stage of succession, tidal energy, salinity, nutrient supply, namely nutrient uptake and N fixation, oxygen release, and nutrient production and losses due to mineralization and nitrification-denitrification, among others (Valiela et al., 2000; Eyre and Ferguson, 2002; Boorman, 2003, McGlathery et al., 2004). Primary production and organic N burial may locally trap the N, while denitrification constitute a process which transfers N to the atmospheric compartment (Valiela et al., 2000), reducing its export from the estuarine system (*e.g.* Flindt et al. 1997, 2007, Salomonsen et al. 1997, 1999). On the other hand, in salt marshes P may be incorporated into plants biomass (primary production), trapped by organic P burial, and by inorganic P sorption to sediment particles (*e.g.* Coelho et al., 2004, Lillebø et al., 2007a, Hou et al., 2008). In this chapter, we will follow the qualitative marsh classification described in Valiela et al. (2000), i.e., young salt marshes correspond to marshes with much open water and relatively simple tidal outlets to the sea, while mature ones are characterized as marshes whose surfaces are largely covered with vegetation and whose channels and inlets are relatively more complex. According to Boorman (2003) revision, in the younger salt marshes, there is a great need for a well-developed root system to anchor the halophytes securely from tidal action. As the marsh matures this requirement decreases, and the aboveground growth increases, facilitating the structural development of the vegetation. In addition, mature marshes have higher levels of nutrients in both the plants and sediment as a result of two major processes: by the accumulation of litter on the sediment surface and by root growth below the surface (Boorman, 2003). These processes lead to the stability of the deposited material and to a steady build-up in the surface level of the marsh (Boorman, 2003). The review by Valiela et al. (2000) show that as salt marsh mature and fill in with vegetation and sediments, they gradually export more materials than young marshes.

As a case study three salt marshes, two young and a mature one, colonised by *Spartina maritima* (Curtis) Fernald will be compared. *Spartina maritima* is a rhizomatous grass with a continuous but very slow growth forming extensive monotypic stands, and occupies intertidal mudflats at Tagus and Mondego estuaries. Both systems are located in the southern European Atlantic margin (Portugal). The Tagus estuary (38°49N, 08°56'W) forms a shallow bay covering an area of about 320 km^2 and the river drains an area of 86 000 km^2 (Figure 1). Seawater enters the estuary through a deep narrow inlet channel and tides are semi-diurnal with average amplitude of 2.4 m ranging from 0.9 m at neap tide to 4.1 at spring tide (Gameiro et al., 2004). This estuary is affected by different pressures, namely navigation (Lisbon harbour), urbanism, industry, fisheries, aquaculture and recreational activities. The hydrographic bay of the Tagus estuary has about 2.5 million people. This means that the estuary receives a high amount of domestic/urban residuals. The Mondego estuary (40°08N, 08°50W) is about 7 km long and is 2-3 km across at its widest part, drains a hydrological basin of 6670 km^2, and is located two hundred kilometres north of the Tagus estuary. This system consists of two arms, northern and southern (Figure 1) with very different hydrographic characteristics, being the intertidal mudflats and salt marshes areas restricted to the shallower southern arm (2-4 m depth during high tide and the tidal range is 1-3 m). The Mondego estuary is relatively small (1 600 ha) and receives agricultural runoff from 15 000 ha of upstream cultivated land, mainly dominated by rice fields (Lillebø et al., 2005). This system is mainly affected by modified riverbed topography, changed hydrodynamics, increased water turbidity and increased concentration of growth limiting nutrients (Martins et al., 2001, Lillebø et al., 2005). In this system *S. maritima* salt marshes colonise 4% of the lower estuarine areas.

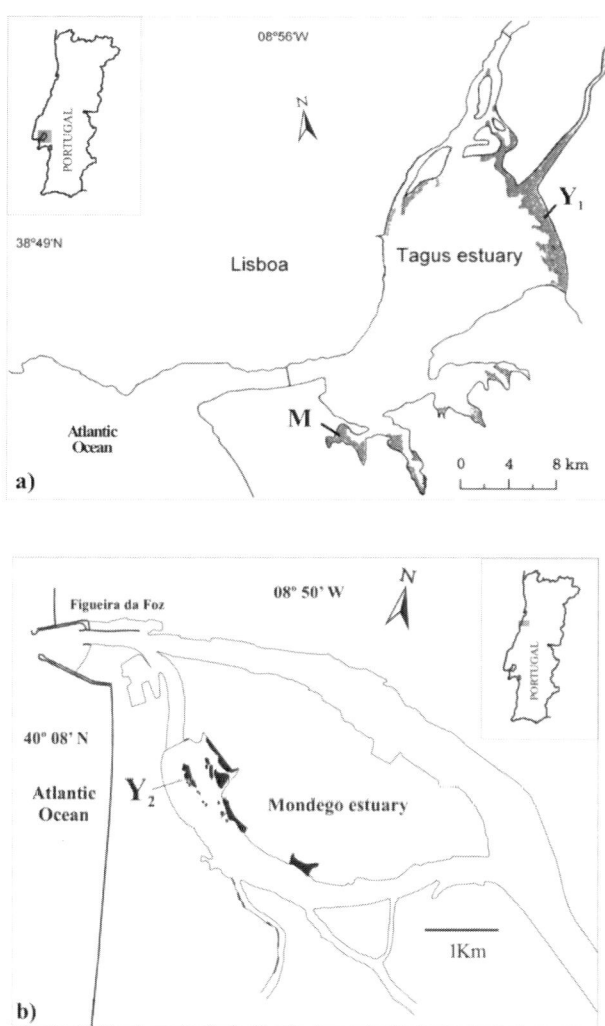

Figure 1. Tagus a) and Mondego b) estuaries with the location of the mature (M) and young (Y_1, Y_2) salt marshes.

The older/mature salt marsh (M) is located in Tagus estuary (Corroios salt marsh, 400 ha) as well as one of the younger ones (Y_1) (Pancas salt marsh, 800 ha), while the second young one (Y_2) is located in Mondego estuary (Gala salt marsh, 10.5 ha) (Figure 1). During one year, monospecific and uniform stands of *S. maritima* were sampled bi-monthly at Mondego (1997-1998) and at Tagus salt marshes (1998-1999). Three replicates of 0.3x0.3 m^2 were collected at M and Y_1 (respectively, old/mature and young salt marsh). There the aboveground material and the detritus accumulated in the same area were collected separately and brought to the laboratory. *S. maritima* belowground material was collected using sediment cores at the same sites as aboveground material for all salt marshes (cores with Ø 7 cm and 25 cm depth). At the Y_2 (young salt marsh), five samples (cores of Ø 13 cm) were randomly collected by clipping the aboveground material at ground level. The belowground material of the same circle was then collected with a circular core (Ø 13 cm and 25cm depth). The percentage of detritus production used in this study was estimated by Castro and Freitas (2000). These authors placed 20 nylon mesh litter traps (100 cm long x 40cm wide), for one month period. The traps were open at the top to allow collection of the senescent aboveground material (leaves and stems). The plant material and detritus, sampled bi-monthly, were rinsed in the laboratory with demineralised water, separated in leaves, stems, belowground material and dried until constant weight at 60°C (for 48h). Since *S. maritima* rhizome biomass is only about 1.4% of total belowground material (roots + rhizomes) (Reboreda and Caçador, 2007), the roots and rhizomes were not treated separately.

Biomass production (net aboveground primary production- NAPP and net belowground primary production - NBPP) was estimated according to the differences between the maximum and minimum biomass recorded during all the year studied, as described by De la Cruz and Hackney (1977) for belowground material. Grazing was not considered since Portuguese salt marshes are not usually used as pastures the way other European salt marshes frequently are (Boorman, 2003, Lefeuvre et al., 2003). Prior to N and P analysis, plant material was ground and homogenised, and samples for P analysis were combusted in a muffle furnace at 500 °C (3 h). Total N was quantified in a CHNS/O analyser (Fisons Instruments Model EA 1108), while total P was quantified according to the method described in Flindt and Lillebø (2005).

N and P production were estimated in the same way considering, respectively, maximum and minimum N and P pool values. The pools were calculated by multiplying the biomass per the N and P concentrations of *S.*

maritima. The turnover rates for biomass (aboveground and belowground) were calculated taking into account the ratio between biomass production and the maximum biomass.

Table 1. Sediment organic matter content (% LOI, loss on ignition) and granulometry in *Spartina* rooted sediment in the mature (M) and young salt marshes (Y_1 and Y_2) (data from Sousa et al. (2010a))

Sediment characteristics		M	Y_1	Y_2
Organic Matter (% LOI)	Jun	26.9	9.5	7.3
	Aug	26.2	9.1	10.4
	Oct	26.9	9.8	8.7
	Dec	27.3	9.9	8.1
	Feb	28.4	9.8	6.0
	Apr	27.6	9.7	6.5
	Annual mean	27.2±0.8	9.6±0.3	7.8±1.6
Granulometry	Silt	60%*	60%*	
	Clay	38%*	38%*	6%
	Fine sand 63µm-125µm	2%*	2%*	56%
	Fine sand >125µm			38%

* Data from Caçador et al. (2004).

Table 2. Annual biomass production and turnover rate for aboveground and belowground material of *Spartina maritima* at the mature (M) and young (Y_1, Y_2) salt marshes

Salt marshes				
		M	Y_1	Y_2
Biomass Production (gDW.m^{-2}.y^{-1})	Aboveground	120 (3%)	319 (32%)	2833 (76%)
	Belowground	3490 (97%)	667 (68%)	895 (24%)
	Total	*3610*	*986*	*3728*
Turnover rate: Biomass (y^{-1})	Aboveground	0.33	0.66	0.50
	Belowground	0.49	0.56	0.51

Bold numbers within brackets represent the percentage of the above- or belowground biomass productions, in relation to the total biomass production.

Turnover rate is shown in terms of biomass (data from Sousa et al. 2008, 2010a,b).

In order to analyze the decomposition of belowground vegetation, samples of belowground material were randomly collected in both systems at the three studied salt marshes (M and Y_1 - February 1999, and Y_2 - June 1997), and rinsed and dried in the lab. *S. maritima* belowground material (about 5 g in each bag, which was then individually weighed) was put into 10x10 cm^2 nylon mesh bags with 450-μm diameter holes and buried at a depth of 10 cm in their own salt marshes. This procedure intended to reproduce their original conditions and to analyze the decomposition of belowground material. At M and Y_1 salt marshes three bags were collected from February to September after 31, 59, 87, 118, 150, 180 days, while at Y_2 salt marsh, five replicates (bags) were collected after 22, 43, 71, 99, 134 and 183 days from June to December. In order to calculate the decomposition rate of the belowground material, the biomass of the remaining belowground material was linked to an exponential decay model (first order decay function), $X_t=X_0*e^{-kt}$, where X_t is remaining dry weight in litterbags, X_0 is initial dry weight, t is time in days and k is the decay rate (see Curcó et al., 2002). Then, N and P content in the belowground material, after 6 months of decomposition, were estimated. Rhizosediment samples (sediment among plant roots and rhizomes (Almeida et al., 2006) were collected to determine the organic matter content (% LOI, loss on ignition at 450 °C for 8 hours), granulometry and total N and P. Previous to analysis, sediment samples were air dried, separated from roots and passed through a 0.25 mm mesh and homogenised. Total N and P were quantified following the same procedure described for plant material.

Results show that sediment organic matter content (% LOI, loss on ignition) is comparatively higher at the mature (M) salt marsh, even though the granulometry in *Spartina* rooted sediment in the mature (M) is similar to the young salt marshes (Y_1) (Table 1). Table 2 shows that the annual biomass production of belowground material is comparatively higher (97%) in the mature marsh (M). In the young salt marshes the annual biomass production of belowground material is 68% and 24%, respectively at Y_1 and Y_2. However, the turnover rate for aboveground and belowground biomass was similar between the young salt marshes (Y_1, Y_2) and comparatively higher than at the mature (M) salt marsh (Table 2). The decomposition rates (k) for belowground biomass were also similar between the young salt marshes (Y_1, Y_2) and comparatively higher than at the mature (M) salt marsh (Table 3). In addition, the amount of N annually retained in the upper 5 cm of *Spartina* rooted sediment was also comparatively higher in the mature salt marsh (M) and is similar for the two young salt marshes (Y_1, Y_2) (Table 4). However, P annually retained in the sediment does not show the same tendency, i.e., differences between marshes do not seem to be related to the maturity of the marsh. In, fact, although Y_1 seem to retain higher P amount than Y_2 and M, the associated standard deviation is much higher (Table 4), conditioning further interpretations. Results concerning N are in agreement with the revision carried out by Boorman (2003), where the author conclude that mature marshes have higher nutrients content in both the plants and the rhizosediment due to the accumulation of litter on the sediment surface and to NBPP, which enhance the steady build-up in the surface level of the marsh. Moreover, Edwards and Mills (2005) verified that the NBPP of *S. alterniflora*, in a constructed salt marsh, increased with the increasing age of the marsh followed by a decreasing trend of the NAPP. Another study (Caçador et al., 1999) highlighted that under environmental stress salt marsh plants respond via investing in the NBPP due to the need of a greater root surface. Thus, the studied mature salt marsh may also be under a higher environmental stress, namely by its geographic location (close to the densely populated city of Lisbon) and through the comparatively higher sediment salinities (Sousa et al., 2008), which has been pointed out as a determinant factor conditioning the productivity of salt marsh plants (e.g. Edwards and Mills, 2005). In addition, the competition for nutrients in younger marshes is lower, concerning their physical and chemical characteristics, which in turn reduces the NBPP vital for the plant (Caçador et al., 1999).

Table 3. Decomposition rates (k) for *Spartina maritima* belowground biomass at the mature (M) and young (Y_1, Y_2) salt marshes during a 180 days period, according to the equation $X_t=X_0*e^{-kt}$. (X_t is the remaining dry weight in the litterbags (%), X_0 the initial dry weight and t the time in days)

M		Y_1		Y_2	
t (d)	K	t (d)	k	t (d)	k
31	0.0076	31	0.0179	22	0.0087
59	0.0032	59	0.0045	43	0.0087
87	0.0027	87	0.0068	71	0.0081
118	0.0024	118	0.0038	99	0.0061
150	0.0017	150	0.0038	134	0.0036

| 180 | 0.0024 | 180 | 0.0038 | 183 | 0.0043 |

Data from Sousa et al. 2008.

The marsh elevation involves the colonization by bacteria and fungi which are involved in biogeochemical processes controlling the breakdown of organic matter and the cycling of plant nutrients (Boorman, 2003). In mature marshes, the higher organic matter content (source of carbon) and higher percentage of clay in the sediment (which favours water retention) should enhance decomposition (e.g. Costa et al., 2007). However, in the studied mature marsh (M) NBPP litter decomposition rates were slower, which suggests that other environmental factors may be involved. Costa et al. (2007) studied the microbial activity profiles in Tagus estuary salt marsh sediments, concluding that microbial activities were generally higher at mature salt marshes due to comparatively higher organic carbon sources. However, the same study showed that higher activities occurred in surface horizons (top 2 cm) with potentially easier degradable litter than in deeper horizons (8–10 cm) with higher content of refractory litter. As the litterbag experiment was carried out at a depth of 10 cm, to reproduce the decomposition of belowground material at a depth with active roots/rhizomes, a possible higher content of refractory litter, may explain differences in decomposition rates. Considering the results obtained from the litterbag field experiment it can be observed that after 6 months the young salt marshes present a higher biomass mineralisation, while in the mature (M) marsh 65% of the belowground biomass still remains in the form of litter. These results indicate a tendency for higher accumulation of organic matter in the rhizosediments of mature salt marshes (Pereira et al, 2007, Sousa et al., 2008), which is in agreement with the revision by Boorman (2003). Even though, differences between marshes concerning P annually retained do not seem to be related to systems maturity. Figure 2 and 3 shows respectively, a schematic representation of *Spartina maritima* biomass and N and P productions, detritus moved by tides and N and P retention in the sediment at mature (M) and young (Y_1, Y_2) salt marshes. Results show that the highest total biomass production of *S. maritima* also corresponded to the highest N and P pools in the plant. Nutrient pools in the belowground plant material were higher at the mature (M) salt marsh, followed by Y_2 and Y_1, whilst the pool of N and P in the aboveground plant material followed the opposite trend. In addition, the N retained in the rhizosediment of the mature salt marsh is 2- to 3-fold higher, when compared to the younger ones. The P retained in the rhizosediment does not seem to be closely related to the maturity of the salt marshes.

Table 4. N and P annually retained in the sediments of the mature (M) and young (Y_1, Y_2) salt marshes, concerning sedimentation rate and N and P content in the upper 5 cm of Spartina rooted sediment

	M	Y_1	Y_2
Sedimentation rate (cm.yr^{-1})	1.0 **	1.0 **	0.7 *
Sediment N (mgN.gDW) (average±SD; N=6)	6.13±0.25	2.93±0.23	3.24±0.74
N retained (gN.m^{-2}.yr^{-1})	61	29	21
Sediment P (mgP.gDW) (average±SD; N=6)	0.53±0.07	0.87±0.18	0.59±0.05
P retained (gP.m^{-2}.yr^{-1})	5	9	4

Data on N from Sousa et al. 2008; * Data extrapolated from Castro (2005); ** data from Caçador et al. (2007).

The amount of nutrients (N and P) from external sources is obtained by subtracting, respectively, the N and P produced by *S. maritima* belowground material from the N and P annually retained in the sediment (Sousa et al., 2008). Results show that in young salt marshes most of the N and P in the in the rhizosediment come from external sources, while in the mature (M) salt marsh the greater percentage of N and P content in the rhizosediment comes from the *S. maritima* belowground system.

From figures 2 it is clear that the mature salt marsh have higher N retention capacity. In fact, the marsh elevation following marsh maturity is accompanied by parallel developments of salt marsh function, characterised by the processes whereby organic matter and nutrients are exchanged between the marsh and their adjoining areas (Boorman, 2003). However, although it has been observed that mature salt marshes export more material than the youngest ones (Valiela et al., 2000), in the studied marshes the amount/percentage of the exported detritus does not seem related to the maturity of the marshes (Sousa et al., 2008). In these southern European Atlantic systems tidal inundation occurs twice a day, contributing to the washing out of detritus. The importance of tidal excursion, as a possible driving force to the export-import balance was pointed out by Valiela et al. (2000). This means that the N and P mineralization of NAPP takes place mostly outside the salt marsh. This process is more relevant in the younger studied salt marshes since they have higher NAPP (Figure 2 and 3). At the mature marsh (M) the main percentage of N and P retained in the rhizosediment comes from the belowground production (NBPP) of *S. maritima*. This is also in agreement with the lower decomposition rates and higher NBPP, which contributes to the higher N and P retention/accumulation in the rhizosediment, and thus acting as a sink for these nutrients. As pointed out by Valiela et al. (2000) salt marshes may be involved in the natural maintenance and protection of other vulnerable estuarine habitats. In fact, as complex ecotones salt marshes ecosystems show strength interactions with other estuarine habitats, namely the upstream fresh water habits and the marine down stream habits, providing valuable ecosystem services

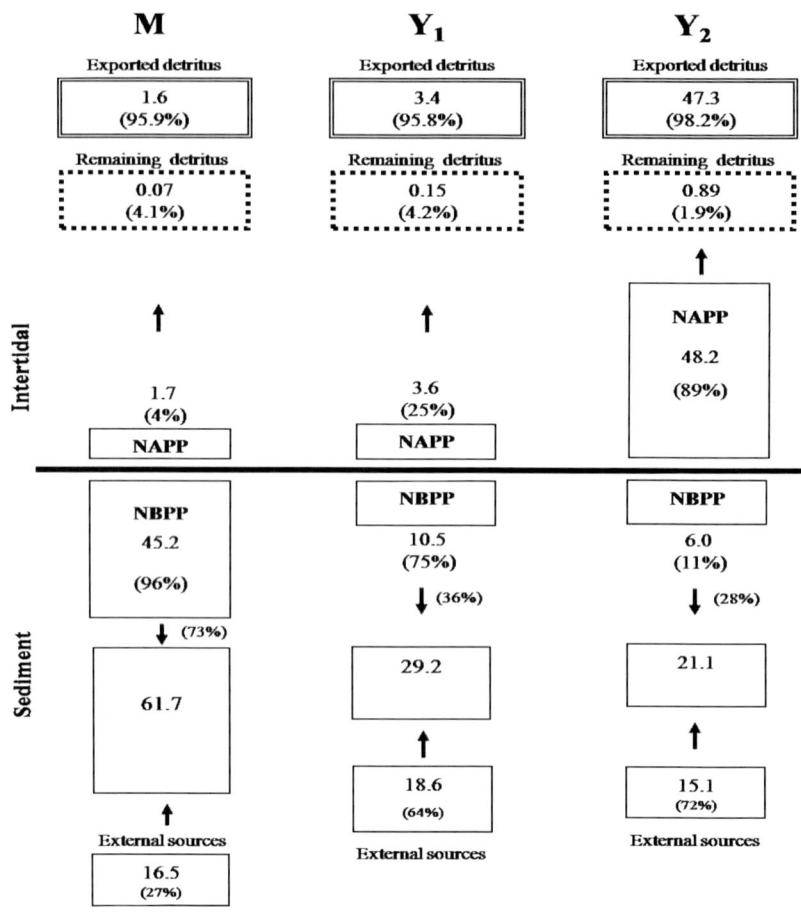

Figure 2. Schematic representation of *Spartina maritima* N productions, detritus moved by tides and N retention in the sediment at mature (M) and young (Y_1, Y_2) salt marshes. (NAPP-Net Aboveground Primary Production and NBPP-Net Belowground Primary Production (g N.m^{-2}.y^{-1})) (data from Sousa et al. 2008).

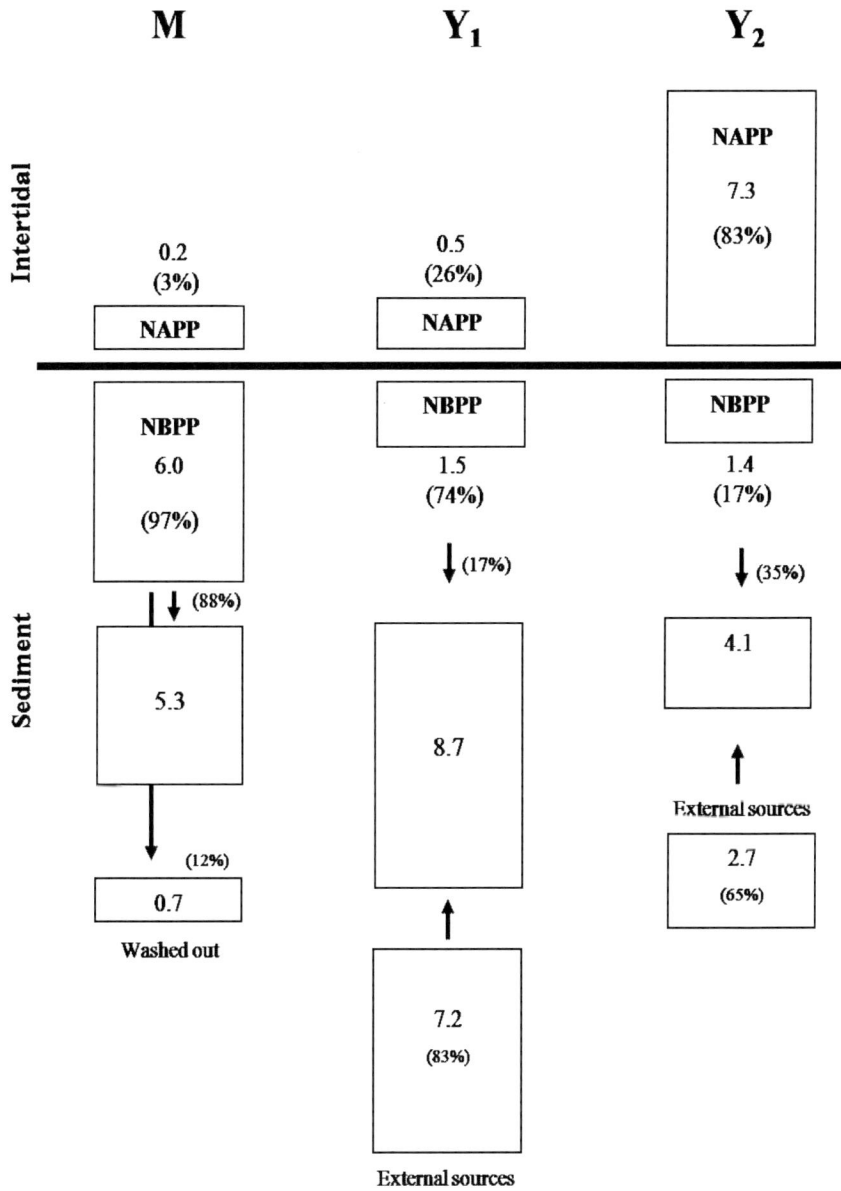

Figure 3. Schematic representation of *Spartina maritima* P productions, decomposition of belowground material and P retention in the sediment at mature (M) and young (Y_1, Y_2) salt marshes. (NAPP-Net Aboveground Primary Production and NBPP-Net Belowground Primary Production (g $P.m^{-2}.y^{-1}$)).

N AND P CYCLING AND SEQUESTRATION IN SALT MARSHES: CASE STUDY OF TWO HALOPHYTES WITH DISTINCT LIFE CYCLES (*SPARTINA MARITIMA* AND *SCIRPUS MARITIMUS*)

Salt marshes are among the most productive systems of the biosphere, however in natural salt marshes, the halophytes diversity and the biomass production (NAPP and NBPP) varies according to marsh maturity (e.g. Valiela et al., 2000, Boorman, 2003, Lefeuvre et al., 2003, Sousa et al., 2008). In temperate estuaries, salt marshes are often colonized by halophytes that are adapted to different physico-chemical characteristics, colonizing upper, middle or lower marshes. Although different species may differ in their physiology and annual biological cycle, they may all have an important role in nutrient cycling in these systems, contributing to their high production (e.g. Ibañez et al. 1999, Lillebø et al., 2002, 2004, Caçador et al., 2004, 2007, Sousa et al. 2008). As a case study two salt marshes, one colonised by *Spartina maritima* (Curt.) Fernald and another colonised by *Scirpus maritimus* L. will be compared with respect to their role on N and P sequestration capacity, since different plants may have different specific effects, and consequently different contributions to the system nutrient dynamics as a whole (Lillebø et al., 2006).

Spartina maritima, is an herbaceous perennial plant distributed in the coasts of western, southern and southeastern Europe and western Africa. *Scirpus maritimus*, usually forms dense monospecific stands in shallow brackish marshes and is widely distributed in Europe and North America. Although both halophytes are perennial, they differ in their physiology and annual biological cycle, and are adapted to different physicochemical characteristics. *Spartina maritima* has a continuous but slow growth and colonises the lower marsh, whilst *Scirpus maritimus* shoots are active during the growing season, showing a seasonal die back for aboveground material, and colonises the middle marsh. In the Mondego estuary this species growing season occur from January to April/May (Lillebø et al., 2003). Like other flooding-tolerant plants, these halophytes respond to oxygen deficiency by forming a well developed aerenchyma system, which confers them the ability to transport oxygen to the belowground parts, down to 20 cm of depth into otherwise impermeable sediments, where it is used for root respiration and oxidation of the rhizosphere (Adams & Bate, 1995). Therefore, these plants may interfere with benthic nutrient cycles, namely with nutrient availability versus sorption to particles (*e.g.* Coelho et al., 2004, Lillebø et al., 2004, 2006, Hou et al., 2008), but also influencing several steps of the N cycle (ammonification, nitrification, denitrification and N-fixation) (*e.g.* Valiela et al., 2000, Pedersen et al., 2004). Both halophytes were sampled each two months, for one year (1997-1998), at monospecific and homogeneous stands of the Mondego estuary (40°07'11.87''N, 8°50'25.96''W), located in the southern European Atlantic margin (Portugal). In this system, salt marshes habitats occupy about 18 % of the south arm of the estuary, where the *Scirpus maritimus* population occupies the inner mud-flats areas, and *Spartina maritima* occurs in the higher downstream mud-fats and sand-flats areas (Figure 4).

Plant material as well as rhizosediment samples were collected, processed and analysed as described in the previous section for Y_2 salt marsh. In *Scirpus maritimus* litterbag experiment, five replicates (bags) were collected following the same periodicity as mentioned in the previous section, but from May to October due to the life cycle of the halophyte. The calculations of halophytes' biomass production, decomposition and turnover rates, N and P productions, turnover rates and N and P retention in the sediment were also performed as described in the previous section for Y_2 salt marsh. In addition, a comparative study of *S. maritima* and *S. maritimus* effect on the rhizosediment profiles concerning the dissolved inorganic nutrients (PO_4-P, NH_3-N, NO_3-N) was done in 2000, followed by an estimation of the total amount of these nutrients during day and night conditions; and finally the potential net-fluxes were compared (see Lillebø et al., 2006). This comparison took place in May, because spring corresponds to the season where *S. maritimus* reaches maximum biomass (NAPP) (Lillebø et al. 2003). The profiles of PO_4-P, NH_3-N and NO_3-N in the rhizosediment were studied by placing vertically dialysis chambers at plants' rhizosphere (for a more detailed description of the field assessment and analytical procedure see Lillebø et al., 2006). Estimates of the amount of nutrients in the rhizosediment at each depth were done considering the loss on ignition (% LOI), the nutrient concentration in the interstitial water, the sediment sample specific mass and the water volume fraction, whilst the total amount was obtained by integration of the amounts through depth. Possible night efflux rates were calculated taking into account the difference between the night and day total amount plus the estuarine area occupied by each salt marsh species (*S. maritima* = 105 ha, and *S. maritimus* = 106 ha).

Furthermore, to calculate the seasonal/annual net internal loading of phosphorus in *S. maritima* and *S. maritimus* salt marshes, flux measurements were performed during 24 hours cycles, in order to cover a complete tidal cycle under day and night situation (Lillebø et al. 2004). Two methodologies were applied to asses for P-flux measurements at each tidal cycle: a) the low tide pools during ebb (between 1999 and 2000), and b) flux chambers during high tide (between 2000 and 2001). Calculations of the mean seasonal phosphate efflux rates were performed taking into account mean daily efflux rates (mg m^{-2} d^{-1}) at each site (day and night) and considering high and low tide, and the correspondent estuarine area covered by each salt marsh (for a more detailed description of the field assessment and analytical procedure see Lillebø et al. 2004). It was assumed that the mean efflux rates in May and July/August represented an average value for spring and summer respectively, and that the mean efflux rates in November and January represented an average value for autumn and winter, respectively (Lillebø et al. 2004).

Sediment organic matter content (% LOI, loss on ignition) is comparatively higher at *S. maritimus* salt marsh, due to its location at the most inner estuarine areas, with lower hydrodynamics and higher sedimentation of fine sediments (Figure 4). Table 5 shows that the annual biomass production of belowground material is comparatively higher (85%) at *S. maritimus* salt marsh, while the aboveground biomass is higher in *S. maritima* (76%). The turnover rate for aboveground biomass was 0.50 for *S. maritima* and 0.92 for *S. maritimus*, whilst the turnover rate for belowground biomass was, respectively, 0.51 and 0.42 (Table 5). The decomposition rates (k) for belowground biomass after 6 months of decomposition were 0.0043 and 0.0031, respectively for *S. maritima* and *S. maritimus* (Figure 5). However, from figure 5 it seems that the initial phases of belowground material decomposition are faster at *S. maritimus* salt marsh. From figures 6 and 7 we can also see that the amount of N annually retained in the upper 5 cm of *S. maritima* and *S. maritimus* rhizosediment was identical (21 gN.m^{-2}.yr^{-1}) (Figure 6), as well as the amount of P annually retained, respectively 4 and 5 gP.m^{-2}.yr^{-1} (Figure 7). The amount of nutrients (N and P) from external sources is obtained by subtracting, respectively, the N and P produced by the halophytes belowground material from the N and P annually retained in the sediment (Sousa et al., 2008). Results show that most of the N and P in the *S. maritima* rhizosediment come from external sources (72% and 65%, respectively), while in *S. maritimus* salt marsh all the N and P content in the rhizosediment come from its belowground system. Although *S. maritimus* belowground material turnover rate is slightly lower, comparatively to *S.*

maritima, it seems that it has a comparatively faster decomposition during its first steps. Decomposition includes several different temporal phases that can be summarised: i) initial leaching of easily degradable low molecular cellular substances, ii) intermediate decomposition of the structural parts, iii) slow degradation of the lesser labile structural parts (Godshalk & Wetzel, 1978). In fact, by having high NAPP and NBPP, salt marshes enhance secondary production and, in these ecosystems, the organic detritus/decomposition pathway represents the basic source that maintains the abundance and productivity of benthic invertebrates (*e.g.* Raffaelli, 1992; Dolbeth et al., 2003, Lillebø et al., 2007b). However, the decomposition of plant litter is mostly regulated by the C:N and N:P ratios of plant material, and by the lability of carbon (*e.g.* Flindt et al., 1999, Costa et al., 2007). A high initial N and P content is often related to higher mineralization rates, whilst a high content of structural compounds such as fibres is correlated with lower mineralization rates (*e.g.* Enriquez et al., 1993; Flindt et al., 1999). The median C:N and N:P ratios of belowground plant material is 36 and 39, and 11 and 3 (N=6), respectively for *S. maritima* and *S. maritimus*. Concerning the aboveground material of *S. maritima* and *S. maritimus*, the decomposition period, under similar experimental mesocosmos conditions (Lillebø et al., 1999, 2007b) and estimated according to 90% of mass loss, was respectively 57 days and 99 days, while initial C:N ratio was 16 (2.3%N and 38%C) and 16 (2.5%N and 40%C). Although this seems contradictory, fast-growing plants tend to decompose quickly because of the adequacy of their litter as substrate for microbial growth (Enriquez et al., 1993). These results are in agreement with the *S. maritimus* higher biomass turnover rate of the aboveground material.

Table 5. Annual biomass production and turnover rate for above ground and belowground material in the sediments of *S. maritima* and *S. maritimus* salt marshes

Salt marshes			
		S. maritima	S. maritimus
Biomass Production ($gDW.m^{-2}.y^{-1}$)	Aboveground	2833 (76%)	325 (15%)
	Belowground	895 (24%)	1858 (85%)
	Total	*3728*	*2183*
Turnover rate:	Aboveground	0.50	0.92

| Biomass (y⁻¹) | Belowground | 0.51 | 0.42 |

Bold numbers within brackets represent the percentage of the above- or belowground biomass productions, in relation to the total biomass production. Turnover rate is shown in terms of biomass. (data from Sousa et al. 2008, 2010a, b)

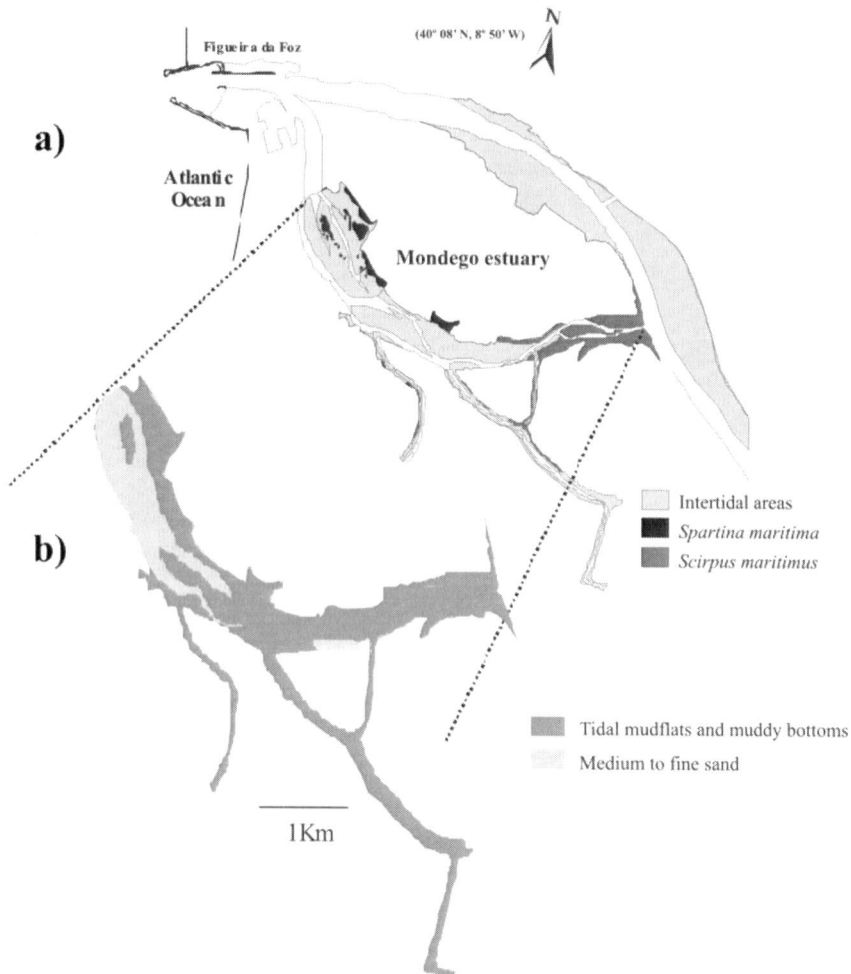

Figure 4. a) The Mondego estuary with the distribution of *Spartina maritima* and *Scirpus maritimus* salt marsh areas; b) representation of the sediments grain-size distribution in the south arm of the estuary (adapted from Coelho et al., 2004).

Results show that the highest total biomass production also corresponded to the highest N and P pools in the halophytes. Thus, nutrient pools in the belowground plant material were higher in *S. maritimus*, whilst the pools of N and P in the aboveground plant material were higher in *S. maritima* (Figure 7).

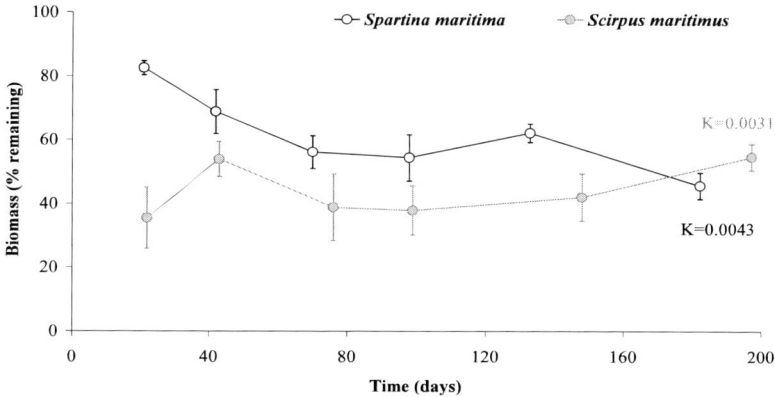

Figure 5. The remaining biomass of *S. maritima* and *S. maritimus* during the litterbag experiment (five replicates (bags) were collected after 22, 43, 71, 99, 134 and 183 days). To calculate the decomposition rate of the belowground material after six months, the biomass of the remaining belowground material was linked to an exponential decay model (*S. maritima* data from Sousa et al. 2008).

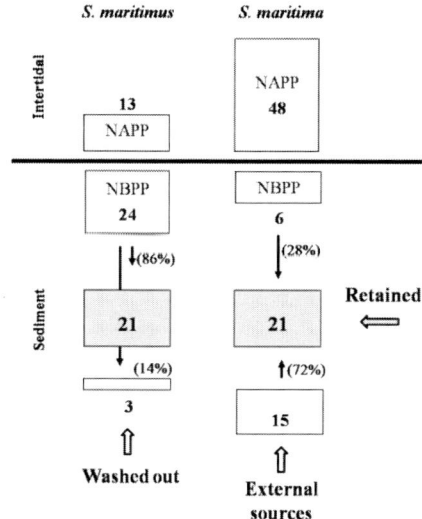

Figure 6. N cycling in *Spartina maritima* and *Scirpus maritimus* salt marshes. NAPP (net aboveground primary production), NBPP (net belowground primary production), and the nitrogen sequestration in the rhizosediment (due to the belowground plant

production and some external sources) are shown in the scheme. The numbers in bold refer to g N.m^{-2}.y^{-1} (data from Sousa et al. 2008, 2010b).

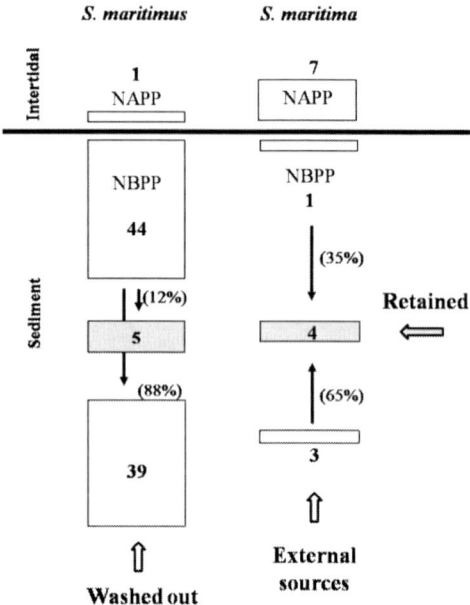

Figure 7. P cycling in *Spartina maritima* and *Scirpus maritimus* salt marshes. NAPP (net aboveground primary production), NBPP (net belowground primary production), and the nitrogen sequestration in the rhizosediment (due to the belowground plant production and some external sources) are shown in the scheme. The numbers in bold refer to g P.m^{-2}.y^{-1} (data from Sousa et al. 2010b).

Results on the effect of *S. maritima* and *S. maritimus* on sediment nutrient profiles show that the concentrations of PO_4-P, NH_3-N and NO_3-N, under day and night situations were statistically different between salt marshes (non-parametric Mann-Whitney tests, Table 6). In addition, day-night profiles were statistically different for NO_3-N *S. maritimus* rhizosphere, whilst in *S. maritima* rhizosphere there were no statistically significant differences between day-night profiles considering the three nutrients analysed (non-parametric Mann-Whitney tests, Table 6). In figure 8 it can be seen that the concentrations of PO_4-P is comparatively higher at *S. maritima* rhizosphere, whilst, concerning the dissolved inorganic forms of nitrogen, NH_3-N was the dominant form at *S. maritima* rhizosphere and NO_3-N was the dominant form at *S. maritimus* rhizosphere, especially during the photosynthetic active period. The calculations of PO_4-P, NH_3-N and NO_3-N total amounts (mg m^{-2}) at the top 20 cm of *S. maritimus* and *S. maritima* rhizospheres, under day and night situations, evidence those differences between salt marshes (Figure 9a). The oxygen diffusion to the sediment is driven by photosynthetic oxygen production (Azzoni et al., 2001) enhancing the phosphate adsorption capacity of the rhizosediment (Berner & Berner, 1996) by means of the precipitation of Fe and Mn oxides. Additionally, the likely comparatively higher oxidised surface area of *S. maritimus* rhizosphere, due to higher NBPP and the fact that during this period (May) *S. maritimus* is reaching maximum density and NAPP, may enhance both biotic and abiotic reoxidation of reduced compounds. This explains the comparatively higher concentration of NO_3-N, especially during the day. This also suggests a higher nitrification rate in *S. maritimus* rhizosphere and possibly a higher coupled nitrification-denitrification, which may be stimulated by high quality dissolved organic carbon released by the roots (Flindt et al., 1999). The calculations of the possible night efflux rates, taking into account the difference between the night and day total amount plus the estuarine area occupied by each species salt marsh, evidences that during this period (May) *S. maritimus* may enhance the uptake of nutrients for growth purposes and promote a more oxidized rhizosphere (Figure 9b). Concerning P, these results suggest a potential efflux of P during the night at *S. maritima* rhizosphere, during the period in which respiration is not compensated by primary production. This is in agreement with previous results, namely Lillebø et al. (2002). However, this does not mean, in an annual basis, that *S. maritima* salt marshes have a comparatively higher contribution to the release of P from the sediment into the water column. In fact, calculations of the annual net internal loading of phosphorus in *S. maritima* and *S. maritimus* salt marshes, taking into account seasonal flux measurements during high and low tide and under day and night situation (Figure 10a), show that both species have a similar contribution to the system P internal loading (Figure 10b). Figure 10 also evidences the P adsorption capacity of salt marshes comparatively to unvegetated mudflats (Lillebø et al., 2004). Seasonal differences shown in figure 10, are explained by differences in *S. maritimus* and *S. maritima* annual cycle, *e.g.* during summer, which corresponds to the die back of *S. maritimus* aboveground material. Although this species is able to allocate nutrients to the belowground material, the adsorption capacity of the rhizosphere is diminished, contributing to a higher efflux of PO_4-P (Figure 10b). Finally, these results are in agreement with the similar amount of P annually retained by *S. maritimus* and *S. maritima* salt marshes respectively 5 and 4 g $P.m^{-2}.yr^{-1}$ (shown previously in figure 7).

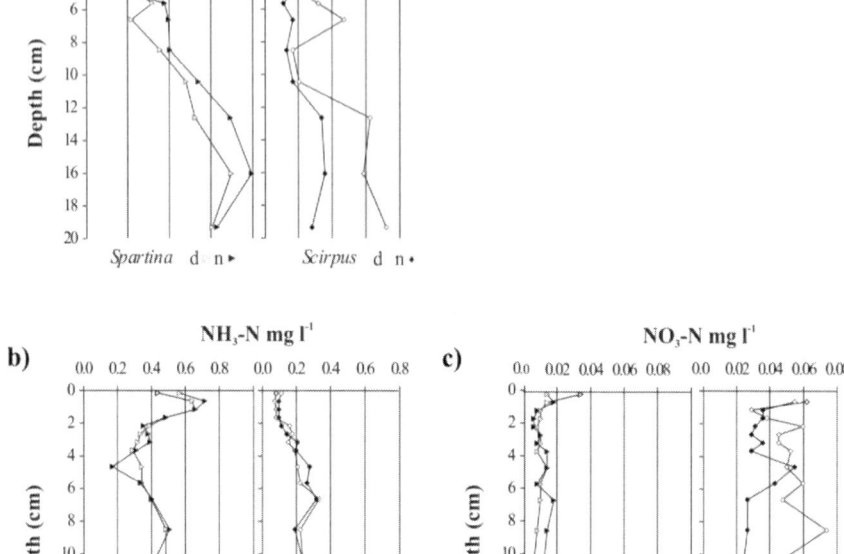

Figure 8. Sediment profiles of *Spartina maritima* and *Scirpus maritimus* a) % LOI, b) phosphate, c) ammonia, d) nitrate (data from Lillebø et al. 2006).

This study highlights that several factors influence N and P cycling and sequestration in salt marshes and consequently the nutrients internal loading at the system level. Besides the species-specific characteristics, namely biomass NAPP and NBPP, physiology and annual biological cycle, the area occupied by each marsh is important when considering the retention capacity of nutrients in salt marshes and consequently the reduction of nutrients internal loading at the system level. In the studied system *S. maritimus* and *S. maritima* salt marshes occupy a similar area and, on an annual basis, both salt marshes contribute to the retention of N and P, which is in agreement with previous studies (Caçador et al., 2004, Coelho et al., 2004, Lillebø et al., 2004, 2006,

Hou et al., 2008, Sousa et al., 2008). Thus, both species have an important role in nutrient cycling, contributing to the high production of salt marshes. Particularly in European temperate estuaries, were *Spartina matitima* and *Scirpus maritimus* are quite common.

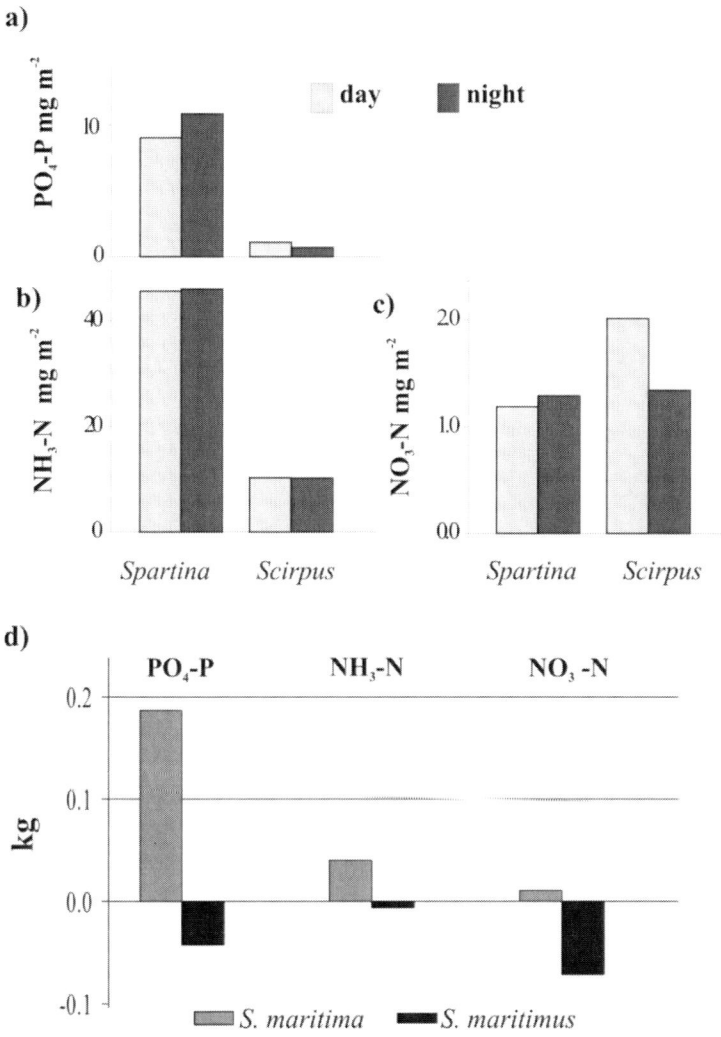

Figure 9. Total amount of nutrients in *Spartina maritima* and *Scirpus maritimus* rhizosphere, a) phosphate; b) ammonia; c) nitrate, and d) the potential night efflux of phosphate, ammonia and nitrate from *Spartina maritima* and *Scirpus maritimus* rhizosphere (data from Lillebø et al. 2006).

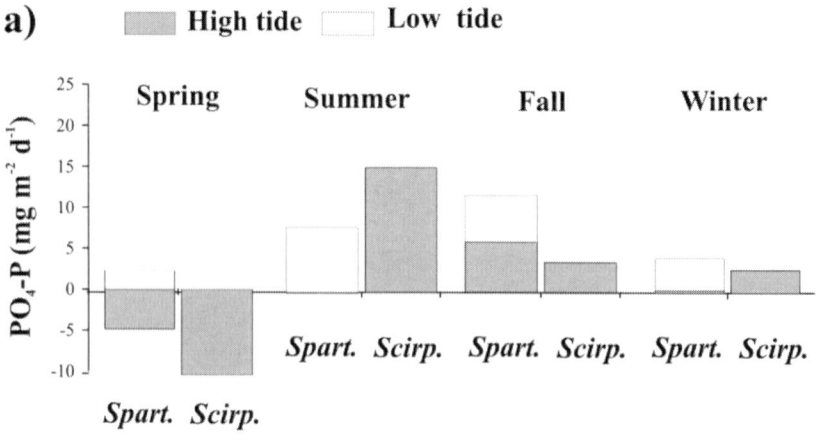

Figure 10. a) Seasonal variation of daily phosphate efflux rates from *Spartina maritima* and *Scirpus maritimus* salt marshes, during high and low tide. b) seasonal and annual P-effluxes (kg PO_4-P ha-1) from *Spartina maritima* and *Scirpus maritimus*, and rhizosphere adsorption capacity (data from Lillebø et al. 2004).

FINAL REMARKS

The contribution of salt marshes to the retention of nutrients (N and P), i.e., salt marshes as sinks for nutrients, has been discussed in this book chapter. Plants uptake and transform the N and P inorganic forms into organic forms, which can then be retained in the rhizosediment. Our results show that nutrients are intensely exchanged within the rhizosediment, allowing to a more comprehensive and environmentally correct understanding of estuarine systems functioning. Overall, the case studies reveal differences between salt marshes: either attributed to salt marsh maturity or to salt marshes species-specific characteristics. The present chapter highlights that biomass production by salt marsh plants constitutes an important service provided by these ecosystems. In addition, N and P uptake from rhizosediment interstitial waters and incorporation into plant biomass enhance nutrient sequestration and retention, decreasing its availability to the water column, thus potentially reducing eutrophication.

Table 6. Results from the non-parametric Mann-Whitney expressing the significance of differences (p value, n.s. means non-significant differences; 95% confidence level) in sediment PO_4-P, NH_3-N and NO_3-N profiles: a) between day-night concentrations; b) between concentrations during day; c) between concentrations during night

a)	Day		*Spartina maritima*
PO_4-P			0.0000
NH_3-N		*Scirpus maritimus*	0.0007
NO_3-N			0.0000
b)	Night		*Spartina maritima*
PO_4-P			0.0000
NH_3-N		*Scirpus maritimus*	0.0016
NO_3-N			0.0000
c)	Day /Night		*Scirpus maritimus*
PO_4-P			n.s
NH_3-N		*Scirpus maritimus*	n.s
NO_3-N			0.0017

Data from Lillebø et al., 2006.

ACKNOWLEDGMENTS

Authors acknowledge funding from the Portuguese FCT (Foundation for Science and Technology) to CESAM - Centre for Environmental and Marine Studies, and the FCT grant given to A.I. Sousa (Ref. SFRH/BD/23634/2005).

REFERENCES

Adams, J. B. & G. C. Bate, 1995. Ecological implications of tolerance of salinity and inundation by *Spartina maritima*. *Aquatic Botany.* 52: 183-191.

Amos, C., Cappucci, S., Bergamasco, A., Umgiesser G., Bonardi, M., Cloutier, D., Flindt, M.R., De Nat, L. &Cristante, S. 2004. The stability of tidal flats in Venice Lagoon – the results of in situ measurements using two benthic annular clumes. *Journal of Marine Systems*, Volume 51, Issues 1-4, November 2004, Pages 211-241.

Azzoni, R. G. Giordani, M. Bartoli, D. T. Welsh & P. Viaroli, 2001. Iron, sulphur and phosphorus cycling in the rhizosphere sediments of an euthrophic *Ruppia cirrhosa* meadow (Valle Smarlacca, Italy). *Journal of Sea Research* 45: 15-26.

Berner, E.K., Berner, R.A. 1996 Marginal Marine Environments: Estuaries. *In The Global Environment: Water, Air and Geochemical Cycles*. Prentice-Hall, Upper Saddle River, NJ pp 284-311.

Best, M., Massey, A., Prior A. 2007. Developing a saltmarsh classification tool for the European water framework directive. *Marine Pollution Bulletin* 55 (2007) 205–214.

Boorman, L.A., 2003. Saltmarsh Review. An overview of coastal saltmarshes, their dynamic and sensitivity characteristics for conservation and management. JNCC, Peterborough. On-line version at http://www.jncc.gov.uk/pdf/jncc334.pdf assessed at 14th October 2009.

Bricker, S.B., C.G. Clement, D.E. Pirhalla, S.P. Orlando, and D.R.G. Farrow. 1999. *National Estuaryne Eutrophication Assessement: Effects of Nutrient Enrichment in the Nation's Estuaries.* NOAA, National Ocean Service, Special Projects Office and the National Centers for Coastal Ocean Science. Silver Spring, MD, 71 p.

Caçador, I., Vale C., Catarino F.M., 1993. Effects of plants on the accumulation of Zn, Pb, *Cu and Cd in sediments of the Tagus estuary salt marshes*, Portugal J-P. Vernet (ed). Studies In Environment Sciences Environment Contamination, Elsevier Science Publisher B.V., Amsterdam. 55:355-364.

Caçador, I., Vale C. Catarino F.M., 1996. Accumulation of Zn, Pb, Cu, Cr and Ni in Sediments Between Roots of the Tagus Estuary Salt Marshes, Portugal. *Estuarine, Coastal and Shelf Science* 42:393-403.

Caçador, I., Mascarenhas, I., Mascarenhas, P., 1999. Biomass of *Spartina maritima, Halimione portulacoides* and *Arthrocnemum fruticosum* in

Tagus estuary salt marshes. In: Leith, H., Moschenko, M., Lohmann, M., Koyro, H.-W., Hamby, A. (Eds.), *Halophyte Uses in Different Climates* I. Backhuys Publishers, Leiden, The Netherlands, pp. 33–41.

Caçador, I., Costa, A.L., Vale, C., 2004. Carbon storage in Tagus salt marsh sediments. *Water, Air, and Soil Pollution:* Focus 4, 701-714.

Caçador, I., Costa, A.L., Vale, C., 2007. Nitrogen Sequestration Capacity of Two Salt Marshes from the Tagus estuary. *Hydrobiologia* 587, 137-145.

Castro, P., Freitas, H., 2000. Fungal biomass and decomposition in *Spartina maritima* leaves in the Mondego salt marsh (Portugal). *Hydrobiologia* 428, 171–177.

Castro, P.C.O., 2005. Assessing key-habitat loss due to eutrophication in the Mondego and Mira estuaries. *PhD Thesis,* University of Coimbra, Portugal.

Coelho, J.P., M.R. Flindt, H.S. Jensen, A.I. Lillebø & M.A. Pardal 2004 Phosphorus speciation and availability in intertidal sediments of a temperate estuary : relation to eutrophication and annual P-fluxes. Estuarine, *Coastal and Shelf Science* 61:583-590.

Costanza, R., d'Arge, R., de Groot, R., Farber, S., Grasso, M., Hannon, B., Limburg K., Naeem, S., O' Neill, R.V., Paruelo, J., Raskin, R.G., Sutton P., van den Belt, M.,1997. The value of the world's ecosystem services and natural capital. *Nature* 387, 353-360.

Costa, A:L., Carolino M., Caçador I. 2007 Microbial activity profiles in Tagus estuary salt marsh sediments. *Hydrobiologia,* 587:169–175.

Council Directive 92/43/EEC, of 21 May 1992, on the conservation of natural habitats and of wild fauna and flora; *On-line version of the Official Journal 1992L0043* http://eur-lex.europa.eu/LexUriServ/, assessed at 14th October 2009.

Crouzet, P., J. Leonard, S. Nixon, Y. Rees, W. Parr, L. Laffon, J. Bøgestrand, P. Kristensen, C. Lallana, G. Izzo, T. Bokn, J. Back, and T.J. Lack. 1999. Nutrients in European ecosystems. In: Thyssen, N., (Ed.), Environmental Assessment Report n°4. European Environmental Agency, p. 82. On-line version available at http://www.eea.europa.eu/publications/ ENVIASSRP04, assessed at 9th November 2009.

Curcó, A., Ibañez, C., Day, J.W., Prat, N., 2002. Net primary production and decomposition of salt marshes of the Ebre Delta (Catalonia, Spain). *Estuaries* 25, 309-324.

Deegan, L.A. 2002 Lessons Learned: The Effects of Nutrient Enrichment on the Support of Nekton by Seagrass and Salt Marsh Ecosystems. *Estuaries* 25, 727-742.

De la Cruz, A.A., Hackney, C.T., 1977. Energy value, elemental composition, and productivity of belowground biomasa of a *Juncus* tidal marsh. *Ecology* 58, 1165-1170.
Dolbeth, M., M. A. Pardal, A. I. Lillebø, U. Azeiteiro & J. C. Marques, 2003. Short term and long term effects of eutrophication on the secondary production of an intertidal macrobenthic community. *Marine Biology* 143:1229-1238.
Edwards, K.R., Mills, K.P., 2005. Aboveground and belowground productivity of *Spartina alterniflora* (smooth cordgrass) in natural and created Louisiana salt marshes. *Estuaries* 28, 252–265.
Enriques, E., C. M. Duarte & K. Sand-Jensen, 1993. Patterns in decomposition rates among photosynthetic organisms: the importance of detritus C:N:P contend. *Oecologia* 94: 457-471.
Flindt, M.R., M. Carrer, J. Salomonsen, M. Bocci & L. Kamp-Nielsen. 1997. Loss, growth and transport dynamics of Chaetomorpha aeraa and Ulva rigida in the Lagoon of Venice during an early summer field campaign. *Ecological Modelling*. 102: 133-142.
Flindt, M. R., M. A. Pardal, A. I. Lillebø, I. Martins & J. C Marques, 1999. Nutrient cycling and plant dynamic in estuaries: a brief review. *Acta Oecologica* 20: 237-248.
Flindt, M.R., Lillebø, A.I., 2005. Determination of total nitrogen and total phosphorus in leaf litter, in: Graça, M.A. (Ed), *Methods to Study Litter Decomposition*. Springer, Dordrecht, Holland, pp. 53-58.
Flindt, M.R., Pedersen, C.B, Amos, C.L, Levy, A., Bergamasco, A. & Friend, P.L.. 2007. Transport, sloughing and settling rates of estuarine macrophytes: Mechanisms and ecological implications. *Continental Shelf Research.* 27: 1096-1103.
Gameiro, C., Cartaxana, P., Cabrita T., Brotas, V., 2004. Spatial and Temporal Variability in the Phytoplankton Composition of an Estuarine System. *Hydrobiologia* 525, 113-124.
Godshalk, G. L. & R. G. Wetzel, 1978. Decomposition of aquatic angiosperms. III. *Zostera marina* L. and conceptual model of decomposition. *Aquatic Botany* 5 329-354.
Green B.C., Smith D.J., Earley S.E., Hepburn L.J., Underwood G.J.C. 2009 Seasonal changes in community composition and trophic structure of fish populations of five salt marshes along the Essex coastline, United Kingdom Estuarine, *Coastal and Shelf Science* 85, 247–256.
Hauxwell, J. and I. Valiela. 2004. Effects of nutrient loading on shallow seagrass-dominated coastal systems: patterns and processes. In Nielsen, G.

Banta, and M. Pedersen (Eds.), Estuarine Nutrient Cycling: *The influence of Primary Producers.* Kluwer Academic Publishers, London, pp 59-92.

Hou, L. J., M. Liu, D. N. Ou, Y. Yang, and S. Y. Xu 2008, Influences of the macrophyte (*Scirpus mariqueter*) on phosphorous geochemical properties in the intertidal marsh of the Yangtze Estuary, *J. Geophys. Res.,* 113, G04038, doi:10.1029/2008JG000780.

Ibañez, C., Curcó, A., Day Jr, J.W., Prat, N. 2000. Structure and productivity of microtidal Mediterranean coastal marshes, in: Weinstein M.P., Kreeger, D.A., (Eds.), *Concepts and Controversies in Tidal Marsh Ecology.* Kluwer Academic Publishers, Netherlands, pp. 107-136.

Ibañez, C., Day Jr., J.W, Pont, D., 1999. Primary production and decomposition of wetlands of the Rhône Delta, France: Interactive impacts of human modifications and relative sea level rise. *Journal of Coastal Research* 15, 717-731.

Jin B., Fu C, Zhong J., Li B., Chen J., Wu J. 2007 Fish utilization of a salt marsh intertidal creek in the Yangtze River estuary, China. *Estuarine, Coastal and Shelf Science* 73, 844e852.

Lefeuvre, J-C., Laffaille, P., Feunteun, E., Bouchard, V., Radureau, A., 2003. Biodiversity in salt marshes: from patrimonial value to ecosystem functioning. The case study of the Mont-Saint-Michel bay. *Comptes Rendus Biologies* 326, s125-s131.

Lillebø, A. I., M. R. Flindt, M. A. Pardal & J. C. Marques, 1999. The effect of macrofauna, meiofauna and microfauna on the degradation of *Spartina maritima* detritus from a salt marsh area. *Acta Oecologica*, 20 (4): 249 – 258.

Lillebø, A. I., M. A. Pardal, J. M. Neto, M. R. Flindt & J. C. Marques 2002 The role of *Spartina maritima* and *Scirpus maritimus* to sediment porewater profiles. Possible implications to the Mondego estuary nutrient dynamics. In: *Aquatic Ecology of the Mondego River Basin.* Global Importance of Local Experience, Scientific Editors M. A. Pardal, J. C. Marques and M. A. Graça, Coimbra, Imprensa da Universidade de Coimbra. pp 325-338.

Lillebø, A. I., M. A. Pardal, J. M. Neto & J. C. Marques 2003 Salinity as the major factor affecting *Scirpus maritimus* annual dynamics. Evidence from field data and greenhouse experiment. *Aquatic Botany* 77 (2): 111-120.

Lillebø, A.I., J.M. Neto, M.R. Flindt, J.C. Marques, and M.A. Pardal. 2004. Phosphorous dynamics in a temperate intertidal estuary. *Estuarine, Coastal and Shelf Science* 61: 101-109.

Lillebø, A.I., J.M. Neto, I. Martins, T. Verdelhos, S. Leston, P.G. Cardoso, S.M. Ferreira, J.C. Marques, and M.A. Pardal. 2005. Management of a shallow temperate estuary to control eutrophication: the effect of hydrodynamics on the system nutrient loading. *Estuarine, Coastal and Shelf Science* 65: 697-707.

Lillebø A. I., M. R. Flindt, M. A. Pardal & J. C. Marques 2006 The effect of *Zostera noltii*, *Spartina maritima* and *Scirpus maritimus* on sediment pore-water profiles, in a temperate intertidal estuary. *Hydrobiologia*, 555:175-183.

Lillebø, A.I., J. P. Coelho, M. R. Flindt, H.S. Jensen, J. C. Marques, C. B. Pedersen & M. A. Pardal 2007a *Spartina maritima* influence on the dynamics of phosphorus sedimentary cycle in a warm temperate estuary (Mondego estuary, Portugal). *Hydrobiologia*, 587:195–204.

Lillebø, A. I., M. R. Flindt, M. A. Pardal, P. Cardoso, S. Ferreira & J. C. Marques 2007b. The faunal role on the degradation of the common intertidal salt-marsh plant *Scirpus maritimus*. *Hydrobiologia*. 579, 1, 369-378.

Maricle, B.R., Lee, R.W., 2002. Aerenchyma development and oxygen transport in the estuarine cordgrasses *Spartina arteniflora* and *S. anglica*. *Aquatic Botany* 74, 109-120.

Martins, I., M. A. Pardal, A. I. Lillebø, M. R. Flindt & J. C. Marques 2001. Hydrodynamics as a major factor controlling the occurrence of green macroalgae blooms in an eutrophic estuary: a case study. *Estuarine Coastal and Shelf Science* 52: 165-177.

McGlathery, KJ., Sundbäck, K., Anderson, I.C., 2004. The importance of primary producers for benthic nitrogen and phosphorus cycling, in: Nielsen, S., Banta, G., Pedersen, M., (Eds.), *Estuarine nutrient cycling: The influence of primary producers*. Kluwer Academic Publishers, The Netherlands, pp. 231-261.

Nedwell, D.B., Jickells, T.D., Timmer, M., Sanders, R., 1999. Nutrients in estuaries, in: Nedwell, D.B., Raffaelli, D.G., (Eds), Estuaries. *Advances in Ecological Research* 29, 43-92.

Pedersen, M.F., Nielsen, S.L., Banta, G.T., 2004. Interactions between vegetation and nutrient dynamics in coastal marine ecosystems: an introduction, in: Nielsen, S., Banta, G., Pedersen, M., (Eds.), *Estuarine nutrient cycling: The influence of primary producers*. Kluwer Academic Publishers, The Netherlands, pp. 1-15.

Pereira, P., I. Caçador, C. Vale, M. Caetano & A.L Costa, 2007. Decomposition of belowground litter and metal dynamics in salt marshes (Tagus, Estuary, Portugal). *Science of Total Enviroment* 380:93-101.

Raffaelli, D., 1992. Conservation of Scottish estuaries. *Proceedings of the Royal Society of Edinburgh*, 100B: 55-76.

Reboreda, R., Caçador, I., 2007. Halophyte vegetation influences in salt marsh capacity retention for heavy metals. *Environmental Pollution* 146, 147-154.

Simas T.C., J.G. Ferreira, 2007 Nutrient enrichment and the role of salt marshes in the Tagus estuary (Portugal). Estuarine, *Coastal and Shelf Science* 75, 393-407.

Salomonsen, J., M.R. Flindt & O. Geertz-Hansen. 1997. Significance of advective transport of Ulva lactuca for a biomass budget on a shallow water location. *Ecological Modelling*. 102: 129-132.

Salomonsen, J., Flindt, M.R., Geertz-Hansen, O. 1999. Modelling advective transport of Ulva lactuca i(L) n the sheltered bay, Møllekrogen, Roskilde Fjord, Denmark. *Hydrobiologia*. 397: 241-252.

Sousa AI, AI Lillebø, I Caçador, M Pardal 2008. Contribution of *Spartina maritima* to the reduction of eutrophication in estuarine systems. *Environmental Pollution* 156: 628–635.

Sousa AI, AI Lillebø, M Pardal & I Caçador 2010a. The influence of *Spartina maritima* on carbon retention capacity in salt marshes from warm-temperate estuaries. *Marine Pollution Bulletin* 61:215–223.

Sousa AI, AI Lillebø, M Pardal & I Caçador 2010b. Productivity and nutrient cycling in salt marshes: Contribution to ecosystem health. *Estuarine, Coastal and Shelf Science* 87: 640-646.

Tappin A.D. 2002 An examination of the fluxes of nitrogen and phosphorus in temperate and tropical estuaries: current estimates and uncertainties. *Estuarine, Coastal and Shelf Science* 55, 885–901.

Valiela, I., Cole, M.L., Mcclelland, J., Hauxwell, J., Cebrian, J., Joye, S.B., 2000. Role of salt marshes as part of coastal landscapes. In: Weinstein, M.P., Kreeger, D.A. (Eds.), *Concepts and Controversies in Tidal Marsh Ecology*. Kluwer Academic Publishers, Netherlands, pp. 23–38.

INDEX

A

access, ix, 50, 78
acid, 85
acidic, 23, 24, 25, 38
adaptations, 30, 51, 127
adsorption, 151, 154
Africa, 124, 144
age, 139
agencies, 65, 73
aggressive behavior, 73
agricultural crops, ix, 50, 73
agriculture, 57, 120, 121, 131
Alaska, 24, 42
alcohol, 117, 127
alfalfa, 58, 73
algae, 32, 65, 131
altered aquatic ecosystems, ix, 50
ammonia, 5, 37, 38, 42, 152, 153
ammonium, 5, 7, 16, 19, 26, 33, 34, 35, 37, 40, 43, 46
amphibians, 72
amplitude, 3, 134
anchoring, 132
angiosperm, 124
annuals, 124
anoxia, x, 103
anthropogenic nutrient loading, viii, 2
anthropogenically enriched groundwater, vii, 1
anticoagulant, 79, 82
aquaculture, 120, 134
aquatic habitats, vii, viii, 49, 58
aquatic systems, 52
aquatic vegetation, ix, 50, 52, 54, 57, 87
aquatic weeds, ix, 50
aquifers, 43
Argentina, 53, 54, 83
Asia, 54, 120
assessment, 65, 78, 145
atmosphere, vii, 1, 3, 4, 6, 22, 24, 29, 30, 34, 35, 42
atmospheric deposition, 16
attachment, 84
Australia, 122
Austria, 54
authorities, 54
authors, 110, 116
availability, 117

B

bacteria, 3, 5, 7, 8, 17, 25, 27, 30, 37, 40, 42, 140
ban, 75

banks, 58, 72, 73
barriers, 24, 63, 121
base, 63, 67, 80
BD, 155
bedding, 67
beef, 63
behaviors, 53
Belgium, 13, 54
benefits, 69, 75, 133
benthic invertebrates, 147
biodiversity, x, 130, 133
biomass, viii, 18, 21, 26, 31, 32, 40, 49, 58, 62, 63, 71, 124, 132, 133, 136, 137, 138, 139, 140, 144, 145, 146, 147, 148, 149, 152, 155, 157, 161
biosphere, 144
biotic, viii, x, 49, 103, 104, 112, 118, 128, 151
biotic factor, 118, 128
birds, 59, 64
births, 56
blood, 58
body weight, 52
Bolivia, 53
Botswana, 54
Brazil, 53
breakdown, 140
breeding, 54, 70, 78, 121
Britain, 54, 83
Brittany, 102
Bulgaria, 54

C

cables, 68
canals, 52, 79
captive populations, 55, 58
carbon, vii, 1, 3, 5, 7, 30, 31, 34, 36, 38, 40, 41, 42, 44, 45, 46, 92, 125, 140, 147, 151, 161
carbon dioxide, 41, 44

Carbon dioxide (CO_2), vii, 1
carbon sinks, vii, 1, 3
case studies, x, 59, 84, 130, 155
case study, 76, 88, 134, 144, 159, 160
catchments, 131
changing environment, 35
channels, 116
character, 112
chemical, x, 33, 38, 103, 104, 105, 112, 118, 122, 131, 132, 139, 144
chemical characteristics, 132, 139, 144
chicken, 63
children, 73
Chile, 53
China, 9, 12, 31, 38, 41, 44, 47, 48, 54, 159
chlamydia, 58
cholesterol, 88
chromatography, 85
citizens, 74
City, 72
classification, 71, 134, 156
cleaning, 58, 121
climate, vii, 1, 3, 16, 19, 34, 36, 42, 88, 104, 119, 130
climate change, viii, 2, 19, 34, 36, 42, 88, 130
climates, 34
cluster analysis, 105, 109
clustering, 107, 109, 110
clusters, 107, 109
CO_2, vii, 1, 3, 4, 7, 8, 10, 19, 24, 26, 27, 34, 35, 36, 38, 40, 43, 47
coastal ecosystems, 4, 6, 15, 16, 35, 117, 123, 125, 131, 133
colonisation, 127
colonization, 94, 99, 118, 140
commercial, 64, 65, 68, 75, 76, 84
communities, 5, 24, 30, 32, 34, 35, 36, 41, 52, 56, 58, 75, 104, 105, 109,

110, 111, 112, 113, 115, 116, 117, 118, 122, 123, 124, 132
community, 17, 31, 35, 38, 44, 48, 72, 88, 104, 112, 113, 114, 115, 116, 118, 131, 132, 158
competition, 17, 23, 31, 75, 87, 110, 117, 118, 126, 132, 139
competitor, 116
competitors, 110
complexity, 21
composition, 17, 31, 32, 33, 35, 38, 44, 48, 62, 105, 107, 109, 158
compounds, 7, 23, 37, 79, 82, 119, 122, 131, 147, 151
computer, 82
concentration, 118
conceptual model, 158
conditioning, vii, x, 103, 113, 115, 119, 122, 139
conductivity, 104, 113, 114, 115, 116
configuration, 122
conservation, vii, viii, 2, 54, 81, 82, 84, 85, 120, 130, 156, 157
constituents, 40
constructed wetlands, 48
construction, 34, 120, 121
consumers, 52
consumption, viii, 2, 4, 8, 14, 15, 18, 21, 22, 28, 29, 32, 63, 65, 79, 120
contamination, viii, 50
Continental, 158
control, 119, 120, 121
control measures, 70
copper, 5
correlation, 113
correlations, 26, 100
cost, 4, 56, 77, 87
Costa Rica, 13
cost-benefit analysis, 87
covering, 62, 134
crabs, 35, 118

crop, 54, 73
crops, ix, 50, 54, 55, 57, 58, 73, 120
cues, 78, 80
cycles, x, 29, 130, 131, 133, 145, 146
cycling, vii, x, 30, 37, 40, 41, 43, 44, 130, 132, 133, 140, 144, 149, 150, 152, 156, 158, 160, 161
cytochrome, 5
Czech Republic, 54

D

daily C sequestration, vii, 2
damages, 72
danger, 51
DEA, 24
deaths, 78
decay, 138, 149
decomposition, 29, 38, 42, 138, 140, 142, 144, 145, 146, 149, 157, 158, 159
deficiency, 127, 144
deficit, 124
degradation, 147, 159, 160
Delta, 47, 88, 121, 157, 159
denitrification, 3, 5, 6, 8, 14, 16, 19, 20, 22, 23, 25, 26, 27, 28, 29, 33, 35, 37, 39, 40, 41, 42, 44, 45, 46, 47, 48, 133, 145, 151
denitrifying, 27, 37, 38, 46, 47
Denmark, 54, 129, 161
Department of Agriculture, 66, 85
deposition, 16, 17, 48
deposits, ix, 33, 91, 92, 94, 99, 100, 101
depth, 20, 22, 33, 112, 113, 114, 116, 124, 128, 134, 136, 138, 140, 144, 145
detection, x, 66, 67, 91, 92
deviation, 106, 114, 139
dialysis, 145
diet, 53, 54, 56, 62, 65

diffusion, 22, 24, 151
direct measure, 20
discharges, 48
discriminant analysis, 113, 115, 116
diseases, ix, 50, 53, 58, 73, 84, 87, 121
dispersion, 121
displacement, 117, 126
disposition, 104
dissolved oxygen, 21
distribution, x, 21, 32, 38, 41, 46, 47, 55, 67, 81, 83, 84, 86, 99, 101, 103, 114, 116, 117, 119, 122, 124, 125, 127, 128, 148
diversity, viii, 48, 49, 72, 92, 97, 98, 100, 105, 119, 127, 132, 144
DNA, 8, 78, 81
dogs, 67, 68, 79
DOI, 43
dominance, 25, 128
donors, 27, 37, 47
drainage, 52, 70, 94, 116, 118, 121, 125, 131
drought, 52, 133
dumping, 122
dynamic systems, 132
dynamics, 124, 125, 126, 128

E

East Asia, 120
ecology, vii, ix, x, 15, 48, 51, 53, 89, 123, 124, 126, 130
economic losses, 56, 65, 88
economics, 89
ecosystem, x, 35, 40, 42, 45, 130, 131, 132, 133, 142, 157, 159, 161
effluent, 18, 19, 26
effluents, 131
electrical conductivity, 113, 115
electron, 5, 21, 27, 30, 33, 37, 115

emission, viii, 2, 4, 29, 30, 39, 41, 42, 43, 44, 46, 47, 48
endangered, 64
energy, 5, 7, 45, 52, 117, 121, 131, 133
England, 45, 48, 55, 56, 124, 125
entrapment, 43, 105, 117
environment, 2, 4, 18, 20, 22, 96, 110, 113, 118, 130, 133
environmental change, 36, 92, 102
environmental characteristics, 127
environmental conditions, vii, 1, 5, 6, 35, 45, 112, 118, 122
environmental control, viii, 2, 8, 45
environmental factors, viii, 2, 4, 14, 15, 19, 125, 140
environmental impact, 121
environmental stress, 139
environments, ix, 8, 15, 33, 48, 50, 52, 56, 75, 91, 92, 94, 99, 102, 105, 122, 128, 130, 131
enzyme, 5, 17, 38, 117
enzymes, 17, 41
equipment, ix, 50, 58
erosion, viii, 49, 58, 59, 65, 72, 73, 86
estuarine environments, x, 91
estuarine gradients, 36
estuarine systems, 92, 132, 155, 161
ethylene, 127
Europe, 56, 101, 119, 120, 121, 123, 144
evapotranspiration, 115, 116, 119
evidence, 3, 7, 55, 59, 151
evolution, 99
exclusion, 62
exploitation, 54
exports, viii, 3, 43, 49
exposure, 18, 78, 79, 94
extraction, 120

F

farmers, 60, 70
farms, 54, 55, 57, 65, 70
fat, 63
fauna, 44, 64, 72, 75, 96, 130, 157
feces, 33, 58
feral populations, ix, 50, 55
fertility, 86
fertilization, 17, 18, 47
fidelity, 53
filters, 82
Finland, 13, 54
firearms, 64
fish, 19, 26, 72, 132, 158
Fish and Wildlife Service, 66, 72, 82, 84
fisheries, 2, 65, 134
fishing, viii, 50, 64
fixation, 133, 145
flood control, viii, 49, 50, 58
flooding, 21, 59, 60, 62, 104, 105, 112, 113, 114, 117, 119, 121, 124, 144
floods, 86, 105, 133
flora, 64, 130, 157
flora and fauna, 64
flotation, 67
fluid, 59
fluorescence, 77
food, 45, 53, 54, 55, 59, 63, 77, 78, 80, 82, 86, 89, 92, 131
food chain, 45
food habits, 55, 77, 82, 89
food web, 131
forbs, 71
force, 141
Ford, 58, 62, 82, 83
forest habitats, 64
formation, x, 83, 103, 119
France, 54, 56, 88, 102, 121, 125, 159
freezing, 29
freshwater, 3, 7, 8, 9, 10, 15, 16, 21, 26, 29, 30, 31, 34, 38, 39, 40, 42, 44, 45, 46, 47, 48, 52, 53, 56, 60, 64, 87, 89, 110, 131
friction, 77
funding, 62, 66, 155
funds, 60
fungi, 140

G

generation, 121
genes, 5, 24
genus, 117, 118, 122
Geographic Information System, 68
Georgia, 40, 47
Germany, 54, 56, 78, 126
germination, 110
GHG, 16, 19, 32
GIS, 68
gland, 78, 82
global climate change, viii, 2, 19
global warming, vii, 1, 3, 19, 32, 36, 40
GPS, 68, 84
graduate students, 66
grain size, 92
grass, 134
grasses, 2, 66, 71
grazers, 34, 119
grazing, 34, 123, 126
Great Britain, 54
Greece, 54
greenhouse, vii, 1, 3, 4, 6, 8, 10, 15, 17, 18, 19, 20, 22, 23, 25, 26, 27, 28, 29, 30, 31, 32, 33, 34, 35, 36, 46, 124, 159
groundwater, vii, 1, 16, 17, 18, 19, 20, 33, 40, 43, 112, 113, 115
groups, 107, 109, 113

growth, 19, 42, 75, 115, 117, 123, 124, 125, 126, 127, 131, 132, 134, 144, 147, 151, 158
guidelines, 113
Gulf Coast, 57

H

habitat, viii, ix, x, 50, 52, 59, 64, 71, 72, 77, 87, 124, 127, 130, 157
hair, 67
halophyte, 132, 145
hardwood forest, 41, 125
harm, 121
harvesting, 54, 64
hazards, 76, 80
health, x, 66, 130, 133, 161
heavy metals, 121, 161
height, 106, 113
hemisphere, 8, 122
heterogeneity, viii, 2, 27, 35, 36
history, 53, 56, 61, 71
HM, 97, 98
Holocene, 99, 101, 102
homeowners, 73
hormone, 83
host, ix, 50
hotspots, 24
human, viii, x, 2, 4, 19, 49, 50, 58, 63, 65, 92, 119, 120, 121, 122, 123, 130, 131, 133, 159
human actions, 122
hunting, viii, 49, 65, 68, 83
hurricanes, ix, 50
hybrid, 122
hybridization, 122
hydrogen, 37, 126
hydrogen sulfide, 126
hypothesis, 2, 39
hypoxia, 3, 39

I

ideal, 78, 122
identification, 82
immersion, 22, 132
immigration, 56, 66
improvements, 86
incisors, 51
income, 63, 75
India, 19, 45
indicators, 110, 125
indirect effect, 32, 37
individuals, 51, 53, 55, 67, 77, 96, 99
Indonesia, 25
industries, 65
industry, 59, 60, 61, 65, 70, 134
infection, 82
infertility, 76
infrastructure, 58
ingestion, 82
inhibition, 17, 19, 20, 22, 118, 119
injuries, 78
insects, 121
integration, 118, 145
integrity, 131
interactions, x, 103, 104, 105, 122, 124, 125, 127, 128
interface, vii, viii, 49
interference, 119
intervention, 55, 119
invasions, viii, 2, 34, 35
invasive herbivore impacts, ix, 50
invertebrates, 53, 56, 147
investment, 77
ions, x, 103, 115
Ireland, 54
iron, 8, 27, 30, 116, 126, 127
irrigation, 20, 42, 57, 120
islands, 62, 82, 131
isolation, 26
isopods, 35

Israel, 54
issues, 73, 75
Italy, 54, 55, 56, 81, 87, 88, 156

J

Japan, 11, 25, 41, 54, 119
Jordan, 9, 41, 48, 60, 61, 63, 64, 70, 84, 116, 126
juveniles, 52, 53

K

Kenya, 54
kill, 68, 78
kinetics, 47
Korea, 54
Kyoto Protocol, 46

L

labeling, 82
laboratory studies, 26
lakes, 2, 52, 121
land, 120, 127
landscape, 32, 66, 77
landscapes, 2, 161
laws, 76
leaching, 123, 147
lead, viii, 18, 35, 49, 73, 112, 132, 134
levees, 58, 73, 86
life cycle, x, 130, 145
light, 20, 22, 105, 118, 119
limitation, 126
line, 104
livestock, 57, 58, 73
logging, 21
long distance, 122

Louisiana, ix, 12, 51, 57, 58, 60, 61, 62, 63, 65, 70, 72, 73, 75, 76, 79, 81, 82, 83, 84, 85, 86, 87, 88, 89, 126, 158
low temperatures, 45
Luo, 38
lying, 58

M

machinery, 73
macroalgae, 20, 160
magnitude, vii, 1, 3, 4, 16, 17, 19, 31, 35
majority, 55, 64, 113
malaria, 121
mammals, 51, 81, 82, 83, 84, 85, 86, 88, 89
management, vii, ix, 4, 24, 34, 36, 50, 56, 64, 65, 66, 67, 75, 76, 77, 78, 80, 81, 82, 85, 88, 89, 120, 133, 156
manganese, 116, 126, 127, 128
mangrove forests, 19, 42
mangroves, 3, 15, 120
Marani, 128
marine species, 99
marsh, vii, ix, x, 1, 2, 3, 4, 5, 6, 7, 8, 9, 11, 13, 14, 15, 16, 17, 18, 19, 20, 21, 22, 23, 25, 26, 27, 29, 30, 31, 32, 33, 34, 35, 36, 37, 38, 39, 40, 42, 43, 44, 45, 47, 48, 52, 55, 58, 60, 62, 64, 65, 66, 73, 75, 76, 78, 80, 82, 83, 84, 85, 87, 88, 89, 91, 92, 94, 96, 97, 98, 99, 100, 101, 103, 104, 105, 109, 110, 112, 113, 114, 115, 118, 119, 121, 122, 123, 124, 125, 126, 127, 128, 130, 131, 132, 133, 134, 136, 138,
marsh ecosystems, vii, 1, 3, 17, 19, 27, 32, 36, 47, 52, 80
Marx, 59, 86

Maryland, 9, 30, 40, 49, 59, 60, 63, 64, 65, 66, 68, 69, 72, 73, 75, 81, 82, 84, 85, 87, 88, 89
mass, 85, 145, 147
mass spectrometry, 85
materials, 53, 79, 134
matter, 2, 7, 18, 27, 29, 32, 36, 47, 48, 115, 132, 137, 138, 140, 141, 146
measurements, 3, 4, 15, 16, 18, 20, 21, 26, 29, 36, 41, 146, 151, 156
meat, 54, 63, 88
media, 106, 108
median, 147
mediation, 27
Mediterranean, 119, 122, 123, 159
metabolism, 38
metals, 121, 161
methane (CH4), vii, 1, 42
methanol, 7, 27
methodology, 105
Mexico, 57
microbial cells, 36
microbial communities, 5, 24, 30, 32, 35
microcosms, 42
microenvironments, 20
microhabitats, 8
microorganisms, 39, 42, 44, 115
migration, 78
mineralization, 21, 27, 34, 38, 47, 48, 115, 131, 133, 141, 147
missions, 15, 19, 20, 26, 34, 44
mixing, 100
model, 123, 127
models, 16
modifications, 52, 103, 129, 159
moisture, 22, 25, 118
mortality, 52, 53, 86, 110
mosaic, 48
mosquitoes, 121
movement, 123, 124

multiple factors, 24
muskrat, 51, 59, 60, 61, 72
mussels, 53

N

NaCl, 114
National Academy of Sciences, 43, 47
native species, 35, 37, 64, 71
natural habitats, 130, 157
natural resource management, 65
Natural Resources Conservation Service, 63
negative consequences, x, 130, 131
negative effects, 24, 131
negative relation, 14, 28
Netherlands, 9, 54, 124, 157, 159, 160, 161
network, 127
neutral, 23, 24, 25, 35
New England, 45, 48, 124, 125
nitric oxide, 5, 24
nitrification, 5, 6, 14, 16, 20, 22, 23, 24, 28, 32, 33, 34, 37, 38, 40, 41, 47, 133, 145, 151
nitrifying bacteria, 17
nitrite, 5, 24, 37, 46
nitrogen, vii, x, 1, 5, 9, 11, 13, 16, 18, 23, 25, 26, 29, 31, 32, 34, 35, 37, 38, 40, 41, 43, 44, 45, 47, 48, 117, 126, 130, 131, 132, 133, 149, 150, 158, 160, 161
nitrous oxide, vii, 1, 3, 7, 8, 18, 19, 20, 26, 28, 29, 32, 37, 38, 41, 42, 43, 44, 45, 46, 47, 48
NOAA, 156
North America, viii, 50, 57, 59, 81, 82, 85, 89, 119, 124, 144
Norway, 54
nuisance, 57
nursing, 53

nutrient, vii, x, 1, 16, 17, 18, 20, 23, 33, 39, 45, 125, 130, 131, 132, 133, 144, 145, 148, 150, 153, 155, 158, 159, 160, 161
nutrient enrichment, 23, 39, 131
nutrients, viii, x, 2, 17, 20, 23, 49, 121, 130, 131, 132, 133, 135, 139, 140, 141, 145, 146, 150, 152, 153, 154
nutrition, 123

O

OCS, 39
oil, 7, 39, 46, 123
opportunities, 87
ores, 6, 17, 21, 26, 27, 99, 136
organic matter, 2, 7, 18, 27, 29, 32, 36, 47, 48, 115, 132, 137, 138, 140, 141, 146
ostracod assemblages, ix, 91, 100
ox, 35
oxidation, 5, 8, 16, 18, 19, 20, 23, 25, 27, 33, 35, 37, 41, 45, 121, 124, 126, 145
oxidation rate, 34
oxygen, 5, 6, 14, 18, 20, 21, 22, 23, 29, 30, 32, 33, 36, 44, 127, 132, 133, 144, 151, 160

P

Pacific, ix, 50, 71, 73, 75, 84, 85, 88
paleontology, 101
Paraguay, 53
parallel, 141
parameters, 125
parasites, 53, 58, 119
participants, 63, 64
pasture, 24, 39
pastures, 136
pathogens, 58

pathways, 5, 7, 27, 30, 35
PCR, 8
peat, 38, 41
percentage frequency, 108
periodicity, 114, 145
Peru, 53
pests, 89
Petroleum, 123
pH, 5, 23, 24, 25, 35, 39
phosphate, 146, 151, 152, 153, 154
phosphorous, 159
phosphorus, x, 130, 131, 132, 133, 146, 151, 156, 158, 160, 161
photosynthesis, 6, 40, 127
physical characteristics, 18
physicochemical characteristics, 144
physiology, 32, 105, 144, 152
plants, ix, 2, 4, 18, 20, 21, 22, 30, 31, 32, 34, 35, 44, 50, 52, 54, 56, 65, 71, 78, 79, 83, 84, 105, 118, 119, 122, 124, 125, 126, 128, 132, 133, 139, 144, 145, 147, 155, 156
platform, 59, 67
playing, 132
PM, 89
pneumonia, 86
Poland, 9, 10, 54
policy, 88
pollutants, viii, 50, 121
pollution, 92, 101, 121, 123, 130
ponds, 52, 59, 71, 120
pools, 136, 140, 146, 148
poor, 116
population, ix, x, 17, 50, 55, 62, 64, 65, 66, 70, 71, 75, 76, 77, 80, 81, 85, 130, 131, 145
population density, 85
population growth, 75
population size, 17, 55, 66
population structure, 81
porosity, 127

Portugal, 101, 124, 129, 134, 145, 156, 157, 160, 161
positive correlation, 100
positive feedback, 21
positive relationship, 14, 25, 28, 32
precipitation, 151
predation, 53, 54, 77
predators, 53
predictors, 113, 114
pregnancy, 55
preservation, 130
pressure, 119
prevention, 75
producers, 20, 160
production, 110, 120, 124, 127
professionals, 75
project, 66, 72
prokaryotes, 38
protected areas, 54
protection, 63, 72, 130, 142
public parks, 73
purification, 16
PVC, 113

Q

quality control, viii, 49

R

radio, 66, 67, 77
rainfall, 124
range, 105, 106, 109, 110, 112, 115, 116
recommendations, 81
recovery, 66, 69
recreation, 63
recreational, 64, 134
regeneration, 125
region, 112
regulation, 124

regulations, 73, 76, 79
relationship, x, 103, 104, 105, 112
remote sensing, 32
repair, 73
repellent, 76
reproduction, 70, 75, 87
requirements, 130, 132
researchers, 2, 52, 65, 78
reserves, 54
Residential, 120
residuals, 134
resistance, 117
resource management, 65
resources, ix, 50, 56, 77, 80, 92, 133
respect, 117, 127
respiration, 4, 18, 20, 26, 28, 29, 35, 40, 48, 117, 145, 151
response, viii, 2, 6, 16, 17, 19, 22, 25, 26, 28, 34, 35, 40, 121, 127
restoration, viii, 2, 36, 62, 72, 86, 119
rhizome, 136
rice field, 134
risk, ix, 50, 54, 58, 66, 67, 68, 73, 77, 79, 89
risks, 58
rodents, ix, 50, 51
Romania, 54
root, 59, 65, 127, 132, 134, 139, 145
roots, 6, 17, 21, 30, 34, 42, 53, 65, 124, 136, 138, 140, 151
rowing, 144
Royal Society, 161
rules, 71
runoff, 131, 134

S

saline water, 25
salinity, x, 12, 15, 25, 26, 28, 36, 37, 91, 92, 100, 101, 103, 104, 111, 113,

114, 115, 117, 119, 122, 123, 124, 125, 126, 127, 133, 156
salinity levels, 26
salmonella, 58
salt, x, 103, 104, 105, 118, 119, 122, 123, 124, 125, 126, 127, 128
salt concentration, 118
salt marshes, vii, x, 2, 3, 4, 7, 15, 18, 25, 28, 39, 92, 101, 103, 119, 123, 124, 125, 127, 130, 131, 132, 133, 134, 135, 136, 137, 138, 139, 140, 141, 143, 144, 145, 146, 147, 149, 150, 152, 154, 156, 157, 158, 159, 161
salts, x, 103, 119
saltwater, 83
sampling, 112
saturation, 66
scent, 67, 82, 85
scope, 66
sea level, viii, 2, 26, 34, 36, 43, 92, 99, 102, 105, 125, 126, 159
sea-level, 43, 101
sea-level rise, 43
seasonal flu, 151
seasonality, 7
sediment, 6, 17, 20, 21, 22, 26, 27, 37, 42, 58, 82, 92, 96, 99, 105, 113, 117, 118, 121, 124, 125, 131, 132, 133, 136, 137, 138, 140, 141, 143, 144, 145, 146, 150, 155, 159, 160
sedimentation, 92, 141, 146
sediments, vii, viii, 1, 5, 6, 7, 8, 16, 17, 18, 19, 20, 21, 22, 27, 28, 29, 32, 33, 35, 37, 38, 40, 41, 42, 43, 44, 45, 46, 47, 49, 65, 94, 132, 134, 140, 141, 145, 146, 147, 148, 156, 157
seed, 73, 110, 125
seeding, 110
seedlings, 62, 118
senses, 51

sensing, 32, 51
sensitivity, 156
septic tank, 18
services, viii, x, 49, 130, 133, 142, 157
sheep, 126
shellfish, 64
shoots, 118, 144
shortage, 132
showing, 22, 144
shrubs, 118, 119, 125
Slovakia, 54
SO_4^{2-}, 115
social group, 52
social perception, 54
social structure, 53
soil, 105, 112, 113, 115, 116, 118, 119, 122, 123, 124, 125, 126, 127
soil type, 20
sorption, 133, 145
South Africa, 124
South America, ix, 50, 53, 54, 120
South China Sea, 38
South Korea, 54
SP, 104, 114, 115, 116, 117
Spain, ix, 11, 19, 40, 55, 91, 99, 101, 102, 103, 112, 122, 123, 127, 157
specialists, 66, 68
speciation, 157
species, viii, ix, x, 31, 32, 35, 37, 39, 48, 49, 50, 51, 53, 54, 56, 58, 59, 60, 61, 62, 64, 71, 72, 75, 77, 78, 84, 88, 91, 96, 99, 100, 105, 106, 107, 108, 109, 110, 112, 116, 117, 118, 119, 120, 121, 122, 126, 127, 128, 130, 132, 144, 145, 151, 152, 155
species richness, viii, ix, 49, 50, 62, 105
Spring, 94, 156
stability, 71, 134, 156
stabilization, viii, 49
stabilizers, 68
standard deviation, 106, 109, 114, 139

standard error, 9, 10, 12
starvation, 53
state, 61, 63, 65, 71, 73, 75, 76, 79
states, ix, 32, 50, 57, 60, 63, 70, 71, 73, 75
stimulation, 29, 31
stock, 70
stock price, 70
storage, 46, 157
storm buffering, viii, 49
storms, 70
stratification, 18
stress, 110, 118, 139
structure, 25, 33, 35, 53, 78, 81, 83, 84, 88, 126, 127, 158
subsidy, 45
substrate, 7, 92, 104, 122, 147
succession, 32, 52, 124, 133
sugar beet, 73
sugarcane, 58, 60
sulfate, 3, 8, 25, 26, 28, 30, 36
sulphur, 116, 156
summer, 116
Sun, 38, 47, 48
suppression, ix, 50
surface area, 35, 151
surplus, 121
survival, 72, 81
susceptibility, 83
Sweden, 55
Switzerland, 12, 13, 54, 85

T

Tanzania, 11, 54
target, 76, 78, 79
taxa, 56
techniques, 8, 20, 22, 66, 67, 75, 77, 78, 120, 121, 125
technology, 36
temperature, 7, 28, 29, 47

terrestrial ecosystems, 15
testing, 66
texture, 33
Thailand, 54
threats, 88
threshold, 117
threshold level, 117
tides, 22, 26, 34, 92, 132, 134, 140, 143
time periods, vii, 1, 17, 22
tissue, 132
toxic effect, x, 103
toxicity, 116, 117, 128
tracks, 67
transformation, viii, 15, 40, 41, 49
transformations, 5, 23, 25, 26
transgression, 42
transition, 110
transmission, 35, 57, 73, 75, 86
transport, 6, 24, 29, 30, 31, 42, 92, 144, 158, 160, 161
trauma, 53
treatment, 17, 78
trial, 89
tundra, 24, 25
Turkey, 54
turnover, 137, 138, 145, 146, 147

U

U.S. Department of Agriculture, 85
UK, 37, 87, 101, 123
uniform, 136
United, v, ix, 43, 47, 49, 50, 55, 56, 58, 59, 60, 64, 65, 70, 76, 79, 80, 86, 89, 158
urban, viii, 19, 50, 54, 56, 74, 78, 81, 87, 121, 131, 134
urban areas, 54, 56
urea, 33
urine, 58
Uruguay, 53, 82, 88

USA, 1, 9, 10, 11, 12, 40, 48, 49, 85, 88
USDA, 49, 71, 73, 74, 75

V

vaccine, 83
variables, x, 103, 104, 113, 114
variance, 113, 115
variations, x, 38, 91, 100, 101
vegetables, 58
vegetation, vii, ix, x, 31, 38, 42, 50, 51, 52, 54, 56, 57, 59, 60, 62, 64, 67, 69, 71, 72, 75, 82, 84, 86, 87, 89, 103, 104, 105, 109, 110, 112, 113, 114, 115, 118, 119, 123, 124, 125, 126, 127, 128, 132, 134, 138, 160, 161
vehicles, 19
vertebrates, 88

W

Washington, 43, 44, 57, 70, 71, 73, 75, 81, 82, 83, 84, 85, 126
waste, 131
waste water, 131
wastewater, 17, 32
water, vii, viii, ix, 7, 15, 16, 18, 21, 22, 24, 26, 27, 29, 30, 33, 34, 37, 47, 48, 49, 50, 51, 52, 53, 54, 55, 56, 57, 58, 59, 60, 64, 65, 71, 73, 77, 112, 113, 116, 120, 123, 124, 126, 128, 130, 131, 134, 135, 136, 140, 142, 145, 151, 155, 156, 159, 160, 161
water purification, 16
water quality, viii, 49, 58
watershed, 18, 36, 48, 67
watertable, 113, 114, 116
waterways, 67, 68, 79
wear, 58
wetland restoration, 4, 86
wetlands, 2, 3, 10, 25, 28, 30, 33, 34, 36, 37, 38, 39, 41, 42, 43, 44, 46, 47, 48, 53, 63, 64, 66, 68, 83, 89, 126, 133, 159
wildlife, viii, 49, 59, 64, 65, 66, 68, 71, 73, 75, 76
wildlife watching, 65
winter, 124
worldwide, viii, 2, 81, 92, 99, 130, 131

Y

yield, 25, 96
Yugoslavia, 54

Z

Zimbabwe, 54
zinc, 79, 87, 89
zonation of saltmarsh vegetation, x, 103